Understanding & Applying Science 5

Sandra Baggley
Formerly GRIST Science Organiser for Manchester, now Curriculum Manager for Manchester Hospital School Service

Jennifer Gow
TVEI Coordinator, Burnage High School, Manchester

Philip Noone
Science Teacher, Burnage High School, Manchester

Series Consultants
Joe Boyd
Walter Whitelaw

JOHN MURRAY

Pupils' Book 5 ISBN 0–7195–5197–8
Teachers' Resource Book 5 ISBN 0–7195–5198–6

© Sandra Baggley, Jennifer Gow, Philip Noone 1993

First published 1993
by John Murray (Publishers) Ltd
50 Albemarle Street, London W1X 4BD

Layout by Amanda Hawkes
Typeset by Wearset, Boldon, Tyne and Wear
Printed in Great Britain by Butler & Tanner Ltd, Frome and London

A catalogue entry for this title can be obtained from the British Library

ISBN 0–7195–5197–8

Contents

Take notes 6

Acknowledgements 8

Unit 1

Plants
Fair testing

1.1 Plants and photosynthesis 10
1.2 Transport in plants 16
1.3 Plant reproduction and growth 20
1.4 Plants and recycling 24
1.5 Problem — How does a plant grow? 28
1.6 Talkabout — Deforestation 29
1.7 Questions 30

Unit 2

Sound and music
Designing and applying information

2.1 Sound facts 32
2.2 Making music 36
2.3 Sound communication 40
2.4 Microelectronics 44
2.5 Problem — The capacity to store electricity 48
2.6 Talkabout — Sound may help to save the ozone layer 49
2.7 Questions 50

Unit 3

Genetics and biotechnology
Examining issues

3.1 Inheritance 52
3.2 Chromosomes and DNA 56
3.3 Genetic engineering 60
3.4 Problem — Pedigree analysis 64
3.5 Talkabout — Testing time 65
3.6 Questions 66

Unit 4

From Earth to the stars
Looking at evidence

4.1 The moving Earth 68
4.2 Rock around the world 74
4.3 A lot of hot air? 78
4.4 Earth beginnings 82
4.5 Problem — Identifying rocks 88
4.6 Talkabout — Spin-offs from space 89
4.7 Questions 90

Unit 5

Making materials
Looking at applications

5.1 Petrochemicals	92
5.2 Agrochemicals	96
5.3 Industrial electrolysis	100
5.4 Colloids	104
5.5 Construction materials	108
5.6 Problem — Profit and loss	112
5.7 Talkabout — Setting up a factory	113
5.8 Questions	114

Unit 6

The quality of life
Extracting information

6.1 Head start	116
6.2 Affairs of the heart	120
6.3 Diet, digestion and disease	124
6.4 Reproduction and development	128
6.5 Sport and fitness	132
6.6 Problem — Preventing tooth decay	136
6.7 Talkabout — Drug abuse	137
6.8 Questions	138

Unit 7

The Periodic Table
Looking for patterns

7.1 How many substances?	140
7.2 Element groups	146
7.3 Periodicity	150
7.4 Radioactivity	154
7.5 Problem — Investigating an element	158
7.6 Talkabout — The nuclear industry	159
7.7 Questions	160

Unit 8

Chemical calculations
Performing calculations

8.1 Mass and number	162
8.2 Formulae	164
8.3 Chemical equations	166
8.4 Moles in a solution	170
8.5 Moles of a gas	172

Throughout the book, this symbol refers to a page in Unit 8 where help may be found with chemical calculations.

Extensions

1.1	Chlorophyll and light	175
1.2	Transport in phloem and xylem	176
1.3	Improving plant growth	177
1.4	Global warming — can our planet cope?	178
2.1	Echoes	179
2.2	How do we hear?	180
2.3	Making use of interference effects	181
2.4	Microelectronic components	182
3.1	True breeding	184
3.2	Cell division	185
3.3	Genetic disorders	187
4.1	Earth shattering	188
4.2	Geological time	190
4.3	Save the planet!	191
4.4	Space debris	192
5.1	Identifying plastics and fibres	193
5.2	Nitrogen and plant growth	194
5.3	Calculating coulombs	195
5.4	Making a cold cream	196
5.5	Investigating concrete and cement	197
6.1	The human eye	198
6.2	The blood and immunity	200
6.3	Enzymes	202
6.4	The human endocrine system	203
6.5	Helpful machines	204
7.1	Extracting metals from their ores	205
7.2	Group II metals	207
7.3	Ionisation energy	208
7.4	Radioactive decay	209

Glossary 210

Index 214

Why is notemaking important?

Making notes is important when you start to study seriously for exams. You will find that there are a great many new facts and ideas to be learnt. Often you will need to use a variety of textbooks and printed material. The process of making good notes helps to **focus** your attention and so you **learn** more effectively.
The very act of **writing** something down helps you to **remember** it, and it can also be used to refresh your memory. Making notes requires **summarising** skills and practice with these can be found on resource sheets. Making notes also helps you to **organise** the material.

How do you start?

You need to read the material carefully, deciding first what the main theme is and then what the **key points** are. Often headings give clues to these. When you have a clear idea about the topic, decide upon the best way of summarising it.

What should your notes be like?

Notes should be shorter than the original text! They should be brief but contain all the **important facts** and **key ideas**. Points should be arranged **logically** and follow on from each other. Reorganising the material mentally and then putting it in your own words helps you to understand and remember the information.

Which layout should you choose?

There are several ways of making notes. Which method you use depends partly on the subject content and partly on your own preference.
Notes can take the form of sentences but often it is not necessary to include every word or item of punctuation. Instead punctuation can be used to highlight your notes by, for example, putting full stops at the end of phrases and capitals at the beginning of important words. Underlining and highlighting with colour are useful ways of bringing out the key points and subsidiary and linked ideas. **Flow diagrams** (spidergrams) are useful for summarising a description of a process, or a sequence of ideas or instructions. **Tables** are good for making comparisons or bringing together lots of small items of information. **Diagrams** are essential for naming the parts of an object and for showing how they are related. Use colour to make your notes more attractive and to show relationships. It is sometimes helpful to mentally visualise the page of notes as a memory jogger in exams so the more personal and varied the better—as long as they make sense.

How should notes be used?

Notes should be referred to frequently so that the information is fixed in your mind. If you cannot understand your notes when you come back to them then either they are too brief or you did not understand the topic or make an effort to clarify any problems. Notes should be **memory joggers**.

Opposite: two examples of notes made from page 122 of this book.

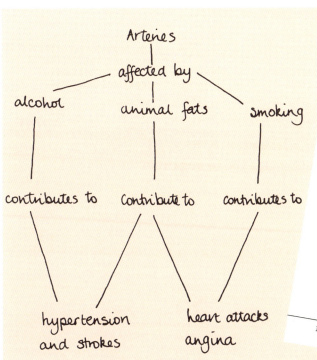

Arteries affected by

- alcohol
- animal fats
- smoking

alcohol **contributes to** → hypertension and strokes

animal fats **contribute to** → hypertension and strokes / heart attacks angina

smoking **contributes to** → heart attacks angina

Avoidable damage

There is a great deal of evidence to suggest that drugs, alcohol, smoking and stress can have a serious damaging effect on many of the body organs. These factors are thought to be instrumental in the development of heart disease, cancer, strokes and other diseases. Obviously if these damaging factors are avoided, the chances of developing disease will be significantly reduced.

Your heart needs food and oxygen to keep its muscle working continuously. A network of **coronary arteries** is spread over the surface of the heart bringing oxygen to the capillaries. Oxygen diffuses into the muscle cells of the heart and carbon dioxide diffuses from the cells into the blood. If one of these coronary arteries becomes wholly or partially blocked the heart muscle can be starved of oxygen, causing the heart to stop beating or to beat irregularly. This can cause a **heart attack** or **angina**. Sometimes surgeons can replace the damaged blood vessel with one taken from a patient's leg. It is, of course, much better if the damage could be avoided in the first place.

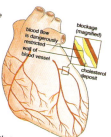

A blockage in a coronary artery.

An artery can become blocked or hardened anywhere in the body. Blockages are caused by deposits of a fatty substance called **cholesterol** building up around the walls of blood vessels (rather like a domestic kettle 'furring' up with chalk deposits). Blood flow is slowed down as a result of the narrowed vessel and may eventually stop due to the formation of a **blood clot**. The blood clot may become dislodged and cause a blockage elsewhere in the body. Oxygen can then no longer reach the areas that are served by that artery.

One common problem found with the circulation of the blood is that of high blood pressure or **hypertension**. The pumping action of the heart through narrowed blood vessels results in a build-up of pressure in the arteries. Blood pressure needs to be fairly high to keep blood circulating around the whole body efficiently. Blood pressure can be raised by exercise, anger or excitement.

People who have continuously high blood pressure have extra strain placed on their heart which may eventually lead to heart failure. Raised blood pressure also pushes the sides of arteries out and may cause them to burst. If this happens in the brain the leaking blood kills some of the brain cells and results in a **stroke**. Strokes can kill or leave a person partially paralysed or unable to speak.

There are thought to be many causes of high blood pressure: over-eating, eating foods high in cholesterol, drinking too much alcohol, and stress all contribute. Scientists also think there may be a hereditary link to high blood pressure.

Other diseases of the circulatory system can be caused by bacteria and viruses, which produce toxins that poison the body. Antibiotics are drugs widely used to kill bacterial infections anywhere in the body. However, antibiotics do not kill viruses so viral infections are difficult to cure.

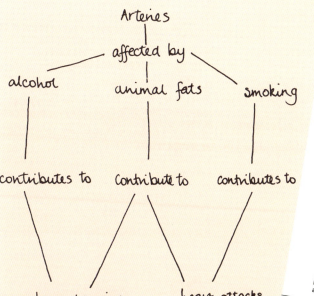

Transverse section of a normal human coronary artery, about × 20.

Transverse section of a human coronary artery showing almost total blockage due to a fatty deposit and a blood clot, about × 20.

122

Illness	Causes	Affect on body	Avoidance strategies
Heart attack	• High cholesterol building up causing blockage then blood clot. • Less oxygen to heart muscles	Coronary artery blocked	avoid animal fats and smoking.
Hypertension	• Cholesterol building up, arteries reduced so pressure increases • Alcohol • Stress	Narrowed vessels so build up of blood pressure, could cause arteries to burst leading to a stroke	avoid animal fats, alcohol practise relaxing
Stroke	Severe, continual hypertension – as above	Burst blood vessels in the brain. Leaking blood kills brain cells. Could lead to paralysis or lack of speech.	avoid animal fats, alcohol and very stressful situations
Bacterial or viral	Bacteria or viruses	toxins in the blood stream, affects circulation.	difficult to avoid, antibodies kill bacteria but not viruses

Acknowledgements

CARTOONS: Richard Duszczak
COLOUR ARTWORK: David Cook, Jane Pickering (medical illustrations)/Linden Artists Ltd
LINE DRAWINGS: Art Construction, Taurus Graphics, Sean Humphries
COVER PHOTO: © D.Noton/Telegraph Colour Library

The following have provided photos or given permission for copyright photos or extracts to be reproduced:

p.9 ZEFA
p.10 top ZEFA; *bottom* Trevor Hill
p.15 Dr Jeremy Burgess/Science Photo Library
p.16 Dr Jeremy Burgess/Science Photo Library
p.19 top left K. Goebel/ZEFA; *top middle* Stephen J. Krasemann/NHPA; *top right* N. G. Blake/Bruce Coleman Ltd; *bottom right* John Durham/Science Photo Library
p.21 ACM/Photos Horticultural Picture Library
p.22 *top* Claude Nuridsany and Marie Perennou/Science Photo Library; *middle* Biophoto Associates; *bottom* Dr Jeremy Burgess/Science Photo Library
p.27 *top* Dr Morley Read/Science Photo Library; *middle* Sheila Terry/Science Photo Library
p.28 *top* Moira Savonius/NHPA; *middle* G. S. F. Picture Library; *bottom left* Photos Horticultural Picture Library; *bottom right* Physics Department, Imperial College/Science Photo Library
p.29 *top* Alex Bartel/Science Photo Library; *middle* Vaughan Fleming/Science Photo Library; *bottom* Alain Compost/Bruce Coleman Ltd; *right* Konrad Wothe/Bruce Coleman Ltd
p.31 ZEFA
p.36 *top* Trevor Hill; *middle* John Murray/Bruce Coleman Ltd; *bottom* Robert Harding Picture Library
p.38 *top* Institute of Mining Engineers
p.39 M. J. Thomas/Frank Lane Picture Agency; *top* Fisons Scientific Equipment
p.40 *bottom* James Stevenson/Science Photo Library
p.41 Trevor Hill
p.42 Dr Jeremy Burgess/Science Photo Library
p.44 Adam Hart-Davis/Science Photo Library
p.45 Trevor Hill
p.46 *top* and *bottom left* Trevor Hill; *bottom right* David T. Grewcock/Frank Lane Picture Agency
p.49 Daniel Clery, *New Scientist*, 4 April 1992
p.51 Eric Crichton/Bruce Coleman Ltd
p.52 *top* and *bottom* ZEFA
p.53 Science Photo Library
p.54 *top* CNRI/Science Photo Library; *bottom* Biophoto Associates
p.57 *top* Jackie Lewin, Royal Free Hospital/Science Photo Library; *bottom left* ZEFA; *bottom middle* ZEFA; *bottom right* A. J. Roberts/Frank Lane Picture Agency
p.58 M. W. F. Tweedie/NHPA
p.61 Julia Kamlish/Science Photo Library
p.65 *left* Will and Deni McIntyre/Science Photo Library; *right* Bob Gelberg/ZEFA

p.67 A. T. Matthews/Frank Lane Picture Agency
p.68 *top* J. Guest/Frank Lane Picture Agency; *bottom* US Geological Survey/Science Photo Library
p.69 Peter Menzel/Science Photo Library
p.70 *top* Science Photo Library; *bottom* Heilman/ZEFA
p.74 N. Nimmo/Frank Lane Picture Agency
p.75 *top* Adam Hart-Davis/Science Photo Library; *bottom left* G. Mabbs/ZEFA; *bottom right* G. S. F. Picture Library
p.76 *top* Eric Crichton/Bruce Coleman Ltd; *bottom* Simon Fraser/Science Photo Library
p.80 weather map *The Guardian* 6 October 1992
p.81 University of Dundee/Science Photo Library
p.82 Hank Morgan/Science Photo Library
p.84 *top, left to right* Bruce Coleman Ltd; NASA/Science Photo Library; European Space Agency/Science Photo Library; *middle, left to right* US Geological Survey/Science Photo Library; Photri/ZEFA; NASA/Frank Lane Picture Agency; *bottom, left to right* Voyager 1986/ZEFA; *Voyager 2*/ZEFA; NASA/Science Photo Library
p.86 ZEFA
p.87 ZEFA
p.88 *top left* G. S. F. Picture Library; *top right* Adrian Davies/ Bruce Coleman Ltd; *bottom* G. S. F. Picture Library
p.91 Nigel Cattlin/Holt Studies International
p.92 Martin Bond/Science Photo Library
p.93 M. J. Thomas/Frank Lane Picture Agency
p.95 Fisons Scientific Equipment
p.96 *top* M. J. Thomas/Frank Lane Picture Agency; *bottom* Francisco Erize/Bruce Coleman Ltd
p.97 Robert Harding Picture Library
p.99 Peter Dean/Frank Lane Picture Agency
p.100 *top* Phototake/ZEFA; *bottom* G. S. F. Picture Library
p.106 article Andy Coghlan/*New Scientist*; 2 September 1992 photo Lawrence Livermore National Laboratory/Science Photo Library
p.108 *top* Austin James Steven/Bruce Coleman Ltd; *middle* John Markham/Bruce Coleman Ltd; *bottom* Michael Freeman/Bruce Coleman Ltd
p.109 *top* G. S. F. Picture Library; *middle* G. S. F. Picture Library; *bottom* John Worrall/Bruce Coleman Ltd; *left* Robert P. Carr/Bruce Coleman Ltd
p.110 *left* David Goulston/Bruce Coleman Ltd; *right* John Worrall/Bruce Coleman Ltd; *bottom* US Department of Energy/Science Photo Library
p.112 Eric Crichton/Bruce Coleman Ltd
p.115 Rettinghaus/ZEFA
p.120 Biophoto Associates
p.121 Science Photo Library
p.122 *top* Science Photo Library; *bottom* Biophoto Associates/Science Photo Library
p.123 Fisons Scientific Equipment
p.124 *three photos* The Nutrition Revolution *article* May 1991 *Slimming Magazine*

p.125 *left* Biophoto Associates/Science Photo Library; *right* St Mary's Hospital Medical School/Science Photo Library
p.126 Marrowfat Processed Peas in Water *food label* Brooke Bond Foods Ltd, Croydon
p.130 *top* Photri/ZEFA; *bottom* Larry Mulvehill/Science Photo Library
p.134 ZEFA
p.136 *left to right leaflet* Stafford-Miller, Welwyn Garden City; *article The Messenger* July 1992; *leaflet* Dentsply, Weybridge
p.137 *article Manchester Evening News*, Carl Johnson, April 1992; *top* ZEFA; *bottom* Alexandre/ZEFA
p.139 US Department of Energy/Science Photo Library
p.144 Novosti/Science Photo Library
p.154 C. Powell, P. Fowler and D. Perkins/Science Photo Library
p.155 ZEFA
p.157 *top* Martin Dohrn/Science Photo Library; *bottom* Jerry Mason/Science Photo Library
p.159 *article* Jeremy Webb *New Scientist* 14 November 1992
p.161 ZEFA
p.170 *top* John Topham/WIL/Bruce Coleman Ltd; *middle* St Bartholomew's Hospital/Science Photo Library; bottom ZEFA
p.174 Dave Curry/NHPA
p.175 Physics Department, Imperial College/Science Photo Library
p.177 George Gainsburgh/NHPA
p.178 *top* NASA/Frank Lane Picture Agency; *bottom* Silvestris Fotoservice/NHPA
p.179 ZEFA
p.181 *article* Peter Hadfield *New Scientist* 28 March 1992
p.182 Fisons Scientific Equipment
p.183 Robert Harding Picture Library
p.184 *top* Hans Reinhard/Bruce Coleman Ltd; *bottom left* Jane Burton/Bruce Coleman Ltd; *bottom right* Colin Molyneux/Bruce Coleman Ltd
p.185 G. S. F. Picture Library
p.188 *top and bottom* S. McCutcheon/Frank Lane Picture Agency
p.189 *left article Planet Earth: Earthquake*, Bryce Walker and the Editors of Time Life Books, © 1982 Time Life Books Inc.; *right article Knutsford Guardian* 18 February 1992
p.191 *left, middle and right* Mark Edwards/Still Pictures
p.192 NASA/Science Photo Library; *graph* Science Issues
p.194 Fisons Horticulture
p.196 John Townson
p.200 G. S. F. Picture Library
p.204 G. S. F. Picture Library
p.206 Gary Gladstone/The Image Bank

The publishers are grateful to the following examining groups for allowing reproduction of examination questions:

Midland Examining Group (MEG)
Northern Examinations and Assessment Board (NEAB)
Southern Examining Group (SEG)

1
Plants

Plants and photosynthesis

The importance of plants

Biologists classify plants into several main groups — mosses and liverworts, club mosses, horsetails, ferns, conifers and flowering plants. You are probably familiar with these (if not, look up in *US 3*). Most plant species grow on land. Can you think of any exceptions?

mosses and liverworts

horsetails

conifers

club mosses

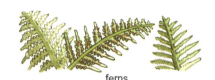

ferns

flowering plants

The main plant groups.

Flowering plants provide fruits and vegetables.

The cotton plant flower provides a very valuable raw material.

Flowering plants (**angiosperms**) are found all over the world in practically every habitat and are represented by more than 250 000 living species. (The rest of the plant kingdom includes about 34 000 living species.) We are particularly interested in flowering plants because of their great economic importance. They provide a food source for humans and animals, a wide variety of raw materials and enhance our environment, whether they are wild or cultivated.

Plants are essential for life because they **photosynthesise**. Chlorophyll in green plants harnesses energy from sunlight which the plants use to build glucose molecules from carbon dioxide and water. Oxygen is also produced.

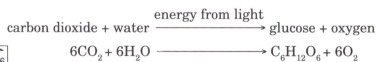

$$\text{carbon dioxide} + \text{water} \xrightarrow{\text{energy from light}} \text{glucose} + \text{oxygen}$$

$$6CO_2 + 6H_2O \longrightarrow C_6H_{12}O_6 + 6O_2$$

Oxygen is essential for living organisms because it is used in **respiration**. Respiration is the process by which living cells produce energy from the combination of foods, such as glucose, with oxygen. Plants also use glucose molecules made from photosynthesis as a starting point for making other more complex substances. These are passed up the food chain when plants are eaten by animals.

Photosynthesis in flowering plants

We can discover if photosynthesis has taken place in a plant by looking for products of the reaction. One of these products is starch. Glucose, made in the leaves during photosynthesis, is rapidly built into starch and stored in leaf cells and other organs in the plant for later use. As we have seen, oxygen is a product of photosynthesis, so we can also test for this gaseous molecule.

Test leaves for starch

Iodine solution turns from brown to dark blue or black when it combines with starch. Iodine does not penetrate plant cells readily and the green colour of the leaf caused by chlorophyll masks any colour change. Therefore, to test the leaf for starch the cells in the leaf are made permeable to iodine and chlorophyll is extracted.

1 Half-fill the beaker with water and heat until the water boils.

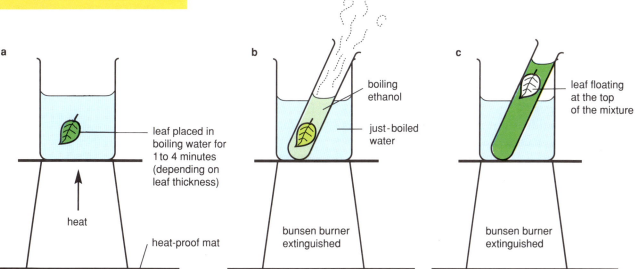

a — leaf placed in boiling water for 1 to 4 minutes (depending on leaf thickness)
heat
heat-proof mat

b — boiling ethanol
just-boiled water
bunsen burner extinguished

c — leaf floating at the top of the mixture
bunsen burner extinguished

2 Using forceps, submerge the leaf in the water for 1 to 4 minutes as shown in the diagram. (If your leaf is thick, leave it in a little longer.)

3 Turn off the bunsen burner.

4 Half-fill the test tube with ethanol and stand it in the beaker of hot water. The ethanol will boil. Quickly transfer the leaf to the test tube of ethanol. Leave the leaf in until it has lost most of its green colour.

5 Either carefully pour out the hot chlorophyll and ethanol mixture or add cold water until the leaf floats to the top of the test tube. Remove the leaf using forceps.

6 Spread the leaf on a petri dish and cover it with iodine solution using a pipette. What do you observe?

after testing a variegated leaf for starch

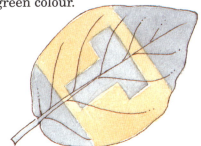

a living leaf was covered with a 'T'-shape for several days and then tested for starch

Collect oxygen from Canadian pondweed

Your teacher may demonstrate this experiment.

1 The experiment is set up as shown in the diagram. Sodium hydrogencarbonate is added to the water to increase the amount of carbon dioxide available.
2 The apparatus is left in a well-lit place for several days.
3 Any gas produced is tested for oxygen.

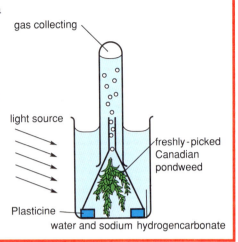

Collect

- test tubes and rack
- filter funnel
- beaker (250 cm³)
- Canadian pondweed
- distilled water
- sodium hydrogencarbonate
- spatula
- Plasticine
- wooden splint

Plan your own experiments

1 Use your knowledge of photosynthesis and the diagrams here and on pages 11 and 13 to plan experiments to show that carbon dioxide, light and chlorophyll are necessary for photosynthesis in plants.
2 Carry out at least one of your experiments. Remember that each experiment will need a control.
3 Now plan and perhaps set up a series of experiments to investigate how changing one of the variables listed below affects the rate of photosynthesis. Remember to plan a control. How can you be sure your investigation is fair?

- light
- temperature
- concentration of carbon dioxide.

IT You could use a computer and sensors to measure light intensity and temperature.

Soda lime absorbs carbon dioxide and sodium hydrogencarbonate produces carbon dioxide.

Is light necessary for photosynthesis?

Q1 Prepare a presentation of your investigations, giving reasons for your methods. Be ready to share your findings with the class.

Q2 Write a report including results from other investigations to show the conditions needed for photosynthesis and how varying these conditions affects the rate of photosynthesis.

How do plants affect the levels of carbon dioxide and oxygen in their surroundings?

From the equation for photosynthesis (page 10) we can see that plants take up carbon dioxide and produce oxygen. At the same time, plants are respiring. During respiration oxygen is taken up and carbon dioxide is produced.

To investigate how plants affect the amounts of carbon dioxide in their surroundings it is best to use a water plant. This is because carbon dioxide dissolves in the water, which can then be tested. Bicarbonate indicator is used to test for dissolved carbon dioxide. As the concentration of carbon dioxide dissolved in the water changes, the indicator changes colour.

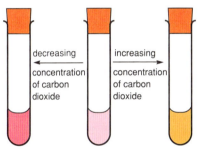

The cycling of oxygen and carbon dioxide during photosynthesis and respiration.

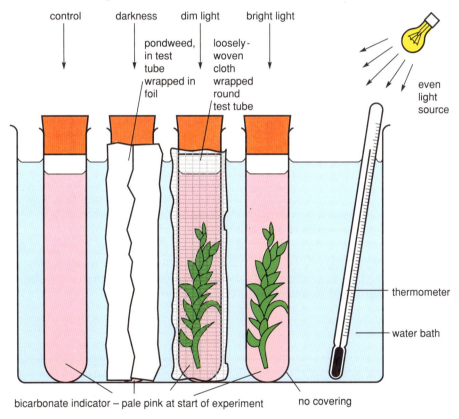

control   darkness   dim light   bright light

pondweed, in test tube wrapped in foil

loosely-woven cloth wrapped round test tube

even light source

thermometer

water bath

bicarbonate indicator – pale pink at start of experiment

no covering

Bicarbonate indicator turns yellow with increasing acidity and purple with decreasing acidity.

decreasing concentration of carbon dioxide

increasing concentration of carbon dioxide

Collect • results table

Test for carbon dioxide
Read the results table carefully.

✎ *Take notes*

Explain how temperature, carbon dioxide concentration and light intensity affect photosynthesis and how gas exchange in a plant depends on the amount of light falling on its leaves. 🏁 CHECKPOINT

The rate of respiration in a plant is unaffected by changes in light intensity. However, the rate of photosynthesis is affected (see page 12 for activity on photosynthesis). It is fast in bright light, slow in dim light and ceases in darkness.

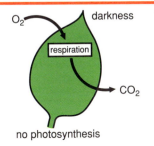

darkness

O_2

respiration

CO_2

no photosynthesis

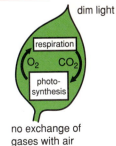

dim light

respiration

O_2 CO_2

photo-synthesis

no exchange of gases with air

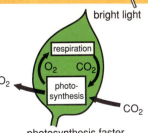

bright light

respiration

O_2 CO_2

photo-synthesis

O_2

CO_2

photosynthesis faster than respiration

Leaf structure

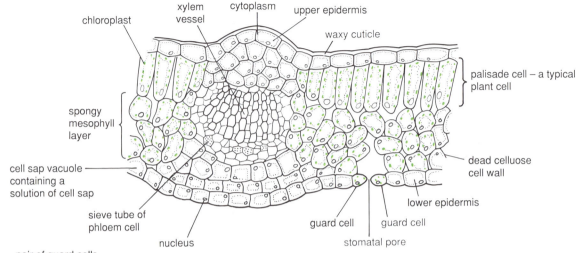

A transverse section through a typical leaf.

The diagram above shows the different cellular layers of a leaf, each layer containing the same type of cell. Most of these cell types have the features of a typical plant cell. However, the size and shape of the cells and the number of chloroplasts in the cells vary from layer to layer. The different layers of cells have different functions.

Guard cells have a specialised function. A pair of guard cells surrounds each small air pore, called a **stomatal pore**, which leads into the spongy **mesophyll layer**. The stomatal pores enable carbon dioxide and oxygen to diffuse in and out of the leaf. The carbon dioxide used in photosynthesis diffuses through the spaces in the mesophyll layer to reach all of the cells. In general the pores are open during the hours of daylight and closed during the hours of darkness.

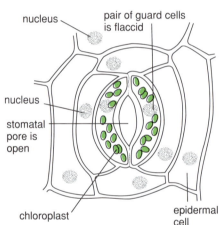

A pair of guard cells. When the cells are turgid the stomatal pore closes and when they are flaccid the pore opens.

Look for stomatal pores

Collect

- leaves (several)
- microscope (low power)
- slide and coverslip
- iodine solution
- clear nail varnish and brush
- forceps
- distilled water
- dropping pipette

1 Paint a thin layer of clear nail varnish on a small area of the lower surface of a leaf.
2 When the nail varnish is dry, carefully peel it off with a pair of forceps and mount it on a slide with distilled water.
3 Examine your sample under the microscope. Make a careful drawing of what you see. Repeat the experiment using the upper surface of a leaf. Try to decide which surface has more pores.
4 Strip off the lower epidermis of a leaf and make a slide of it. Stain the leaf with a few drops of iodine solution using a pipette.
5 Examine the slide under the microscope and make a labelled drawing to show any stomatal pores.

Q1 Why do you think there is a difference in the number of stomatal pores on the upper and lower surfaces of a leaf?

Xylem vessels and phloem cells are tubular structures that transport substances through a plant. Xylem transports water and mineral salts to the leaf and phloem transports sugars (such as sucrose) and amino acids away from the leaf to higher or lower parts of the plant (see page 19).

Photosynthesis in leaves occurs in **chloroplasts**. They look green because of a mixture of different **pigments** known as **chlorophyll**. The chlorophyll molecules are arranged in membranes in the inside of the chloroplast and trap energy from light, which is then used in photosynthesis. Most chloroplasts are found in cells of the **palisade layer**, which are near to the upper surface of the leaf and so receive most light.

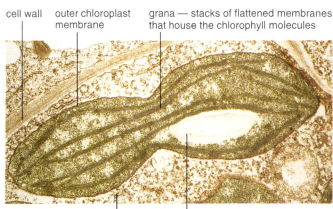

cell wall   outer chloroplast membrane   grana — stacks of flattened membranes that house the chlorophyll molecules

cytoplasm   a large starch body — one of the products of photosynthesis

A chloroplast in the leaf of a pea plant, *Pisum sativum*, × 14 700.

Investigate chloroplasts

Moss leaves are very small but they have the advantage of being very thin and translucent (allow light to pass through).

Collect

- moss (small piece)
- forceps
- iodine solution
- microscope (high power)
- slide and coverslip
- filter paper
- plain paper
- distilled water

1 Remove a single leaf with forceps and mount it on a slide with distilled water.
2 Examine it under the microscope. Try to distinguish different types of cell. Make a drawing of any cells you see. (Remember that chloroplasts are green.)
3 Remove your slide from the microscope. Put two drops of iodine solution at one edge and 'draw' the solution across the slide by touching the opposite edge with a piece of filter paper.
4 Examine your slide again. Black specks indicate starch grains. Add them to your drawing.

 *Take notes*

Make sure you have a clearly labelled drawing to show the structure of a leaf.

Indicate the different functions of each cell layer and say how the structure of the cells in each layer suits their function.

 *Project*

Look round your sitting room. Which objects and materials are made from plants? If an object is made from a synthetic material find out if a plant could be used to make it and, if so, name the plant.

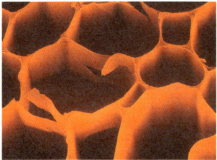

Air-filled strengthening cells in the trunk of a tree, × 230.

Osmosis

Water molecules enter, or leave a cell by osmosis. This is the movement of water molecules across a semi-permeable membrane from an area where the concentration of water molecules is high to an area where the concentration of water molecules is low. (*UAS 4*, page 137.)

Movement of water

Plants contain a large proportion of water. A potato (tuber) contains about 77% water, while a soft fruit like a strawberry is almost 90% water and lettuce is nearer 95%. Most plants need a regular supply of water. Without it, leaves start to droop and curl, then the stem becomes floppy and the whole plant wilts. The plant is then described as **flaccid**. This condition is usually reversible if the plant is watered in time but beyond a certain point, the plant dies.

The following give support to the root, stem and leaves of flowering plants:

- cellulose contained in cell walls
- thick-walled xylem vessels
- the turgidity of cells.

If a plant is short of water, the water content of the **cell sap solution** in the vacuole of each cell drops leaving the cell flaccid. Small, soft-stemmed plants wilt because the xylem vessels alone are not strong enough to support the weight of the plant. Trees and smaller woody shrubs have xylem vessels with extra strengthening material in their walls. This material is called **lignin**. This is why they do not wilt as easily.

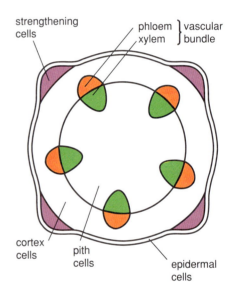

Schematic drawing of a plant stem in transverse section.

Turgor and plasmolysis

Collect

- onion (small piece)
- microscope
- slide and coverslip (2)
- concentrated sucrose solution
- distilled water
- filter paper
- pipette

1 Strip off two pieces of onion skin and peal off the inner epidermal cell sheet.

2 Mount one piece on a slide in sucrose solution and examine it under the microscope for several minutes.

3 Mount the other piece in distilled water and cover with a coverslip.

4 Replace the sucrose with distilled water using filter paper to 'draw' water across the slide.

5 Examine both slides under the microscope.

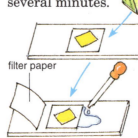

filter paper

inner epidermal cell sheet

control

Q1 Draw and label what you observed through the microscope. Try to interpret your drawings.

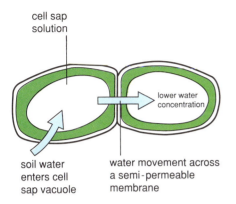

cell sap solution

lower water concentration

soil water enters cell sap vacuole

water movement across a semi-permeable membrane

Osmosis in two plant cells.

Xylem vessels form continuous hollow tubes that transport water *upwards only* in the plant.

Some of the water is used by the plant in photosynthesis but most of it passes out of the plant through the stomatal pores in the leaves to evaporate into the air. This is called **transpiration**.

Plants take up water mainly through the **root hairs**. Each root hair is a single, long cell with a structure similar to the palisade cell shown on page 14. Water in the soil forms a layer around the soil particles. The root hair cells are in contact with the water. The cell sap solution inside each root hair cell is more concentrated than the soil water. Water enters the first layer of root hair cells by osmosis. Each time water enters the vacuole of a living cell, its cell sap solution is diluted. The cell sap solution of the neighbouring cell will now be more concentrated. Water passes, by osmosis, into the neighbouring cell. This process repeats over and over, resulting in the passage of water through the root to reach the xylem vessels. Some water takes a different route to the xylem vessels, passing in or between the cell walls.

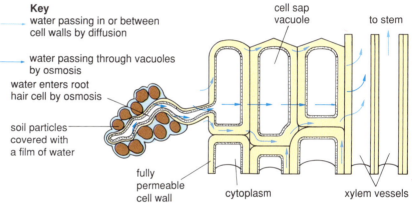

Key

→ water passing in or between cell walls by diffusion

→ water passing through vacuoles by osmosis

water enters root hair cell by osmosis

soil particles covered with a film of water

fully permeable cell wall

cytoplasm

cell sap vacuole

to stem

xylem vessels

Transverse section through a root showing the passage of water from the surrounding soil to the xylem vessels.

As the water evaporates heat is lost so transpiration may help to cool the plant during hot weather. Transpiration is also important because essential mineral salts are transported to all the cells of a plant in the water.

'pulling' force

capillary action

'pushing' force

Transpiration in a plant.

Water transport in plants

Collect

- celery stalk
- Busy Lizzie stem
- seedling
- hand lens
- microscope (low power)
- slide and coverslip
- scalpel

CARE!

1 Examine the roots of the seedling using a microscope. What do you notice about them? Draw a diagram of the root.
2 Examine the piece of celery stalk which has been in coloured water. Slice through the stalk. Draw a diagram of what you see. From these observations can you write something simple about the way water is carried in the plant?
3 Examine the piece of Busy Lizzie stem in the same way. Use a hand lens. If possible, prepare a slide of a transverse section of the stem and look at it under the microscope. Draw a diagram of what you see.

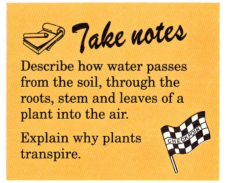

Take notes

Describe how water passes from the soil, through the roots, stem and leaves of a plant into the air.

Explain why plants transpire.

Q1 What is the basic similarity between a Busy Lizzie stem and a celery stalk?

How do changing conditions affect water uptake in a plant?

We can demonstrate that transpiration is taking place by securing a polythene bag over a potted plant. We can measure the rate of uptake of water in a cut shoot using a **potometer**.

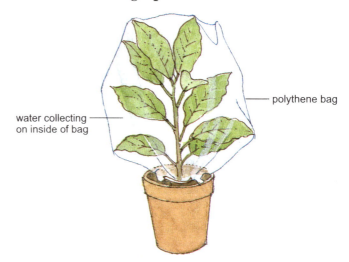

A demonstration of transpiration in a pot plant. A bag should also be secured over a pot of earth but no plant, to act as a control.

freshly-cut plant shoot

3-way tap

top of scale

capillary tube

bottom of scale with water meniscus

A potometer. The level of water gradually rises in the capillary tube, indicating water has been taken up by the plant shoot.

water collecting on inside of bag

polythene bag

Investigate the rate of transpiration

How might the following affect the rate of transpiration?

- temperature
- air humidity
- air movement.

1 Write down your hypothesis.
2 Design a way to test your hypothesis. Which variables will you change and which ones will you keep the same?
3 Show your plan to your teacher. You may be able to carry out your experiment yourself or your teacher may set it up for you.
4 Record your results. Were you able to find out if your hypothesis was correct?

Q1 Write a report on your experiment and be ready to share your findings with the rest of the class.

Q2 Describe and explain the effect of temperature, air humidity and air movement on transpiration.

Q3 Most plants close their stomatal pores at night. What effect does this have on transpiration? What benefits do you think this brings to the plant?

Adaptations for conserving water

Plants that grow in dry environments have developed some structural adaptations to minimise water loss.

This desert plant reduces water loss by storing water in its fleshy stem.

Organ Pipe cactus growing in hot, dry desert of Arizona. Water loss is reduced by having an epidermis with a thick, leathery cuticle.

Marram grass growing on sand dunes has a small surface area to reduce water loss.

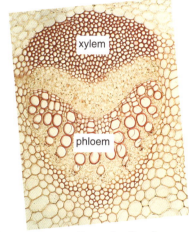

Transverse section of a Sunflower stem showing a vascular bundle, × 60.

Transport of substances

Substances are transported by **phloem**. Phloem cells are joined forming a tube, which runs close to xylem tissue. These two structures together form **vascular bundles**. The phloem tubes run the length of the plant through the stem. The cells that make up the phloem tubes differ from xylem vessel cells in several ways.

- Phloem cells are living, each containing cytoplasm and a nucleus.

- They have thin cell walls and a semi-permeable membrane.

- They carry substances both *up* and *down* the plant.

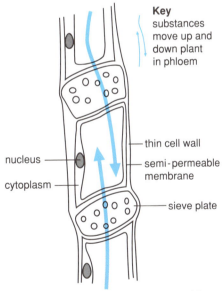

Key
substances move up and down plant in phloem

nucleus
cytoplasm

thin cell wall
semi-permeable membrane
sieve plate

Movement of substances in a phloem tube.

Chemicals such as **glucose** and **amino acids** made in the leaves are transported by the phloem to other regions in the plant for later use. The phloem cells use energy released during respiration to transport these chemicals. Transport in phloem tubes is an active process and is called **translocation**.

 Take notes

Draw a table to compare and contrast the structures and functions of xylem vessels and phloem tubes.

Project

Some house-plants need water more often than others. Do differences in leaf shape and structure affect the amount of water a plant needs?

Plant reproduction and growth

Plants are able to produce new individuals by two types of reproduction.

- **Asexual reproduction** — only one parent is needed, no gametes are involved and the offspring are genetically identical to the parent (clones).

- **Sexual reproduction** — usually two parents are needed, gametes are produced, fertilisation occurs and there is variation amongst offspring and between parents and offspring.

Asexual reproduction

This form of reproduction is also called **vegetative propagation** in plants.

In many cases the organs associated with asexual reproduction also serve as food stores. This food allows very rapid growth in Spring enabling the plant to flower and produce seeds before competition with other plants for water, mineral salts and light reaches a maximum. The potato is an economically important example of a **stem tuber**. As its name suggests the potato tuber is a special kind of underground stem.

Corms and **bulbs** are other types of underground stem storage organs from which buds and new shoots grow.

Collect

- crocus corm
- tulip bulb
- sharp knife or scalpel
- cutting tile

CARE!

Examine a corm and a bulb

1. Examine the crocus corm on the outside and compare it to the illustration on the left.
2. Slice the corm vertically through its centre. Make a clear drawing of what you see. Label as many parts as you can.
3. Examine the bulb on the outside, slice it vertically through its centre and compare it to the diagram (below left). Draw what you see. Label your drawing.

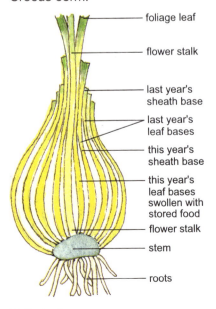

lateral bud will grow into independent plant

new corm forming as stem swells with stored food

scar left by last year's circular leaf base

roots

Crocus corm.

foliage leaf

flower stalk

last year's sheath base

last year's leaf bases

this year's sheath base

this year's leaf bases swollen with stored food

flower stalk

stem

roots

Tulip bulb.

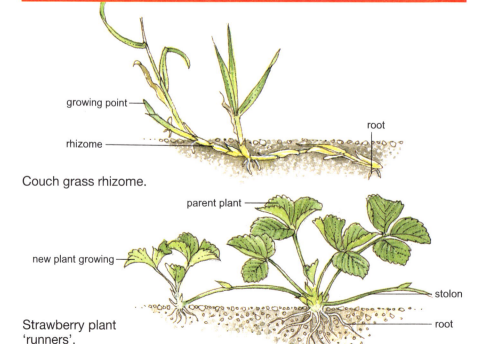

growing point

rhizome

root

Couch grass rhizome.

parent plant

new plant growing

stolon

root

Strawberry plant 'runners'.

Take a stem cutting

A stem has the ability to grow roots. It is possible to cut a piece from a stem and grow a new plant.

Your teacher will demonstrate the best way to take a cutting from the plants that are available to you.

Make your own cutting and look after it carefully over the coming weeks.

Sexual reproduction

Sexual reproduction involves two sex cells fusing to form a new cell. Sex cells are called **gametes**. Plants possess male and female gametes. The gametes are produced by the sex organs. The flowers are the reproductive structures on a plant. They contain the male organs called **stamens**, which produce pollen grains containing the male gametes, and the female organs called **carpels**, which house the ovary and ovules containing the female gametes.

Flowers that possess both male and female organs are called **hermaphrodites** (not all plants are hermaphrodites).

Sexual reproduction in plants can be divided into four stages.

1 Pollination
  The male pollen grains migrate from the **anthers**, where they are made, to the **stigma** (female part) of the same or different flower.

2 Fertilisation
  A male gamete from a pollen grain and a female gamete fuse (join).

3 Seed formation
  After fertilisation, an embryo forms and develops into a **seed**. The seed forms inside an ovary.

4 Dispersal
  Reproduction is complete when the seeds leave the ovary and are carried away from the parent plant.

 **Take notes**

Discuss with a partner and then explain in your own words:

- what is meant by asexual reproduction

- the different methods of asexual reproduction in plants.

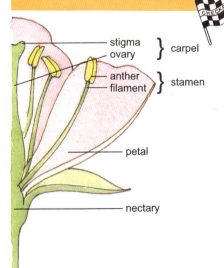

Schematic diagram to show the sexual reproductive organs of a flower.

Pollination

The anthers split open to release pollen grains. In **self-pollinating** plants, pollen that reaches the stigma comes from the same flower or another flower on the *same* plant. In **cross-pollination**, the pollen is carried from the anthers of one flower to the stigma in a flower on *another* plant of the same species.

Self-pollination
Insects usually bring about self-pollination of a flower by transferring pollen from the anther to the stigma in the same flower.

Cross-pollination by insects
Flying insects, for example bees, visit flowers to collect a sugary liquid called **nectar**, which is produced at the base of the flower. As a bee reaches for nectar, pollen grains from the flower's anthers stick to hairs on the insect and are then carried by the bee to the stigma of a flower on a different plant. Flowers that are pollinated by insects in this way have several adaptations to attract the insects and to aid pollen transfer.

The flower of Wild Sage being pollinated by a bee. Note the 'platform' petal.

- Nectar is produced.

- Flowers are large, scented and have brightly coloured petals.

- Pollen is produced in quite small quantities, but it is rough and sticky and large to help it stick to the hairs on an insect.

- Anthers are enclosed inside the flower to increase the chance of the insect brushing against them.

- Stigma is sticky so that pollen will not be dislodged once deposited by an insect.

- Sometimes the petals have a convenient shape for an insect's easy access, for example, one of the petals may form a 'platform'.

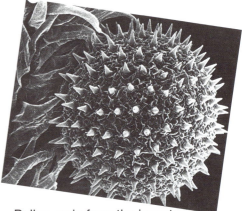

Pollen grain from the insect-pollinated Hollyhock flower showing 'spikes', × 340.

Cross-pollination by wind
The most common family of wind-pollinated plants is the **grass family**, which includes wheat, rice and maize. Many trees common to Britain such as birch, pine and willow are also wind pollinated. Most grasses flower in June and July in Britain. Wind-pollinated flowers also have several adaptations to help pollen transfer.

- Flowers are usually small and lack scent.

- Petals are insignificant and often colourless.

- Nectar is usually absent.

- Anthers dangling on long, hanging filaments allows the pollen to be scattered by wind.

- Stigmas are feathery and hang out of the flower to trap passing pollen being carried by wind.

- Pollen is dry and dusty and produced in large quantities (scattering to the wind is a wasteful process) and is much smaller and lighter than pollen produced by insect-pollinated flowers.

Wind dispersal of pollen from male flowers of the Silver Birch tree.

Fertilisation

Once the pollen grains have been deposited on the stigma during pollination, the process of fertilisation begins. The stigma is joined to the ovary by a solid stalk called the **style**. A pollen tube passes through the style reaching the ovule.

Seed formation

The single cell formed after the male and female gametes fuse during fertilisation is called a **zygote**. This zygote divides to form an **embryo**. There may be several developing embryos within one flower. Unfertilised ovules soon die and degenerate. Still embedded in the wall of the ovary, the embryo gradually develops into a seed. The seed contains the beginnings of the root, stem and leaves as well as a store of food that will be mobilised for use by the growing seed. When the seed is fully developed the ovary changes. In the pea plant it dries and shrivels. In soft fruits it swells and turns into an edible succulent fleshy fruit.

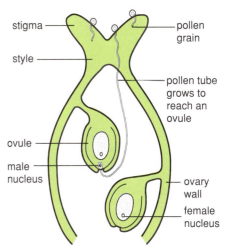

Fertilisation in a flower.

Mature seeds in a swollen ovary.

Collect
- resource sheet

1 Collect a resource sheet and draw and label the stigma, style and ovary on the diagram. Use the diagram on page 21 to help you.
2 Sort the sentences into the correct order to describe the process of fertilisation.

Dispersal

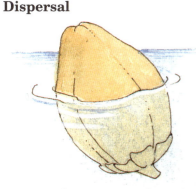

Coconut – water dispersal lightweight seed covered in a tough water-proof husk

Burdock – animal dispersal hooked bracts can attach to animal's fur

Sycamore – wind dispersal fruit 'wings' help seed to float on wind currents

Lupin – explosive dispersal as the ovary wall dries it splits open and ejects the seeds

Young plants have a better chance of reaching maturity if they begin their growth away from the parent plant.

Take notes

Define sexual reproduction and summarise the key steps involved when a flowering plant reproduces.

Project

Visit a garden and collect as many different seeds as you can find. Can you suggest how they were dispersed?

Collect

- revision sheet

Make sure that you understand the following terms:

- food chain
- primary producer
- consumer
- ecosystem
- herbivore
- carnivore
- biotic
- abiotic.

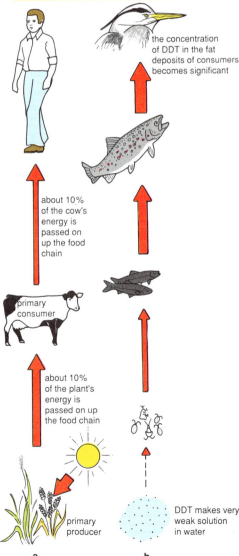

the concentration of DDT in the fat deposits of consumers becomes significant

about 10% of the cow's energy is passed on up the food chain

primary consumer

about 10% of the plant's energy is passed on up the food chain

primary producer

DDT makes very weak solution in water

a   b

Energy transfer (a) and DDT uptake (b) in food chains.

The start of the food chain

Plants are **primary producers**. They use energy trapped from sunlight to build **complex compounds** such as polysaccharides (sugars) and proteins from **simple compounds** such as carbon dioxide, water, nitrates, phosphates and other minerals. The plants use the complex compounds for growth.

The stored energy in these complex compounds is used in different ways. Respiration by the plant releases energy. A further small amount is transferred to other living animals that feed directly on plants. However, most plant material is not consumed. Instead it dies and is **decomposed** by small animals, fungi and bacteria known as **decomposers**. The decomposers harness the energy released during decomposition. The decomposers, in their turn, die and decompose. Energy transfer within food chains is very inefficient. Approximately 10% of the energy in plants is passed on to a **primary consumer**, which passes 10% of the energy from itself to a **secondary consumer** and so on.

If we interfere with this natural cycle using artificial fertilisers, pesticides, fungicides and other synthetic compounds, there may well be a detrimental effect on food chains and even the ecosystem.

Pesticides are used to control insects and agricultural pests. One pesticide that was in widespread use in many countries before the 1970s is dichloro-diphenyl-trichloroethane (**DDT**). It is now banned in the USA and Europe. DDT is a very effective **insecticide** (it kills insects) but has the disadvantage of being absorbed in small amounts by crop plants when applied by spray. The crop is then harvested. The amount of DDT in an individual plant is very small, but because consumers tend to eat large volumes of plant material, the amount of DDT taken up by them becomes quite significant. Another disadvantage of DDT is that it tends to remain in animal tissues, especially fat deposits, and therefore is not excreted easily. DDT is described as a **persistent insecticide** because it lasts a long time without breaking down. As we travel up the food chain the amount of pesticide in consumers increases. Near to the top of the food chain DDT may be present in the tissues in sufficient amounts to prove dangerous.

Take notes

Use flow diagrams to summarise how (a) energy and (b) complex compounds in organisms are transferred through the ecosystem. Can you identify the **biotic** (living or once-living) and **abiotic** (never-living) parts of your diagrams?

Make notes on how pesticides can become concentrated in a food chain.

The nitrogen cycle

Proteins are complex compounds needed by all living organisms and are made by joining simple molecules called amino acids. All amino acids contain nitrogen, carbon, hydrogen and oxygen, and some contain sulphur.

Plants obtain the nitrogen they need to make amino acids from the soil in the form of nitrate ions (NO_3^-) and ammonium ions (NH_4^+). When plants are eaten, the nitrogen in protein progresses further up the food chain. Decomposition of dead organic matter by decomposers releases nitrogen in the form of **ammonia** (NH_3) which is converted to ammonium ions (NH_4^+) and then back to nitrate ions by the action of **nitrifying bacteria** in the soil. Thus, the progression of nitrogen through the food chain is cyclical. Nitrogen compounds are also returned to the soil in faeces and urine.

Q1 Draw a cyclical flow diagram to summarise the information above.

Fertilisers usually contain nitrogen. Fertilisers can be used to increase the yield of crops because they provide plenty of nitrogen. We use fertilisers in an attempt to support the ever-increasing population of our planet. However, a larger proportion of nitrogen is then trapped in living organisms and is therefore unavailable to growing plants.

Nitrogen can enter the cycle in three other ways. The first is direct conversion of nitrogen gas in air to nitrate by **lightning**. The second is as a result of **leguminous plants**, members of the legume family. Examples of legumes are clover, pea and bean plants. In these plants nitrogen in air is converted to ammonia and ammonium compounds by the action of **nitrogen-fixing bacteria** contained in **nodules** (swellings) in the plants' roots. Legumes are very useful plants because they can be ploughed into and hence fertilise the soil.

The third is a result of a group of **nitrifying bacteria**, which produce ammonium compounds from nitrogen in air, for example *Nitrobacter spp.* and *Nitrosomonas spp.*

Direct conversion of nitrogen to ammonia or nitrate is called **nitrogen fixation**. This process is reversed by **denitrifying bacteria** such as *Pseudomonas denitrificans*, which break down nitrates in the soil to release nitrogen gas.

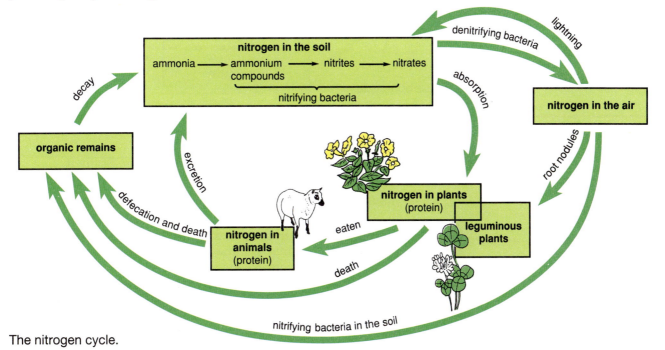

The nitrogen cycle.

Q2 Complete your flow diagram of the nitrogen cycle by drawing the three additional inputs of nitrogen described above.

Q3 Compare your nitrogen flow diagram with the cycle given above.

The carbon cycle

The element carbon is present in many compounds essential to life. Compounds that contain carbon are called **organic compounds**. Organic compounds can contain other elements as well, such as hydrogen, nitrogen and phosphorus. When organisms die and are decomposed they release carbon from carbon-containing compounds.

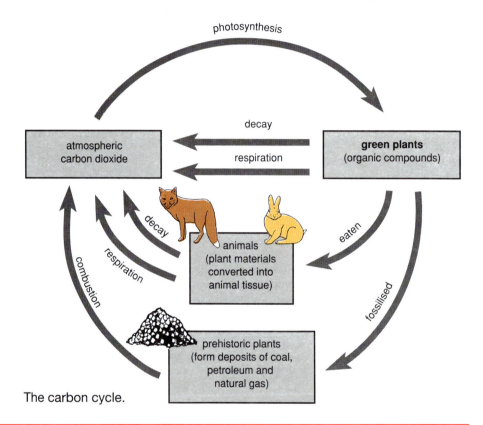

The carbon cycle.

The carbon cycle

The resource sheet shows an incomplete carbon cycle. Study it carefully.

Collect
- resource sheet
- coloured pencils

1 Write the following labels in the correct places: *photosynthesis*, *fossil fuels*, *eaten*, *primary producers*, *decomposition*.
2 Choose a colour and fill in the parts of the cycle that show carbon in biotic (living or once-living) parts of the cycle. Provide a key to the cycle, stating what your colour represents.
3 Use another colour to fill in the parts of the cycle which show carbon in abiotic (never-living) parts of the cycle. Add this to your key.
4 In a third colour, pick out the arrows indicating the build-up of carbon into more complex compounds. Add this to your key.
5 In a fourth colour, highlight the arrows that demonstrate the breakdown of complex carbon compounds to simple carbon compounds. Complete your key.

The greenhouse effect

Widespread destruction of tropical rainforests, with subsequent combustion of the trees, is thought to affect the carbon cycle. The burning of fossil fuels could also be affecting the cycle.

The three major rainforest areas (Congo, Amazon and Malaysia) have an area of 30 to 40 million square kilometres. This area of trees removes a significant amount of carbon dioxide from the air during photosynthesis. When large numbers of trees are felled less carbon dioxide is removed from the air.

Cleared sites provide areas for oil exploration platforms in the Amazonian rainforest of Ecuador.

Coal-fired power station at Didcot, Oxfordshire.

When the trees from the forests and also fossil fuels such as coal are burnt, carbon dioxide is released into the air. We therefore seem to have two processes, the combined effect of which is to raise the level of carbon dioxide in air. The carbon dioxide in the air has an **insulating** (or greenhouse) effect on the Earth. Carbon dioxide reflects the infra red (heat) radiating from the Earth's surface, so an increase in carbon dioxide leads to an increase in temperature. Although this temperature increase is estimated to be very slight, the **global warming** caused by the greenhouse effect is expected to raise the temperature of our oceans and atmosphere and possibly cause a proportion of polar ice caps to melt. On present trends the amount of carbon dioxide will have doubled by the year 2080, though some scientists believe it may double in 40 years.

If this does indeed take place, the level of the oceans will rise. Some people predict the rise to be several centimetres. This is enough to cause serious flooding to low-lying continents. The consequences of flooding are far-reaching and serious. Plant, animal and human life would all suffer.

The effects of global warming are also predicted to cause climatic alterations, including a change in wind patterns, and change in the pattern of water circulation in the atmosphere, and thus a change in our precipitation (rainfall) pattern over the whole world.

 *Take notes*

How do you think polar ice cap melting and widespread flooding could affect the water cycle?

What part does vegetation play in the water cycle?

Project

Collect newspaper articles written about the greenhouse effect and global warming and make a resource file. Do people agree on the causes of global warming?

Problem

A plant bending towards the light.

Dwarf Pea seedlings grown in the light (left), and dark (right).

Differently pigmented leaves.

How does a plant grow?

1 Plan an experiment to find out about one of the following:
   - how plants respond to a change in the direction of light
   - which wavelength of light (colour of light) or combination of wavelengths cause photosynthesis to take place at a high rate
   - how darkness affects growth in plants
   - if an increase in the carbon dioxide level surrounding a plant produces a better plant
   - the effect on the rate of germination of seeds which have been pretreated at varying temperatures
   - if plants of a different species have the same kind of chlorophyll or pigments.
2 If you can think of a different investigation of the factors which affect plant growth, do so. Then discuss your idea with your teacher before beginning.
3 Write your plan. You will need to think about:
   - the precise working of your hypothesis (the idea you want to test)
   - what is likely to happen and the scientific reasons why
   - the kind of plant material to use
   - what variables to control (keep the same)
   - what variable(s) to change
   - what measurements to take to test your hypothesis
   - how to make your measurements fair.
4 Discuss your plan with your teacher who will give you advice on suitable apparatus or materials to use and encourage you to think about your plan critically.

the spectrum of electromagnetic radiation

radio waves	microwaves	infra red (heat)	V I S I B L E	ultra-violet	X-rays	gamma rays

10^2 10^{-0} 10^{-2} 10^{-4} 10^{-6} 10^{-8} 10^{-10}

750   700   600   500

the spectrum of visible light

Spectrums of electromagnetic radiation and visible light.

Talkabout

Bales of waste paper await recycling.

Deforestation

There is much concern felt about the loss of forests in many parts of the world. Perhaps most worry centres on the destruction of tropical rainforest in South America. At present, the rainforests occupy an area about 60 times the total area of England, Scotland and Wales. But an area of rainforest about the size of Britain is being cleared every year. Within your lifetime the rainforests could be destroyed completely. Nobody knows for certain what the effects of this would be on our planet.

As in most situations, we should not forget to think about the 'other side' to this problem. The local people who live near to the rainforests need to find employment to be able to support themselves and their families. Often, the tree-felling companies offer the only possibilities of employment. The local people also practise 'slash and burning' of the trees on a small scale. This provides them with a clearing where they can build dwellings and begin to cultivate food crops and graze livestock.

The situation is very complicated, involving many factors. You should try to think of other factors that may affect the situation — what about the economics of the countries where the rainforests grow, the profits of the multinational felling companies and the existence of the indigenous (native) population of the affected countries?

'Slash and burning' of rainforest.

Erosion after forest felling.

Felling a tree with a hand axe.

Q1 Why are the forests being cleared?

Q2 Besides the vegetation, what else will be lost?

Q3 How does the vegetation affect the soil?

Q4 What happens to the soil after the forests have been cleared?

Q5 How might deforestation affect the global climate?

Q6 How can such destruction be stopped?

1 A student was asked to find if plants need light to make starch. She was given a potted plant which had been kept in a dark cupboard for 48 hours. She covered part of the leaf with aluminium foil as shown in the diagram below.

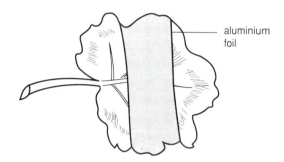

a Why did she cover part of the leaf with aluminium foil? [1]

b The student left the plant in bright sunlight for four hours. Then she took the leaf off the plant, removed the foil, and tested the leaf for starch.

  i Name the solution which is used to test for starch. [1]

  ii The diagram below shows the leaf after the starch test.

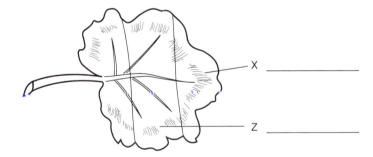

    Copy the figure and label the colours of parts X and Z *after* the test. [2]

c Write a conclusion for the student's experiment. [1]

d Copy and complete the following word equation for photosynthesis.

    ___ + water → sugar + ___

    [2]

Total [7]
(*NEA 1992 The Sciences*)

3 The diagram shows a cell from the epidermis of an onion bulb. The epidermis is in sugar solution.

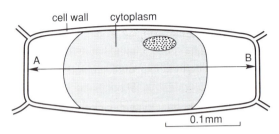

a Before the cell was put in the sugar solution the cytoplasm filled the cell.

  i Explain why the cytoplasm has shrunk in the sugar solution. [3]

  ii Use the scale to work out how much the cytoplasm has shrunk in length along the line AB. (Show your working and give your answer in mm.) [2]

b The figure shows leaves from four types of tree.

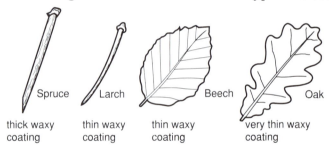

A similar mass of leaves from each tree was weighed. The leaves were hung up separately in a laboratory for 30 minutes. They were then reweighed. The loss in mass from each type of leaf is shown in the table.

Type of leaf	Loss in mass (g)
Spruce	1.0
Larch	1.3
Beech	3.8
Oak	5.1

Explain why the leaves lost different amounts of mass. [2]

c The investigation was repeated with the leaves in a more humid atmosphere.

  i How would this affect the loss in mass? [1]

  ii Explain why. [1]

Total [9]
(*NEA 1992 Biology*)

2

Sound and music

Waves

Energy can be moved from one place to another as waves. There are two kinds of waves, **transverse** and **longitudinal**.

Collect

- Slinky spring

Demonstrate transverse and longitudinal waves

1 Stretch the Slinky spring along the bench.
2 Give one end a quick shake at right angles to the spring. This produces a transverse wave. An example of a transverse energy wave is **light**.

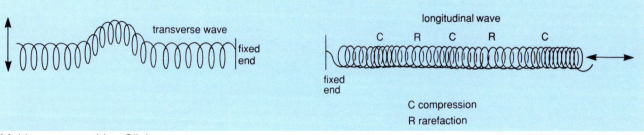

Making waves with a Slinky.

A longitudinal wave.

3 Stretch the spring out again.
4 Give one end a quick shake to and fro along the length of the spring. This produces a longitudinal wave. An example of a longitudinal energy wave is **sound**.
5 Use the Slinky to make more longitudinal waves and look carefully at the distances between the spring coils. At any one time during the wave:
   - parts of the spring are pushed together, called **compression**
   - parts of the spring are pulled farther apart, called **rarefaction**.
6 Try to change the distance between each compression.
7 Now try to count the number of compressions that pass along the Slinky in a given time.

When a sound wave passes through air, in a similar way to the Slinky model, some air molecules are pushed closer together and in some places the molecules are pulled farther apart. These compressions and rarefactions reach your ear and set up vibrations in your eardrum enabling you to hear.

A particular type of sound we call music is also produced by regular vibrations of air. The faster the vibration (in other words, the higher the frequency) the higher the sound. Musicians use the word **pitch** to describe how high or low a note is within the audible range.

When a guitar string is plucked it vibrates to produce sound. The pitch is changed by tightening the string or reducing the length of the part that vibrates. The thickness of the string also affects the rate of vibration.

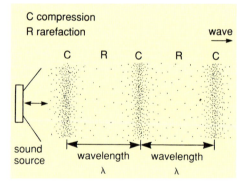

A sound wave in air.

The **wavelength** of a sound wave is the distance between two successive compressions. The number of vibrations every second is termed the **frequency**. The unit of frequency is the hertz (Hz).

Q1 Write a report of your investigation using the Slinky.

Q2 How did you change the wavelength and the frequency?

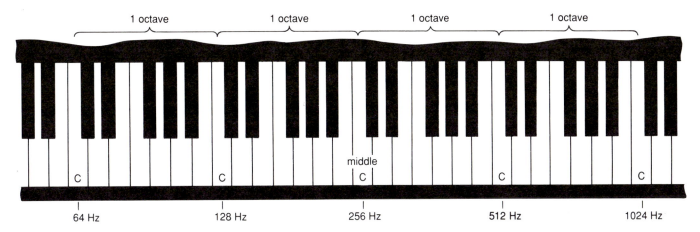

Each time the frequency doubles the pitch goes up one octave.

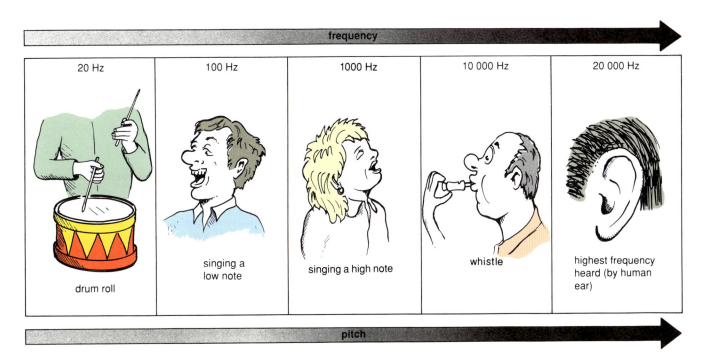

Examples of the range of frequencies we can hear.

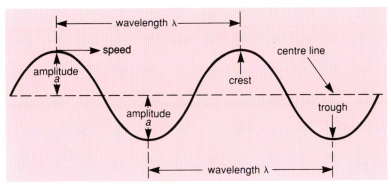

Wavelength and amplitude.

A **cathode ray oscilloscope** (CRO) can be used to investigate sound waves. A longitudinal sound wave is changed into an electrical signal and shown as a transverse wave. As well as measuring the wavelength and frequency we can measure the **amplitude** of the wave. This is the height of a crest or the depth of a trough measured from a centre line.

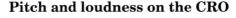

Pitch and loudness on the CRO

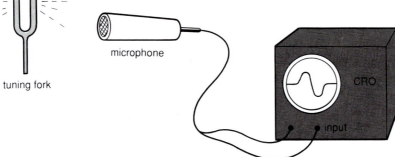

Collect

- CRO
- microphone
- tuning forks (2)
- connecting wires

1 Connect the microphone to the CRO using the connecting wires.
2 Hold a vibrating tuning fork near to the microphone as shown in the diagram. Observe the wave shown on the CRO screen.
3 Use the apparatus to find out what happens to the wavelength and amplitude of the wave shown on the screen when the following are held near to the microphone:
   - high-pitch tuning fork
   - low-pitch tuning fork
   - loud sound
   - soft sound.

tuning fork

microphone

CRO

input

Q1 What happens to the wavelength when different tuning forks are used?

Q2 What happens to the amplitude of the wave when a soft sound compared to a loud sound is held near to the microphone?

SHARK! SHARK!

Sound waves cannot travel through a vacuum because there are no molecules to transfer the energy of the waves. Sound waves travel faster through solids than liquids and faster through liquids than gases. For example, if you are swimming underwater, you will hear a sound earlier than you would if your head were above water. This is because the sound waves travel faster in water than in air. The **speed** of a sound wave is related to its wavelength and its frequency and can be represented by the following equation.

$$\text{speed} = \text{frequency} \times \text{wavelength}$$
$$\text{m/s} \qquad \text{Hz} \qquad \text{m}$$

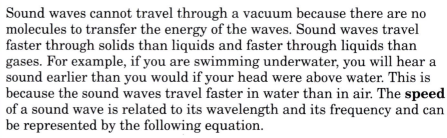

Example

The speed of sound in air is approximately 340 m/s.

What is the wavelength of a sound wave that has a frequency of 170 Hz?
   speed = frequency × wavelength
   340 = 170 × wavelength
   wavelength = 340/170 m
                    = 2 m

The speed of sound

Find the speed of sound in air

1 Connect the loudspeaker to the sweep output of the CRO.
2 Connect the microphone to the Y input and set this at the most sensitive level.
3 Set the time base on the CRO to one millisecond.

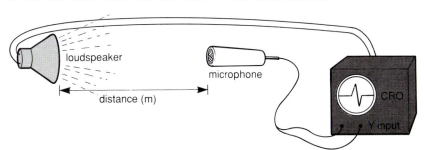

4 A dot sweeps very fast across the screen and a whining sound is produced at the loudspeaker. The microphone picks up this sound. Watch the screen and compare what you observe with the diagram.
5 Measure distance t on the CRO screen and work out the time taken for the sound wave to travel to the microphone.
6 Repeat the experiment several times, placing the microphone at a different distance from the loudspeaker each time.

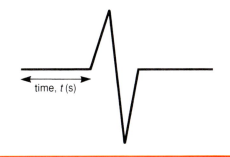

Q1 Write a description of how you did the experiment. Record your results in a table.

Q2 Plot a graph with distance on the vertical axis and time on the horizontal axis. Find the gradient (slope) of the graph, which will give a value of the speed of sound in air under the conditions of your experiment.

Q3 The speed of sound in air is approximately 340 m/s. If a clap of thunder is heard 10 seconds after a lightning flash, approximately how far away is the storm?

Calculating the gradient of a graph

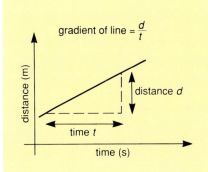

gradient of line = $\dfrac{d}{t}$

Take notes

Write notes on the following:
- two wave types and their differences
- how the energy of a wave travels in air
- a wave diagram, labelling wavelength and amplitude
- how the medium through which a sound wave is travelling can affect its speed.

Project

Find out about dog whistles and how they work.

Making music

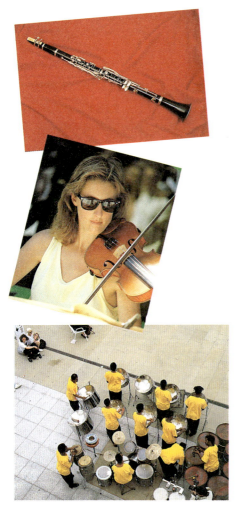

Different sounds

The instruments in an orchestra can be divided into three groups: string, wind or percussion. The groups are based on the method used to produce vibrations, leading to sound waves. We have learnt that music is the name given to sound produced by regular vibrations. A musical note has three properties — pitch, loudness and quality.

The vibrations produced by instruments can be simple or complicated, leading to pure or not so pure notes. A tuning fork has a simple vibration pattern and produces a very pure note but most other instruments do not. Simultaneous (at the same time) vibrations at different frequencies occur, which produce complicated vibrations and impure notes.

The dominating frequency of a mixture of vibrations is known as the **fundamental frequency**. The other frequencies of vibrations are exact multiples of the fundamental and are known as **overtones**. This is shown in the diagram of the vibrating guitar string below.

fundamental wavelength   1st overtone   2nd overtone

N = node

Vibrations are set up when the strings of a violin or cello are stroked with a bow or plucked. A column of air inside a clarinet or trumpet vibrates when blown, and percussion instruments such as drums or cymbals vibrate when struck.

Overtones can be pleasant or unpleasant and a good musician knows how to reduce the bad overtones and strengthen the good ones. The vast variety of popular music available today is a good example to indicate that overtones are a matter of personal taste! Not all instruments produce the same overtones, which is why they sound different. The wave pattern for a piano and violin playing the same note can be compared with the pattern of the fundamental node produced by a tuning fork. They all have the same fundamental shape but the violin has more overtones than the piano.

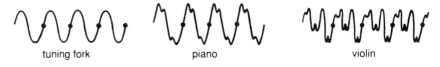

tuning fork   piano   violin

A guitar string does not produce loud music when it is plucked. However, if an **amplifier** is attached to the strings the sound produced is louder. A hollow wooden box on which the guitar strings are mounted acts as the amplifier.

When a guitar string is plucked it vibrates at a **natural frequency**. This vibration is enhanced (increased) by the box and the air inside it vibrating at the same frequency. The effect is called **resonance**.

Many instruments in addition to stringed instruments use resonance. The note from a wind instrument such as the clarinet or trumpet originates from vibrations of the length of air inside the instrument.

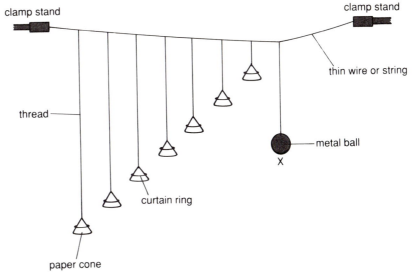

Collect

- thin wire or string
- clamp stands (2)
- thread
- paper cones (7)
- curtain rings (7)
- small metal ball

Barton's pendulums

Investigating what happens when a heavy pendulum is set swinging.

1 Working in groups, set up the apparatus as shown in the diagram.
2 Write down what you expect to happen when you start pendulum X swinging. (Write your own hypothesis.)
3 Set pendulum X swinging.
4 What do you observe? How do the other pendulums swing compared to pendulum X? Which of the pendulums is in resonance with it?
5 Can you explain your observations?

Collect

- plastic tube (80 cm)
- tuning forks (1 set)
- water
- bung
- tube
- clip
- ruler

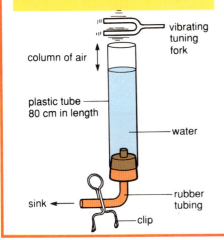

Investigate a column of air using a resonance tube

1 Working in groups, set up the apparatus as shown in the diagram.
2 Fill the tube with water.
3 Starting with the tuning fork of highest frequency, strike the fork, and hold it vibrating near to the open end of the tube.
4 Slowly let out the water by releasing the clip a little until the sound becomes much louder.
5 Close the clip and measure the length of the column of air in the tube.
6 Continue to let out the water to detect if there are any other heights of the air column where the sound peaks.
7 Repeat with the other four tuning forks.
8 Plot a graph of the air column lengths against frequency.
9 Comment on your graph.

Q1 For each tuning fork, what is the wavelength of the fundamental note and any overtones you observed?

Disadvantages of resonance

Most objects can vibrate and we have seen that each has a natural frequency at which it vibrates most easily.

If a glass is tapped gently with a spoon it will vibrate and give off a certain note. A singer who sings exactly this note can provide enough energy to make the glass resonate until it shatters!

Resonance in mechanical objects is quite common. A washing machine can vibrate so much at certain speeds that it moves across the floor. Many cars vibrate noticeably at one particular speed.

Earthquakes cause waves with a range of frequencies. When these match the natural frequency of tall buildings or bridges the damage can be very severe (even in the event of quite mild earthquakes).

In 1940 the Tacoma Narrows Bridge, in Washington State, USA, was destroyed. The wind was blowing in gusts which had the same frequency as the natural frequency of the bridge. The bridge eventually began to resonate with sufficient energy to destroy itself.

Helpful sound

Ultrasound is the term used to describe sound waves that have a frequency above 20 kHz.

Bats use ultrasound to judge distance. They emit high-pitched squeaks (which humans cannot hear) and measure how long it takes for the noise to bounce back after reflection off an object.

Ultrasound is used in industry to detect flaws in welded joints. An ultrasound scanner emits signals that bounce off the object. A computer interprets the return signals and details any faults. Ultrasound can also be used for cleaning objects such as street lamp covers. The covers are placed in a container of water that has an ultrasound vibrator in its base. Ultrasonic vibrators contain quartz crystals that can be set to vibrate at a particular frequency, and clean the lamp covers.

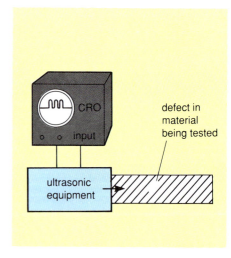

Ultrasound being used to check for faults in a material.

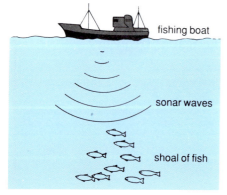

Ships use ultrasonic sonar equipment to measure the depth of the sea or to detect the whereabouts of shoals of fish.

Ultrasound glasses have been designed to aid blind people. As well as emitting ultrasound they contain a receiver that changes the return signal to one that can be heard by the wearer.

Sound is also used by geologists in their hunt for minerals. An explosion or large weight impacting on the Earth's surface transmits sound waves underground into the rock layers. The sound waves are reflected back from the layers at different depths from the Earth's surface. These sound waves are detected by surface instruments and interpreted by a computer. Different layers can be identified because, as we have learnt, sound travels faster through more dense materials (see page 34) and this can give clues to the minerals that may be present. This process is called **seismic surveying.**

The use of ultrasound in medicine is discussed on page 130.

Noise

The **intensity** (volume or loudness) of sound waves is measured in **decibels**. Zero decibel is the smallest change in air pressure that the human ear can detect and is called the **threshold** level. The original unit was the bel, named after the Scot, Alexander Graham Bell (1847–1922) who invented the telephone. The bel is a large unit so decibels (dB) (1/10 bel) are usually used to be able to quantify quieter sound waves. With the threshold level equal to zero dB, a sound ten times louder is 10 dB, one hundred times louder is 20 dB, one thousand times louder is 30 dB. This is because the decibel scale is **logarithmic**.

Q1 What is the threshold level on the decibel scale?

Q2 How many decibels is a sound 10 000 times the threshold level?

Damage to hearing can be caused not only by the intensity of sound waves but also by the *duration* of exposure to the sound waves. Sound waves above 140 dB, heard even for a short time interval, are painful and can cause permanent damage to the ear. Someone using a pneumatic drill, which has a sound level of 90 dB, over a period of time without wearing ear protectors may suffer a permanent loss of up to 25% of their hearing ability.

We use different materials to reduce noise levels. People who live under aeroplane flight paths may have sound insulation fitted to their windows. Double glazing with a 15 cm gap and heavy curtains provide effective insulation against noise. However, many people argue that modern aircraft should be designed to reduce the intensity of noise they emit. For people who live near to motorways, high banks, barriers and trees help to reduce noise levels.

Machinery often vibrates because of its moving parts. The vibrations are passed on to the surrounding casing, which acts to amplify the sound waves as they pass to the air. The level of noise could be reduced if the vibrations passing to the casing were stopped.

Decibel levels of everyday sounds.

A screen erected beside a road helps reduce noise.

 Take notes

Discuss sound and music with a partner and then make notes.

Include the key words shown in bold in your notes. Flow diagrams or spider diagrams could add interest to your notes.

Project

Using suitable reference sources (perhaps you could write to your local airport), find out the size of the area around an airport affected by excess noise and what steps are taken to reduce it.

Audio systems

Sound does not travel very far along a wire, so how is it that we can speak to someone on the other side of the world by telephone?

The telephone is, simply, a **transducer**. A transducer converts a non-electrical energy, such as sound, to an electrical signal. Electrical signals can be transmitted over great distances.

The parts in a telephone carry out four main functions.
1 A microphone containing a diaphragm transduces a sound to electrical signals.
2 A source of energy amplifies the signals.
3 The signals are transmitted.
4 A receiver changes the signals to sound.

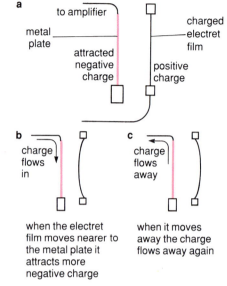

Sound waves vibrate the electret film in the microphone producing electric signals.

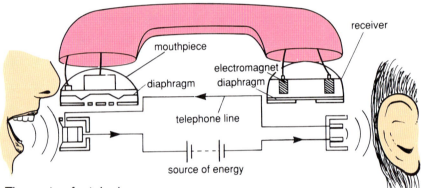

The parts of a telephone.

Microphone
When a person speaks into a microphone, sound waves set up vibrations in a **diaphragm** (thin sheet). This movement produces electrical signals.

Older telephones have a carbon microphone, which responds to frequencies below 4 kHz only. More recent telephones use electret microphones. These use factory-charged plastic film.

There are different types of microphone available. One of the most popular is a **moving coil microphone**. It responds well to the full range of frequencies that we can hear.

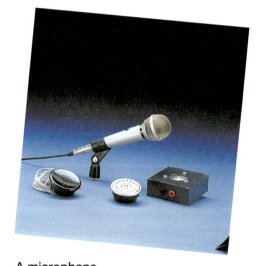

A microphone.

Mobile satellite dish.

Energy source
When energy travels from one place to another there is always some energy dissipated (lost). It is necessary to install **energy boosters** or amplifiers to overcome this problem.

Transmitter
For many years copper wire has been used to transmit electrical signals produced by a microphone. A disadvantage of copper wire is that it has a degree of electrical resistance, resulting in energy loss between emitting and receiving the signal. **Optical fibres** and light are being used to replace copper wire and electrical impulses. The energy loss is much reduced. Satellites, which use radio waves and microwaves, have an even higher efficiency.

Receiver

A receiver changes electrical signals to sound. The receiver works due to the **motor effect**. The changing current, produced by the electrical signal, flows through a coil. The coil moves within a strong magnetic field produced by a permanent magnet. The coil is connected to a diaphragm, which vibrates due to the movement of the coil. This sends out a compression wave that results in sound waves that are a copy of those that first entered the microphone.

Loudspeakers are a type of receiver and are available in a range of sizes for different frequencies. Most hi-fi speaker units contain more than one loudspeaker.

One potential problem in the use of loudspeakers is that at low frequencies sound waves have a long wavelength and tend to 'bend' around corners more easily than at the higher frequencies. If this happens within a speaker box, the compressions and rarefactions cancel out and no sound is heard. This is overcome by surrounding the speaker with absorbent material.

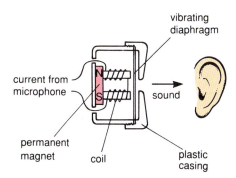

The receiver.

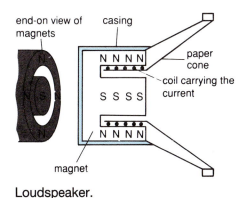

Loudspeaker.

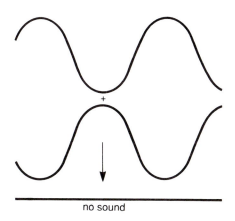

Compressions in one wave and rarefactions in another cancel each other.

In a **headphone set** each earpiece contains a very small loudspeaker. Despite their size the speakers can produce enough energy to damage a person's eardrum permanently and should be used with care. As a rough guide, if another person near to you can hear your music playing on a personal stereo system, the music is too loud!

Stereo hi-fi system.

Compare tape recordings

Design an experiment to compare tape recordings using different kinds of microphone.

What variables should you keep constant? How will you compare the quality of the recordings? Carry out the experiment.

Collect
- microphone (3 types)
- audio tapes
- tape recorder

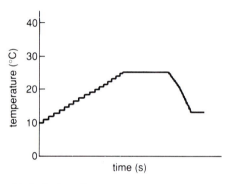

Analogue signal.

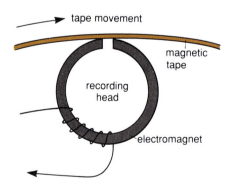

Digital signal.

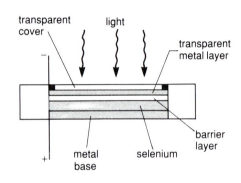

A photocell.

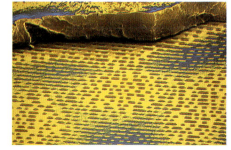

The recording head in a tape recorder.

Analogue or digital?

From whatever source, sound waves start as a continuously changing signal. This is called an **analogue signal**.

Analogue signals cannot be used by computers and microelectronic systems because the systems only respond to numbers. The systems process data digitally.

A **digital system** is based on just two numbers, 0 and 1. This is called a **binary system**.

Music can be recorded using either analogue or digital systems on a vinyl disc, compact disc (CD), tape or film sound track.

The sound track of a film is an analogue recording using different densities of light, which match different sounds. When the film is projected the pattern of light is read by a **photocell**, which converts the light to electrical current and then to a copy of the sound waves used in making the film. A photocell reacts to different light densities by producing a varying current of electricity.

Audio tape is a very thin piece of plastic coated with a magnetic material. A recording head in a tape recorder has a tiny electromagnet which magnetises the tape. The original sound waves are transduced to a varying electric current running through the coil. A small magnetic field is set up around the recording head that changes as the current changes. These changes affect the magnetic material on the tape and a 'copy' of the changes is made. The playback head produces a varying current that is amplified and passed to a loudspeaker. The tapes we buy in shops are analogue. Record companies use a digital recording system on special wide tape to record music.

The grooves on a vinyl record are 'copies' of the original sound. As the record turns the needle follows the groove. This movement sets up a varying electric current that passes through an amplifier and then to a loudspeaker where it is changed to sound waves.

A digital system is used to record on to a CD. Numbers are stored on the disc as a series of very small holes or pits, which are only about a millionth of a metre in diameter. A strong laser beam is used to make the holes. The disc is then coated in a silver compound to make it reflective and is 'read' by a weaker laser beam. Each disc contains millions of pits making it possible to store a large amount of information. It is now possible to buy CDs with both sound and pictures stored on them although they are very expensive!

Surface of a CD magnified to show pits.

Q1 What are the advantages of CDs?

Most modern communication systems are being developed to use digital codes. Analogue information, such as music, speech or pictures, must be converted to numbers using a digital code. The numbers are sent through a medium using a **carrier** and picked up using a **receiver**.

Sensors can be used to measure such variables as temperature or pH. They are analogue systems, producing electric voltages, which can have any value. If a sensor inputs to a computer (which reads digital codes only) the analogue signal needs to be converted to binary numbers. A device called an **analogue-to-digital converter** (ADC) is fitted. The output from the computer is often an analogue device (for example, a lamp) so a **digital-to-analogue converter** (DAC) is fitted also.

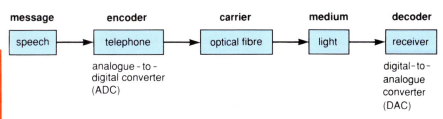

message	encoder	carrier	medium	decoder
speech	telephone	optical fibre	light	receiver
	analogue - to - digital converter (ADC)			digital - to - analogue converter (DAC)

Using a computer to study sound waves

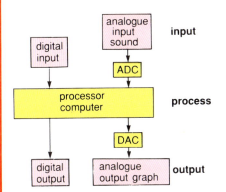

Investigate waveforms of musical instruments

A detailed representation of a note from an instrument can be obtained on a computer screen.

The ADC converts the sound waves produced by an instrument into digital signals which can be interpreted by a computer.

A computer contains a DAC which shows the characteristics of the sound wave on a screen.

1 Either obtain a printout from a computer or sketch some of the waveforms that you observe on the screen.
2 How do the shapes of the waveforms vary for different instruments?

Compare digital and analogue signals

Connect a tape recorder to an oscilloscope.

1 Speak into the microphone. Sketch the waveform you see on the screen.
2 Play a computer tape. Sketch the waveform shown on the screen.

 *Take notes*

Write a short summary on the main topics. Include in your notes:

- how microphones and loudspeakers work
- a comparison of digital and analogue systems
- examples of different types of communication.

Q1 What are the main differences between analogue and digital systems?

 *Project*

How are microwaves used in communication systems?

Decisions, decisions

Microelectronics is an important area of science and engineering. The benefits of microelectronic systems can be seen all around us. Over the last 40 years improved technology has lead to smaller and cheaper radios, televisions, computers and many other everyday items.

The block diagram on the left does not give any information on the role of electronics in the system. A **system** consists of a set of electronic devices, which can be represented in the form of a block diagram. A **decision block** is included to represent the microelectronic part of the system.

Here is an example of a very simple system.

The arrows connecting each block represent a directional flow of electronic information between each block. Other blocks can be added to the diagram.

The decision part of a system is used to process an input signal. For example:

- a **transistor** can switch objects on or off
- a **logic gate** can be used to control part or all of a system
- an **amplifier** can make signals larger.

Q1 Give an example of three microelectronic components that have an electric equivalent.

The transistor as a switch or an amplifier

Transistors form the basic building blocks of microelectronics.

They were invented in the 1950s and since this date, improved technology has made it possible for them to be made smaller and smaller. They are made from specially treated silicon or germanium, which are **semi-conductors** (a semi-conductor conducts electrons only under certain conditions).

A transistor can be used alone or as part of an **integrated circuit** (a circuit containing different components). Many thousands of integrated circuits can be packed into a single **microchip**.

Transistors act as fast switches and as amplifiers.

Modern radios contain several transistors which amplify the current until it is large enough to operate a loudspeaker.

transistor

resistor

light emitting diode (LED)

thermistor

loudspeaker

variable resistor (rheostat)

Symbols for components.

Electronic components.

Collect

- electronics kit

CARE!
Check the connections are correct before switching the transistor on

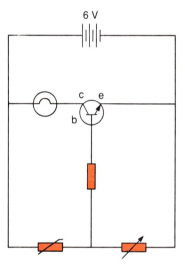

6 V

Investigate the action of transistors

1 Set up the apparatus as shown in the circuit diagram. Ensure that the correct connections are made to the transistor to avoid damaging it.

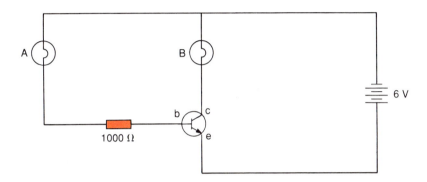

a Comment on the brightness of the lamps.
b Unscrew lamp A and note what happens.
c Replace lamp A and note the brightness again.
d What is happening to the current through lamp B?
e Draw a block or systems diagram to show what happens.

2 A resistor in which the resistance decreases as the temperature increases is called a **thermistor**. Connect a thermistor and a variable resistor to a transistor as shown in the circuit diagram.
a Adjust the resistor until the lamp is just emitting light.
b Heat the resistor with your fingers, a hair dryer or a candle. Note what happens to the lamp.
c What happens when the positions of the thermistor and the variable resistor are exchanged?

Q1 The block diagram on the right can be drawn to represent the circuit used in activity (2).
Draw a block diagram to show what happens if the thermistor is replaced by a photocell. Draw a circuit diagram to represent your drawing and predict what happens if light is shone onto the photocell. How could this circuit be used as a burglar alarm?

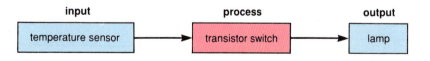

input	process	output
temperature sensor	transistor switch	lamp

There are other switches operated electrically, such as **relays** and **reed switches**, but using transistors as switches has advantages. The transistors can switch on and off millions of times a second, they last a long time, they have no moving parts and they are small, cheap and reliable.

Q2 For each of the circuits in the activity, is the transistor acting as a switch or an amplifier?

Q3 Why are transistors so widely used?

Transistors are also used as switches in digital watches, pocket calculators, computers and telecommunication systems.

Logic gates

Electronic circuits often contain arrangements of switches called **logic gates**.

Logic circuits are most useful when they are made from transistors packed in an **integrated circuit** (IC). However, logic circuits can be built using electrical components to show how they behave.

The following circuit is very simple.

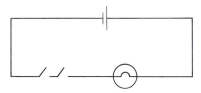

This is the kind of circuit found in a microwave oven. It will only operate if both the power switch is on AND the oven door is closed. This is an **AND gate**. A table, called a **truth table**, is often used to show what will happen at the output for all possible inputs of a logic gate.

Truth table for an AND gate
0 = OFF   1 = ON

A	B	C
INPUT A	INPUT B	OUTPUT
0	0	0
1	0	0
0	1	0
1	1	1

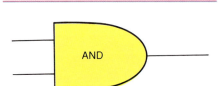

Symbol for AND gate.

Microwave oven.

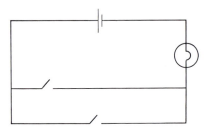

Circuit using OR gate.

At a level crossing, lights begin to flash if a train is coming from the left OR the right. This is an **OR gate**.

Truth table for an OR gate
0=off 1=on

A	B	C
INPUT A	INPUT B	OUTPUT
0	0	0
1	0	1
0	1	1
1	1	1

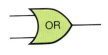

Symbol for OR gate.

Level crossing.

Automatic parking light.

The most simple gate is the **NOT gate**. This has only one input and the gate reverses the input signal. A simple automatic parking light (which comes on when it is dark) is operated by a NOT gate. If there is NOT enough light reaching the **light dependent resistor** (LDR) the bulb lights.

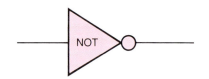

Symbol for NOT gate.

Collect

- electronics kit

Make a parking light

1 Design a circuit similar to that in activity (2) on page 45, connecting an LDR in place of the thermistor. Remember the LDR must light up in the dark but not the light.
2 Draw a circuit diagram.
3 Explain how the circuit acts as a NOT gate.
4 Draw a truth table for a NOT gate.

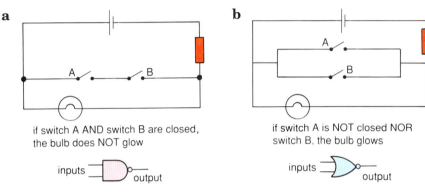

if switch A AND switch B are closed, the bulb does NOT glow

inputs — output

if switch A is NOT closed NOR switch B, the bulb glows

inputs — output

Circuit and symbol for (a) NAND gate and (b) NOR gate.

Q1 Gates can be combined. An AND gate with a NOT makes a **NAND gate**. Combining an OR gate with a NOT gate gives a **NOR gate**. Write down a truth table for each gate.

Q2 For each gate say what happens to the output when:
a both inputs are ON
b both inputs are OFF
c only one input is ON.

Bistable circuits

An electric light switch can be switched either ON or OFF. It stays in one state unless switched to the other. It can be described as a **bistable switch** — it is stable in either of two states.

In electronics a bistable switch can be made from two NAND gates.

The circuit can store information. It 'remembers' or 'latches' on to the last change made to it. It can also be called a **latch**, and is used in computer memories.

Q3 What type of logic gate is used for the switching circuit in an automatic kettle?

Q4 Draw a logic gate circuit diagram for a baby alarm. Draw its truth table.

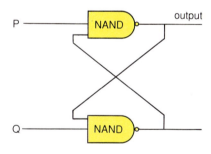

A bistable switch.

Q5 Give another name for a 'latch' and state what it might be used for.

Q6 What does bistable mean?

Take notes

Include in your notes:
- why microelectronics is important
- how transistors work
- types and uses of logic gates.

Project

Choose one of the devices mentioned in this topic. Find out how its design has changed over the last 20 years.

The capacity to store electricity

In 1746 Peter van Musschenbroek tried to electrify the water in a jar. By accident he discovered that the charge could be stored in the jar. This was the first **capacitor** and he called it a Leiden jar after his home town of Leiden in Holland.

Capacitors are devices which can store small quantities of charge. They are used extensively in electronic circuits in radios, televisions, record players and hi-fi systems.

Capacitors are usually made from two metal plates. When one plate is charged the other plate gains an equal and opposite charge. The plates are separated by an insulating material. A change of current can be transferred through a capacitor but a continuous current is prevented from flowing. Capacitors can also be used to make electrons oscillate (flow backwards or forwards between the plates). This oscillating effect can be used in a signal generator.

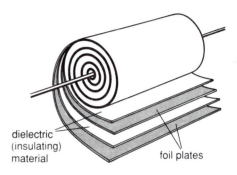

A capacitor made from two metal plates separated by insulating material.

Collect

- electronics kit
- earphones (2 × 21 kHz)
- battery (1.5 bias)
- potential divider (6 kHz, 50 kHz)
- input capacitor (5 μF)
- microphone
- CRO

CARE!
Set up the circuit as shown. Too much voltage will discharge the capacitor too quickly and damage it

Compare two circuits

1 Set up the two circuits as shown in the diagrams.
2 For each circuit in turn place the output microphone near to a microphone connected to a CRO and then:
   a play an instrument or whistle a sound into the microphone
   b sketch the waveform shown on the CRO
   c compare the waveforms of the two circuits.

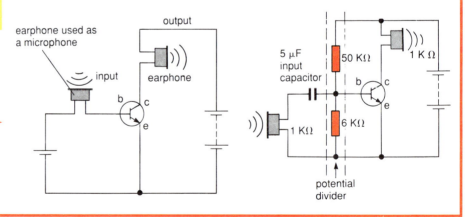

Q1 Which variable did you keep constant for the two circuits?

Q2 Is the transistor in these circuits acting as a switch or an amplifier?

Q3 What effect did the capacitor have on the output waveform?

Q4 Make a list of devices in the home which do not switch off immediately. Why can this be useful?

Sound may help to save the ozone layer

1 Read the following article about an acoustic fridge.
2 Collect a copy of the article.
  a Underline all sentences that include information about CFCs.
  b Put a box around the paragraph that explains how normal fridges work.
  c Use a different colour to underline all passages that include the word 'acoustic'.
  d Put a box around the sentence containing the phrase *resonant cavity*.
  e Pick out and underline any advantages of an acoustic fridge listed in the last two paragraphs.

Acoustic fridge sounds good for the ozone layer

A VERY loud noise is the key to a new refrigeration system that cools without the use of ozone-destroying CFCs. The system uses sound rather than the usual piston pump to compress the refrigerant fluid and its developers claim it will make fridges use 40 per cent less energy.

Tim Lucas developed the system while working at the Los Alamos National Laboratory in New Mexico and has now set up a company, called Sonic Compressor Systems, to develop the system further. Lucas expects to have the system working in a small domestic refrigerator within six months.

Conventional refrigerators work by compressing a refrigerant gas using a piston pump. The compressed gas is cooled and condenses into a liquid. The liquid then expands along a length of fine capillary tubing and evaporates, absorbing heat as it does so, and cooling the interior of the fridge.

The problem is that the most efficient refrigerants are CFCs which destroy ozone in the Earth's stratosphere when the fridge is eventually broken up. Alternative refrigerants exist but they are chemically incompatible with the lubricant used to form a seal around the piston in the pump.

Lucas's system abandons the piston altogether. Instead a linear electric motor vibrates a flexible diaphragm to produce acoustic waves. The diaphragm, which resembles a loudspeaker, projects its waves into an acoustic chamber.

The waves move along the chamber away from the diaphragm and bounce back when they reach the far end of the chamber. The size and shape of the chamber is engineered into a "resonant cavity", so that the reflected wave exactly superimposes itself onto the original wave. The two opposing waves reinforce each other and produce unusually large swings in the pressure of the gas.

"Normally when you try to create acoustic waves with very high pressure amplitudes, a shock wave will form," says Lucas. This causes most of the power to be wasted as heat. "The acoustic chambers designed at Los Alamos provided high pressure amplitudes without the shock waves."

The far end of the chamber from the diaphragm is where the pressure varies most. At this end are two one-way valves and when the pressure is high the outlet valve is pushed open and compressed refrigerant escapes into the rest of the system. This gas is then cooled and condensed in the usual way and expanded through a capillary tube.

The decompressed gas is then drawn back into the acoustic chamber through the inlet valve when the pressure is low and recompressed. The valves open and close at a rate of 340 times a second, about 6 times faster than in a conventional piston compressor.

As there is no piston, and hence no lubricant, CFC refrigerant need not be used. And as the compressor is the only part of the system that differs from a conventional fridge, manufacturers will not have to alter their production significantly.

The efficiency of the acoustic compressor means that an acoustic fridge would use 40 per cent less energy than a conventional model. This could prove to be extremely popular in the US, where as much as 8 per cent of all electric power is consumed by ordinary domestic refrigerators.

(New Scientist 4.4.1992)

Discuss the following.

Q1 What are CFCs and why are they thought to be a problem?

Q2 How do normal fridges work?

Q3 How can sound replace CFCs?

Q4 What is resonance and how is it of use in the acoustic fridge?

Q5 Give three advantages of the new fridge suggested in the article.

1 An observer standing 3000 metres from a church sees lightning strike the steeple. He hears the thunder 9 seconds later. Calculate the velocity at which the sound of the thunder travelled. [3]

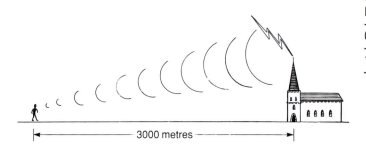

3000 metres

2 A microphone is connected to the Y plates of a CRO.

A note is produced which gives trace 1. How must the note have changed to give trace 2 ? [2]

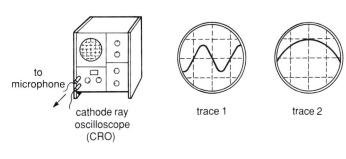

to microphone

cathode ray oscilloscope (CRO)

trace 1   trace 2

3 In this circuit the relay coil is energised and can close switch S if the output of the NOT gate is high.

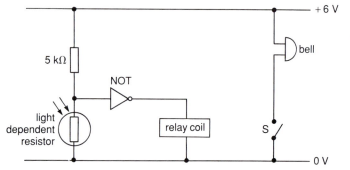

+ 6 V

5 kΩ

NOT

bell

light dependent resistor

relay coil

S

0 V

  a When a bright light is shone on the light dependent resistor the input voltage to the NOT gate falls.
    i Why does this happen? [1]
    ii What happens in the rest of the circuit as a result of this? [1]

  b Suggest a practical use for the circuit shown at the start of the question. [1]

(MEG Physics 1988)

4

Input	Output
0	
1	

input — NAND — output

The symbol shows a NAND gate connected as an inverter. Copy and complete the above truth table for it.

(MEG Physics 1988)

5 The two circuits, A and B, include buzzers, an inverter and switches.

For each circuit say what happens when the switch is closed.

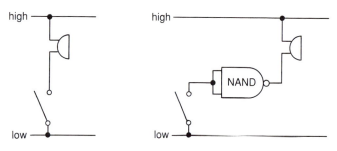

high   high

NAND

low   low

6 In a car, a buzzer sounds when a front seat passenger has not fastened the seat belt. However, the buzzer does not sound when there is no passenger.

Devise a circuit using two switches, an inverter and a buzzer which could be used. Copy and complete the circuit below. The inverter has already been drawn.

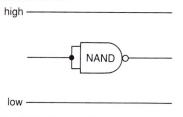

high

NAND

3

Genetics and biotechnology

Inheritance

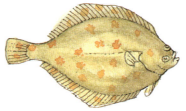
Rabbit

Jelly-fish

Plaice

Buttercup

Similarities and variations

There is an astonishingly large number of different species of living organisms inhabiting the Earth. Each species exhibits **variation**. This may be immediately obvious or become apparent only after closer inspection of a species. Species variation is caused by changes in the environment in which an individual lives (especially during its early growth and development phase) and by inheritance. Small alterations in the 'instructions' that are received from each parent result in variation of offspring. However, we know that when a cat reproduces, it produces more cats, and similarly, pea plant seeds will grow into pea plants. The **similarity** within a species is far greater than the variation.

The distinguishing features of individuals are known as characteristics or **traits**. **Continuously varying** characteristics, such as height, do not fall into sharply defined categories and are greatly influenced by the environment. **Discontinuous variation** means that the characteristic of an individual is either present or absent with no intermediates. For example, a person is normally either right-handed or left-handed.

Inherited variation in coat colour in a puppy litter and acquired variation in corn height.

Distinguish traits

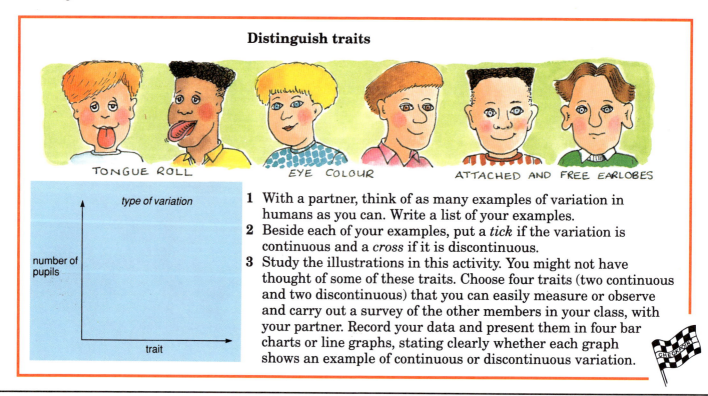

TONGUE ROLL   EYE COLOUR   ATTACHED AND FREE EARLOBES

type of variation

number of pupils

trait

1 With a partner, think of as many examples of variation in humans as you can. Write a list of your examples.

2 Beside each of your examples, put a *tick* if the variation is continuous and a *cross* if it is discontinuous.

3 Study the illustrations in this activity. You might not have thought of some of these traits. Choose four traits (two continuous and two discontinuous) that you can easily measure or observe and carry out a survey of the other members in your class, with your partner. Record your data and present them in four bar charts or line graphs, stating clearly whether each graph shows an example of continuous or discontinuous variation.

The inheritance of characteristics

In 1866, an Austrian monk called Gregor Mendel (1822–84) presented results of his experiments on **inheritance** in the garden pea. Mendel recognised several traits in the pea plants. He chose to study flower colour and whether the pea was wrinkled or not wrinkled. These are discontinuous traits. After studying many, many pea plants and analysing his results using statistics, Mendel proposed a theory to predict whether a trait would or would not appear in the next generation. He developed some basic rules for predicting inheritance.

Mendel's rules can be applied to predict the inheritance of a human trait such as whether earlobes are attached or free. As there are two possible shapes for earlobes, two different instructions may be carried by the genes in the gametes from each parent. Variations in a gene for a particular trait are called **alleles** or **allelic forms**. The earlobe gene has two alleles — one for attached earlobes and one for free earlobes. The different allelic forms are passed on to the offspring by the gametes, each gamete carrying only one allele.

Geneticists give genes and their alleles letters of the alphabet. A letter is selected for each gene and its control of a trait. A capital letter or small letter is used to distinguish the two alleles.

F allele for free earlobe

f allele for attached earlobe

A child receives half of their genes from their mother and half from their father. The mother's egg cells could contain either F or f. The father's sperms could also contain either F or f. The two genes from the parents combine to make up the total number of genes for the child. The full set of possible combinations of genes in the child is called the **genotype**.

It is possible for the genes to combine in different ways as shown in the table.

Gregor Mendel.

Mother's egg cells	Father's sperm cells	Child's genotype	Child's phenotype (earlobes attached or free)
F	F	FF	free
F	f	Ff	free
f	F	fF	free
f	f	ff	attached

Q1 Choose a different discontinuous trait. Choose a letter to represent the trait and write down all the possible genotypes.

The full genotype has two copies of the gene F (FF) or two of the gene f (ff), or Ff and f F. It makes no difference to the genotype which gene is from the mother and which is from the father.

The way a trait is expressed visibly, for example free earlobes, is called the **phenotype**. The genotype FF produces a phenotype of free earlobes and ff produces a phenotype of attached earlobes. The genotype Ff also produces the phenotype free earlobes because the F allele has a greater 'importance' than the f allele. It is called the **dominant** allele. The f allele can only show its effect when both parents' alleles are f. The f allele is the **recessive** allele.

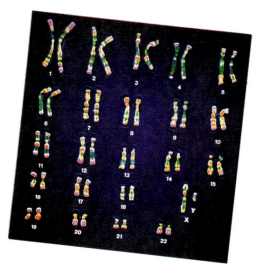

A full set of human chromosomes arranged in homologous pairs.

Genes and inheritance

Almost every cell contains a nucleus and inside the nucleus are thread-like structures called **chromosomes**. Chromosomes carry 'instructions', called **genes,** for producing a particular trait. When a cell is not dividing, chromosomes cannot be seen under the microscope even when the cell is stained. Just before the cell divides, the chromosomes shorten and thicken and can then be seen clearly.

Each species has a fixed number of chromosomes. Fruit flies (*Drosophila spp.*) have been used a lot in genetic research, and have 8 chromosomes. A normal human has 46 chromosomes. The different chromosomes can be identified because they have different shapes and sizes. The chromosomes are always in pairs called **homologous pairs**. This is because when the zygote is formed (see page 129), one chromosome of each pair comes from the female gamete and one from the male gamete. In humans, 23 chromosomes come from the mother and 23 from the father, making up the full set of 46 chromosomes. In 22 out of the 23 chromosome pairs, the chromosomes are identical to each other, but in the last pair one chromosome may be slightly longer. The longer chromosome of the pair is labelled X and the shorter one is labelled Y. Females have two X chromosomes (XX) and males have one X and one Y chromosome (XY).

The number of chromosomes in each body cell of an organism is called the **diploid number**. It is always an even number because the chromosomes are in pairs.

While body cells in humans contain a full set of 46 chromosomes, this is not the case in gametes. A father's sperms and a mother's egg cells have only half the full set of chromosomes — that is 23. This number is called the **haploid number**. Each set contains one of each of the homologous pairs.

These gametes are produced in the male by sperm-producing cells and in the female by ovum-producing cells. The process is called **meiosis** (see page 186). The genes carrying instructions for a particular trait on each of the chromosomes from each parent will be similar (because the parents are from the same species) but they will not be identical, because the parents inherited genetic variation from their parents and may have also acquired genetic variation during their lifetime (see page 52).

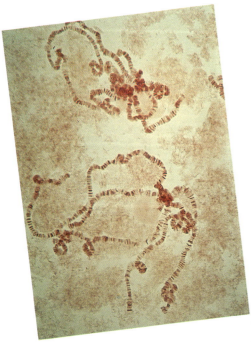

A full set of fruit fly chromosomes.

Sexual reproduction involves the fusion of the male and female gametes (see page 128). At fertilisation, when the gametes fuse, the two half-sets of chromosomes will combine to make up the full set of 46 within the single-celled zygote. These chromosomes provide instructions for an individual that are different from both parents, but which share certain of the parents' characteristics. After fertilisation has taken place, the zygote divides again and again (see page 129). At each cell division, all the chromosomes are copied exactly and the copies passed on to each new cell. This means that every new cell contains the full set of 46 chromosomes. This type of cell division is called **mitosis** (see page 185).

Diploid sex cells produce haploid gametes which fuse at fertilisation to form a diploid zygote.

Finding which alleles are present in a gamete

Look at the phenotype. Work out what the possible genotypes could be.

Phenotype	Possible genotypes	Parent's possible genotypes
attached	ff	f and f
free	Ff or FF	F and f or F and F

If there are two alleles in the genotype, then some gametes will be F and some will be f.

To explore the possible different combinations of the alleles that make up the genotype it is a good idea to use a **Punnet square**. In the Punnet square on the right the father's gametes are ff and the mother's are Ff.

father's gametes   mother's gametes
f   F
f'   free Ff   f
free Ff   attached ff
attached ff

Collect
- resource sheet

Inherited traits

1 The resource sheet gives examples of other traits that are inherited in the same way. Study the information and complete the table.

Take notes

Make your own notes on different types of variation between individuals and between species and give the meaning of the words *chromosome*, *gene*, *allele*, *gamete*, *genotype* and *phenotype*.

Project

Mendel studied garden peas. Find out the colours of pea flowers and how he carried out his famous experiments on inheritance.

Chromosomes and DNA

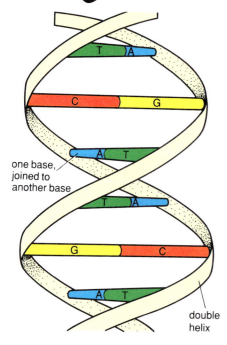

one base, joined to another base

double helix

Part of a DNA molecule showing its double helix structure and a sequence of the four bases.

Where are the genetic instructions?

Each chromosome contains a chemical compound called **deoxyribonucleic acid** (DNA). DNA is sometimes referred to as the 'blue-print' of a cell. It carries the necessary instructions for a cell to function normally. In DNA two long strands twist together to form a **double helix** or **spiral**. Attached to each of the strands is a specific sequence of four differently shaped molecules called bases, which are represented by the letters C, A, T and G. Scientists believe that it is this sequence that holds the key to inheritance.

The structure of proteins made in the body is dependent on the sequence of bases on a DNA strand. The protein may be destined to be a structural protein in muscle or an enzyme in the stomach. If one amino acid in the sequence is changed, or if a mistake happens in 'translating' the DNA code into amino acids, the protein may no longer function.

A gene is a length of DNA that codes for a particular protein. The gene that codes for the same trait appears on the same part of both chromosomes in a pair. Some traits are expressed by several genes. The traits studied on pages 53–55 are expressed by only one gene.

sequence of bases in DNA	amino acids	protein
C A T	VALINE	VALINE
C C A	GLYCINE	GLYCINE
C G A	ALANINE	ALANINE

The sequence of bases along a DNA strand 'code' for amino acids, which join to form proteins.

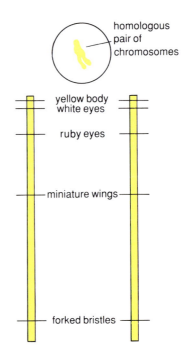

homologous pair of chromosomes

yellow body
white eyes

ruby eyes

miniature wings

forked bristles

Genes that code for the same trait on the same parts of a chromosome pair. This chromosome pair codes for traits in a fruit fly.

Collect ● resource sheet

DNA structure

1 Study the resource sheet on DNA structure and then answer the questions.

A sickle-shaped deformed red blood cell (left) from a person suffering from the disease, × 3250.

A person with sickle-cell disease has damaged haemoglobin in their red blood cells, caused by a mutation, and suffers bouts of anaemia. However, a person who is heterozygous for sickle-cell disease (inherits normal blood trait from one parent and sickle-cell blood trait from the other) is protected from malaria. This has resulted in the sickle-cell trait remaining in the population.

Changes in the genetic instructions

Individuals vary because they have inherited different combinations of alleles from their parents. Further variation may occur because of changes in the genetic code. It may be a slight change such as swapping one kind of base for another in a particular gene or it may be as large as a whole chromosome being damaged. As we have seen, these changes will alter the way the cell makes proteins. These changes are known as **mutations**.

If the mutation is in a liver cell, for example, it will be passed on to any new liver cell formed from the mutated cell. If enough new cells with the mutation are produced it may begin to affect the way the liver functions. If the mutation is in a gamete it may be passed on to offspring and affect the way the whole organism develops.

Mutations are going on all the time and while some of them are harmful others can help the organism. These changes come about slowly but the rate of mutation can be increased by certain chemicals and radiation, such as ultraviolet, X-rays and gamma rays.

Selective breeding

Humans have been making use of **natural variation** (as a result of mutation) for years. They have selected for species of crop plants that will give them improved yields, have good resistance to pests or can cope with harsh climates, in addition to many other useful characteristics. Animals have been selectively bred for centuries to produce highly prized characteristics.

These peppers have been selected for their bright colours, which are appreciated by consumers.

Researching a new hybrid strain of wheat.

A prize-winning bull at a livestock show.

Natural selection

As you have already seen, there is a lot of variation within species that reproduce sexually. Some of this phenotypic variation is due to the genotype and its interaction with the environment. Many species can produce very large numbers of offspring. This leads to competition for the resources needed for survival. Natural selection takes place:

- when organisms having harmful alleles are less likely to survive on account of competition with others
- when environmental conditions change, so that other individuals, with slightly different phenotypes may be able to survive better.

There are two forms of the peppered moth *Biston betularia*. One has a dark and light speckled pattern and the other has a much darker, more uniform pattern. The two patterns are genetically determined. Records show that in 1849 in Manchester there were more of the speckled moths than the dark ones. However, by the end of the nineteenth century, 98 % of these moths had the dark colouring.

Before reading further, try to suggest some environmental factors that might favour one form of moth over the other.

Biston betularia dark and speckled forms on a sooty tree trunk.

Q1 What do you think has happened to the population of peppered moths in more recent years?

Q2 Suggest some natural conditions which could be important in causing selection.

Collect
- resource sheet
- necessary equipment

Bird taste

Read the activity on the resource sheet and plan your method in detail before starting.

Darwin's finches

In 1858 Charles Darwin (1809–82) and Alfred Russel Wallace (1823–1913) both published theories to explain how animals evolve over time as a result of natural selection. Darwin took part in a five-year expedition and sailed round the world on a ship called HMS *Beagle*. On the Galapagos islands off the coast of South America Darwin noticed that each island had a different type of finch.

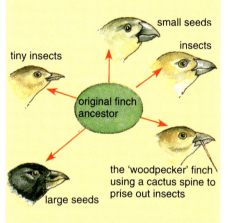

The various species of finch are closely related but are isolated from each other by feeding behaviour, which has affected the shapes of their bills, and by geography; some species living on only one of the islands.

Experiments were carried out 'in the wild', with both forms of moth. The results showed that the dark variety were less conspicuous when they settled on the black tree trunks and were less easily spotted and eaten by birds. The speckled or peppered form was less easily seen on tree trunks covered in lichen. However, Manchester at that time suffered from much air pollution which killed most species of lichen. Since the 1950s the pollution has much reduced.

Squared off . . .

The Sales Manager of a supermarket thinks that customers will buy square potatoes so that they can make chips more easily.

Imagine that you are:

- a research scientist who is trying to develop the new strain of potato
- the farmer who will then grow the square potatoes to sell to the supermarket.

1 For each person, what are the advantages and disadvantages of producing the potatoes by asexual reproduction (page 20), or by sexual reproduction?
2 Design a poster to display your conclusions. You could include illustrations from magazine advertisements that show actual plant characteristics selected for by fruit and vegetable breeders.

 ## Take notes

Make notes on the role of DNA, variation and natural selection in Darwin's theory of evolution. Include flow diagrams to help summarise the information.

Project

Make a list of some common breeds of dog. Try to group them into families that show similar characteristics. Say how a dog's particular characteristics equip it for the job it is bred to do; give examples.

Genetic engineering

Enzymes are used in a wide range of products.

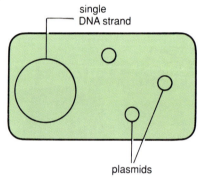

single DNA strand

plasmids

Manufacturing proteins

Throughout the world scientists have been investigating ways to produce certain enzymes and other proteins that are needed on an industrial scale. For example, enzymes which break down fat and grease molecules are used by manufacturers to make biological washing powders. These enzymes are produced by a variety of organisms naturally but not on a large enough scale to be of use in industry. Scientists can now take the specific part of a DNA strand which codes for a particular enzyme from one organism and add it to the existing DNA of a suitable bacterium. This is known as **genetic engineering**. Large numbers of treated bacteria are then grown, all of which produce the enzyme.

One bacterium used widely by genetic engineers is called *Escherichia coli* (*E. coli*). In nature it is found living in large numbers in our intestines. *E. coli* has a single large, circular chromosome made of a single strand of DNA and small rings of DNA called **plasmids**.

Scientists can remove plasmids from one *E. coli* bacterium, insert a section of new DNA that codes for a protein of their choice into the plasmids and then add the genetically altered plasmids to another *E. coli* bacterium. The genetically altered plasmids will be absorbed into the bacterium's genetic material, which will then begin to produce the protein coded for by the altered plasmids.

E. coli is shown on the left, and the stages in a genetic engineering procedure are shown below.

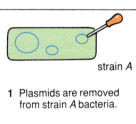

strain *A*

1 Plasmids are removed from strain *A* bacteria.

2 The DNA ring is broken by chemical treatment.

3 A chosen gene is spliced (cut) out of DNA from a different strain of bacteria, or even from a human cell, using special enzymes.

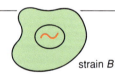

strain *B*

4 This gene is mixed with the open plasmids from strain *A* bacteria.

5 A second chemical treatment causes the ends of the open plasmids to join up with the added gene to form a ring again.

strain *A*

6 The plasmids with the added gene are now mixed with fresh strain *A* bacteria.

protein P

strain *A*

7 The plasmids enter the strain *A* bacteria.

protein P

strain *A*

8 Strain *A* bacteria now make protein P (possibly an enzyme) coded for by the new gene.

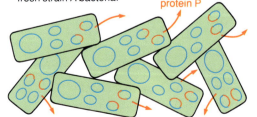

protein P

9 Strain *A* bacteria multiply in number and since they all carry copies of the new gene, they can produce large amounts of protein P.

The genetically altered strain *A* bacteria produce generation after generation of identical cells. That is, they form **clones**, each of which produces protein P.

Genetic engineering in medicine

Many medical tests and treatments of disease rely on chemicals made by genetic engineering.

Diabetes

To understand the disease diabetes, we must first look at how glucose levels in the blood are regulated in a healthy person.

The first part of the small intestine is a U-shaped tube called the duodenum and connected to it by means of the **pancreatic duct** is a leaf-shaped gland called the **pancreas**.

When we eat starchy foods, enzymes in the digestive tract break down the starch molecules into glucose. When the level of glucose entering the blood increases, islet cells in the pancreas release **insulin**, which is a hormone. Insulin controls the rate at which glucose is converted into glycogen for storage in the liver. When there is excess glucose in the blood, some of the glucose is converted into glycogen. When the levels of glucose in the blood fall too low, **glucagon** is released from the pancreas which signals stored glycogen in the liver to be broken down to form glucose which is released into the blood.

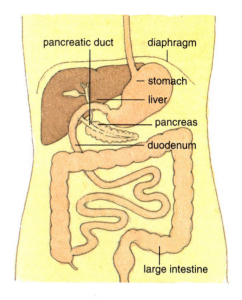

The intestines, showing the position of the pancreas and its duct.

About 2% of the population in Britain suffer from a disease called **diabetes mellitus** where the body is unable to produce enough insulin. As a result, glucose is not converted into glycogen in the liver and remains in the blood. When glucose in the blood passes through the kidneys at a high level the normal reabsorption of glucose in the urine back into the blood is disturbed. Some of the glucose stays in the urine and is excreted. The high glucose level in the urine disturbs the water balance and leads to the production of large quantities of weak urine, which can cause dehydration of the patient. The word *mellitus* means honey. The disease was first given this name by doctors who smelt patients' sugary urine. The most obvious symptoms of this disease are excessive thirst and weight loss.

Diabetes mellitus can be controlled by regular injections of insulin and a carefully monitored diet. Blood sugar must not be allowed to increase too much after a meal. Patients must eat regular meals since there are no glycogen stores in their livers.

For many years insulin for people with this form of diabetes has been extracted from the pancreas of cows or pigs. However, cow and pig insulin can cause problems to humans.

- Some patients do not like using insulin taken from animals.
- Animal insulin has a different chemical structure from human insulin and in some cases patients are allergic to it.
- There are difficulties in getting enough supplies.

Much of the insulin made today comes from genetically engineered bacteria. The gene that codes for human insulin is inserted into plasmids from bacteria, which make and secrete an insulin almost identical, chemically, to human insulin. Insulin is the first genetically engineered protein to be given to humans.

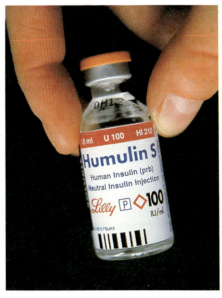

Insulin for human use prepared by genetic engineering.

Design a poster to compare selective breeding and genetic engineering. You will need to consider the starting material, the end products and what happens to the DNA of the organisms in the two different techniques. Include examples of selective breeding and genetic engineering. Use your library to find out more about each of your examples.

Genetic engineering and fertilisers

Legumes (peas, beans and clover) are plants that have root nodules containing nitrogen-fixing bacteria (see page 25). The root nodule bacteria can fix atmospheric nitrogen into nitrate ions (NO_3^-) for use by the plant. This extra nitrate supply acts as a type of fertiliser for the plant. Fields containing legume crops need less artificial nitrate fertiliser. This helps to reduce pollution by fertilisers.

Unfortunately, cereal crops such as wheat, oats and barley do not have nitrogen-fixing bacteria. Attempts to transfer the bacteria from a legume to a cereal plant have failed. Scientists are now using genetic engineering to alter the bacteria. The altered bacteria are able to survive in the roots of cereals and act as built-in fertiliser factories. Scientists are also trying to produce plants that resist disease, high temperature and drought. Genetic engineering is a different approach to that of plant breeding. In genetic engineering new varieties are produced by introducing new characteristics from different plants.

Genetic engineering in the future

There are about 100 000 genes in every human cell. We must know the exact position of a gene on its chromosome if it is to be used in genetic engineering. So far we can locate many of these genes on a particular chromosome. This process is called **gene mapping** (see page 56 for a simplified gene map of a fruit fly). Several years ago the Human Genome Project was set up to identify all the genes carried by the 23 chromosomes in humans. Obviously, this continuing research project is of great medical importance.

Gene therapy is the term given to a particular type of genetic engineering. In theory, it is possible to put genes into certain (but not all) body cells. One inheritable disease that could possibly be treated in this way is **thalassaemia major**. It may be possible to add the normal gene into the DNA of a patient's bone marrow cells. Unfortunately, the defective gene would still be present in the gametes, so children of genetically treated parents could still have thalassaemia and would need gene therapy. Thalassaemia could be completely removed from a family by performing gene therapy on very young embryos. There is still a lot of research to be done and it seems unlikely that gene therapy will be available as a medical treatment in the near future.

normal red blood cells

people with thalassaemia trait are not ill. They are normal, but some of them may have slight anaemia, because of their slightly smaller red blood cells

children with thalassaemia major cannot make enough haemoglobin so they produce nearly empty red blood cells. Sufferers normally die between one and eight years of age. Treatment to alleviate symptoms is available

parent with thalassaemia trait

parent with thalassaemia trait

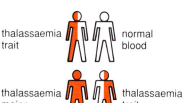

thalassaemia trait

normal blood

thalassaemia major

thalassaemia trait

Thalassaemia major and its inheritance.

Dangers of genetic engineering

The transfer of genes between different bacteria and between different species has often been a cause for concern. When reporters working for newspapers first learnt that gene transfer was possible they produced some sensational headlines. Alarm that uncontrollable diseases could be caused and spread by engineered bacteria usually featured in most of the articles. Worse still, some papers suggested that such bacteria may be deliberately or accidentally released into the environment. The newspaper articles did contain a grain of truth. Genetic engineers have to work under strict guidelines.

MONSTER MICE PRODUCED BY GENETIC TAMPERING

GENES TO STOP THE EFFECTS OF FROST ARE TRANSFERRED TO CROPS

GENETICALLY ENGINEERED BUGS RELEASED INTO OUR ENVIRONMENT

- Genetic engineering or gene therapy can only be done in special laboratories equipped to handle potentially dangerous organisms.

- The bacteria which receive the genes have to be specially treated so that they will only grow under culture conditions in the laboratory. Outside the laboratory they die.

- Genetic engineering can only begin after permission has been granted by a controlling authority.

For or against?

1 Collect newspaper articles on genetic engineering or genetically engineered products. Make a list of the benefits mentioned and the dangers highlighted in the articles. Do you think most journalists are in favour of or against genetic engineering?
2 Design a survey to test public opinion about genetic engineering. How much do people understand what it involves? Do they think the media gives accurate information? Do they think genetic engineering is a good development? Show your teacher the questions you will ask before you carry out your survey.

 *Take notes*

Use step-by-step diagrams to show the main stages in genetic engineering using *E. coli*. List some uses of genetic engineering in medicine and in agriculture. Use your survey results to summarise the fears people have about genetic engineering.

 Project

Find out which cleaning products contain enzymes.

Key

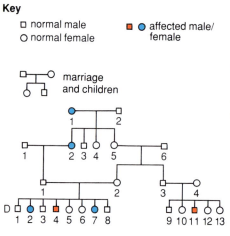

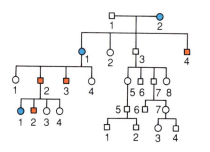

A family tree to show inheritance of Huntington's chorea. All the people married spouses whose families do not have Huntington's chorea.

Pedigree analysis

In order to work out patterns of inheritance of a particular trait, geneticists use organisms that have a short reproductive cycle and large numbers of offspring, for example fruit flies (*Drosophila spp.*) or a species of plant. This allows them to make many crosses (matings) over many generations and answer questions such as how many individuals are affected, which generations show the trait, whether it affects only males, only females or both.

For geneticists who wish to study inherited disorders in humans it is not quite so straightforward for two main reasons.

- It is unethical to perform breeding experiments on humans.
- Humans take a long time before they start to reproduce and do not have many children.

Instead, geneticists gather information enabling them to construct a family tree going back as far as possible and including information about the presence or absence of a particular trait, for example, a disease.

Study the family trees and, for each of the trees, answer the following questions.

Q1 Is every individual affected?

Q2 Is every generation affected?

Q3 Do you think this disease shows a dominant or recessive trait? Why?

Q4 Does the trait affect just males, just females or both sexes equally or unequally?

Q5 What evidence is there for the trait not being carried on the X chromosome?

Q6 Find a piece of evidence which indicates whether or not the trait is carried on the Y chromosome.

Q7 Can you pick out the evidence in the family tree that suggests that interbreeding is not a very good idea?

Testing time

Amniocentesis is a technique that doctors use to find out whether the genes for different traits are present in developed fetuses (unborn babies). They do this by analysing the **amniotic fluid** that surrounds the fetus in the womb. Doctors can look for traits like sex or even something trivial like eye colour. They can also look for a gene that codes for a debilitating disease, such as Down's syndrome or spina bifida. In the future it may be possible to determine much vaguer traits such as personality characteristics or perhaps a tendency to become delinquent.

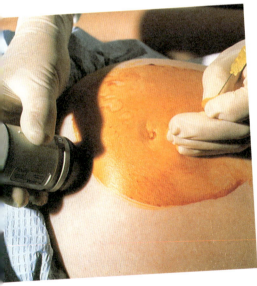

A doctor performing amniocentesis on a woman in the late stage of pregnancy. An ultrasound probe (left) is used to prevent accidental injury to the fetus.

Determination of eye colour, hair colour and personality of offspring may be possible in the future.

Q1 What do you consider to be the dangers in allowing free access to this knowledge?

Q2 How do you think it should be used?

Q3 There are many potentially damaging genes in the population. Probably everybody carries one or more defective genes. What should people do who know they carry a harmful allele? Should they take a risk and have children?

1 Chromosomes contain a substance called DNA which has very large molecules. Apart from identical twins, everybody has different DNA. The DNA molecules in chromosomes can be broken up by enzymes into small pieces. These pieces can be separated in a thin layer of jelly. Radioactive substances are used to make the DNA pieces show up on film. DNA from different cells in the same person, and from identical twins, always produces the same pattern on the film.

The technique can be used to find out whether a sample of blood comes from a particular person. The figure below shows the results of analysing a sample of blood from the scene of a crime, and samples from five suspects.

a Which part of a cell contains the chromosomes? [1]

b The DNA in the blood sample comes from the white cells, not the red cells. Explain why DNA does not come from the red cells. [1]

c i From which of the five suspects, **A**, **B**, **C**, **D** or **E**, did the blood sample come? [1]
   ii Explain how you can tell. [1]

d i Explain why identical twins produce the same DNA pattern. [1]
   ii Explain how identical twins are produced. [3]

Total [8]

(NEA 1992 Biology)

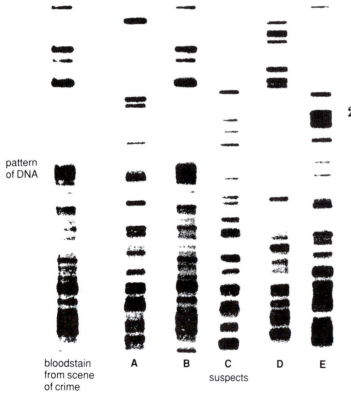

pattern of DNA

bloodstain from scene of crime

A   B   C   D   E

suspects

2 A potato grower wanted to produce a new variety of potato which grows quickly and makes good chips. She has one variety which grows quickly but makes poor chips, and another which grows more slowly but makes good chips.

When plants of these two varieties produce flowers, she crosses the two varieties. Later she collects the seeds and plants them.

a Explain how the grower would cross the two varieties. [3]

b From the seeds she collects, she finds that one of the new plants grows very quickly and produces potatoes which make good chips. How would she produce a crop of potatoes which were exactly the same? [2]

c The grower's daughter takes a new potato and an old potato which is producing shoots. She tests both potatoes for sugar. She finds sugar in the old potato, but not in the new potato.

   i From what substance in the old potato would the sugar have been produced? [1]
   ii Suggest why there is sugar in the old potato but not in the new potato. [2]

Total [8]

(NEA 1992 Biology)

4

From Earth to the stars

The moving Earth

A red-hot lava flow on Mount Etna.

Mount Etna, on the island of Sicily in Italy, is the most active volcano in Europe and erupts every few years. In spite of this, the number of people living in the area of the mountain is high. In December 1991, lava began to flow towards the village of Zafferana. A dam was built in January which diverted the lava flow towards a natural crater. By early April of the following year the lava had filled the crater and began to flow towards Zafferana once again. On 15th April the first of many houses in the village was engulfed by the encroaching lava flow.

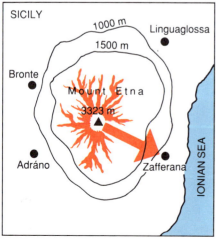

A map of Mount Etna showing the path of a lava flow towards Zafferana.

Solid as a rock?

We sometimes quote the saying 'solid as a rock' to describe the dependability of a person or object. But anyone who lives in the shadow of a volcano or in an earthquake zone will know that rock can be far from 'solid'. There are approximately 500 to 600 active volcanoes in the world.

In the last few years separate geological upheavals have brought fear and destruction to parts of Europe.

On 7th December 1988 an earthquake measuring 6.8 on the **Richter scale** left over 500 000 people homeless in Armenia. The fault line was 10 km long and up to 1.5 m wide and the effect was felt in neighbouring Iran and Turkey. Buildings collapsed and landslides developed killing at least 25 000 and injuring a further 19 000. It is estimated that the damage was worth about $16.2 billion (about £11 billion).

The aftermath of a severe earthquake.

Fortunately, most large volcanic eruptions occur unseen beneath the sea, along mid-ocean ridges (see page 72). Although volcanoes can cause widespread death and destruction they can also be beneficial to humans. Volcanic soils are some of the richest and most fertile. Volcanic regions produce heat that has contributed to important energy resources.

An earthquake is caused by a sudden release of energy in the Earth's **crust** or **upper mantle**. Enormous **strain energy** gradually builds up until the energy is discharged where the rocks are weakest. When this energy is released **shock waves** travel through the Earth in all directions.

Shock waves from earthquakes are recorded on an instrument called a **seismograph**. The Richter scale, which is often quoted in the media, is a measure of the intensity of an earthquake.

Geophysicist sitting by a seismograph.

The Richter scale is a measure of an earthquake's strength, over a range of units 1 to 10.

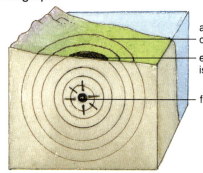

a line connects the points of equal strength detected by the seismograph

epicentre — the point on the Earth's crust that is directly above the focus

focus

When a connecting line is drawn through the points at which the same strength of earthquake is recorded a rough ring shape results. The centre of the ring is called the **epicentre** and this is the **focus** of the earthquake or place from where it originated.

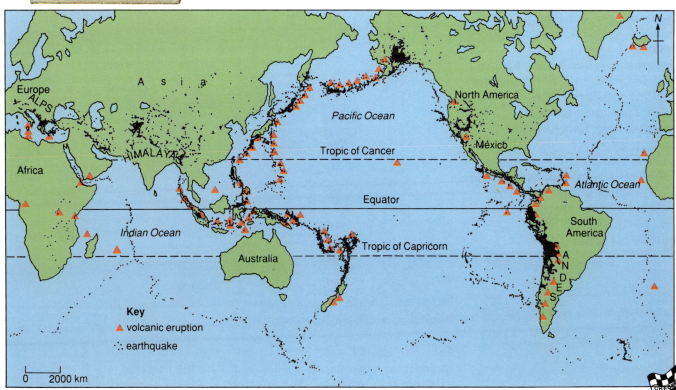

The world map shows the distribution of earthquakes and volcanic zones.

Q1 What do you notice about the pattern of distribution of earthquakes and volcanic zones?

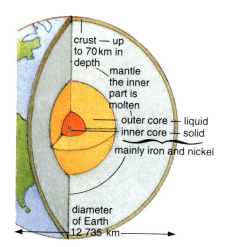

Earth and its believed structure.

Alfred Wegener (1880–1930).

Evidence for continental drift

Geological

The geology of the Atlantic edges of Africa and South America show startling similarity. The Caledonian mountain belt stretches from Greenland and Norway through the British Isles to North America. This evidence and additional geological evidence in other parts of the world eventually led scientists to consider the possibility of continental drift.

A Mesosaurus fossil.

The **core** of the Earth is thought to be made mainly from iron and nickel with a solid inner part and a liquid outer part. Evidence for this comes from the fact that the Earth is magnetic and therefore would be expected to contain a significant proportion of magnetic substances. The density of the layers in the Earth's core can be calculated by transmitting sound waves into the ground and measuring the speed at which they travel. The sound waves travel faster in denser material (see page 34), enabling us to build up a **profile** of the core layers. Because the outer core and inner mantle are liquid, the upper **mantle** and **crust** can be imagined to be 'floating'. Many scientists think that the crust and the upper mantle are composed of several large plates which can migrate over the lower mantle, rather like rafts floating on water.

In the seventeenth century Francis Bacon suggested that the continents may once have fitted together as a whole, in a similar way to a jigsaw. In 1858, the American Antonio Snider-Pelligrini showed how the Americas, Europe and Africa could have fitted together before later separating. Then a German called Alfred Wegener suggested that the continents may have started as one land mass, which then drifted apart. At first the idea was scorned by other scientists and Wegener died in 1930 on a Greenland icecap attempting to find evidence to prove his ideas. At that time scientists did not believe in the idea of **continental drift** because they did not understand how it could have happened.

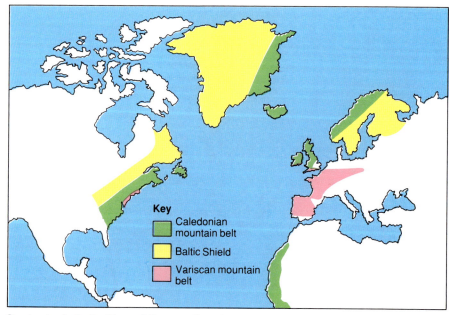

Geological similarities of the continents.

Palaeontological

In addition to geological evidence, **palaeontological** (study of fossils) evidence was produced. For example, fossils of a crocodile-type reptile Mesosaurus have been found in Southern Africa and Brazil. It is extremely unlikely that this reptile could have crossed the Atlantic Ocean so it seems the continents may once have been joined.

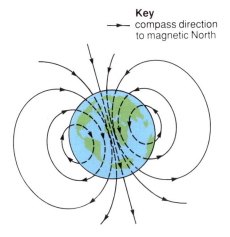

Key
→ compass direction to magnetic North

Magnetic

We have seen that some rock types contain magnetic particles. These are usually oxides of iron (such as magnetite) and titanium. During their formation these rocks became magnetised in the direction of the Earth's magnetic field. Using extremely sensitive instruments, geologists have discovered that very old rocks found in different parts of the world contain magnetic particles which do not point to the position of the present magnetic North Pole. This suggests that the rocks have migrated relative to the Earth's magnetic field since they were first formed.

Earth's magnetic field.

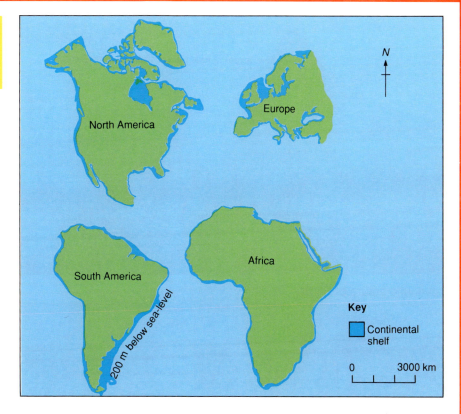

North America

Europe

South America

Africa

200 m below sea-level

Key
▇ Continental shelf

0   3000 km

Collect
● resource sheets

Jigsaw pieces
1 The illustration on the right shows the continents and the extent of continental shelf. (Continental shelf is the area surrounding continents where the water is not more than 200 m deep.)
   a Collect a copy of continent shapes.
   b Cut out the individual shapes.
2 Try fitting the continents together similar to a jigsaw to make one large land mass. (Don't try to be too exact.)

'We didn't get where we are today . . .'
3 It is thought that Britain has not always been in its present position. Geologists believe that as the plates migrated Britain was carried to different locations on the Earth.
   a Collect a copy of the geological time column.
   b Look at the diagram on the right, which shows estimates of the different positions of Britain on the Earth's surface.
   c Construct a table with the headings: *Time period (million years)*, *Estimate of Britain's position*, *Forming rock type*, *Climate*.

Britain's position (million years ago)
A = present
B = 50
C = 170
D = 250
E = 300
F = 380

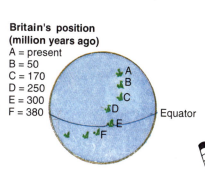

Equator

Movements of the ocean floor

Surveys that map ocean floor magnetism have shown that the direction of the magnetism changes at ocean **ridges** and **trenches**. In 1960 Harry Hess suggested that **convection currents** (movement of heated and therefore less dense material) in the mantle, pushed up ocean ridges and caused new crust to flow off to the sides. This **sea floor migration** has been confirmed by a Deep Sea Drilling Project, which began in 1968. The drillship *Glomar Challenger* found that the ocean floors are relatively young at the ridges and become progressively older with distance.

Material is added to the ocean floor at ocean ridges and destroyed at trenches. The movement of material in this way is described as **dynamic** (the movement is a continuous process). Ocean trenches form when crust slides under an island or a mountain range. This migration can produce earthquake activity.

In 1968 W. J. Morgan put forward a theory of **plate tectonics**. He suggested that the Earth is divided into plates or sections which undergo dynamic movement. This movement slowly parts the plates in different directions. An earthquake or volcanic zone indicates the edge of a particular boundary. The plate tectonics theory is favoured by the evidence we have examined earlier (pages 70 and 71). The ideas of continental drift, ocean floor migration and destruction at ocean trenches all fit Morgan's theory.

layers of rock buckle and form mountains

mid-ocean ridge

ocean plate   ocean trench

hot rock from volcano

continental plate

granite

basalt

solid upper mantle

softer inner mantle

plates come together

convection currents, rising hot rock

rising hot rock

The dynamic nature of Earth.

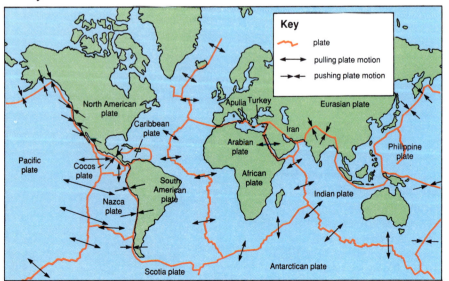

Key

— plate

⟷ pulling plate motion

→← pushing plate motion

North American plate

Caribbean plate

Pacific plate

Cocos plate

Nazca plate

South American plate

Scotia plate

Apulia Turkey

Iran

Arabian plate

African plate

Eurasian plate

Philippine plate

Indian plate

Antarctican plate

The world distribution of tectonic plates.

Faults

Enormous frictional forces are involved when plates meet. The plates move relative to one another at speeds of 1 to 20 cm/year along three types of boundary. A **fault** is produced when two plates slide past one another. When plates collide and crumple at the edge they form **fold mountains** or **trenches**. Plates separate from each other when they are formed in **mid-ocean ridges**. An example of a major plate boundary is the San Andreas fault in California.

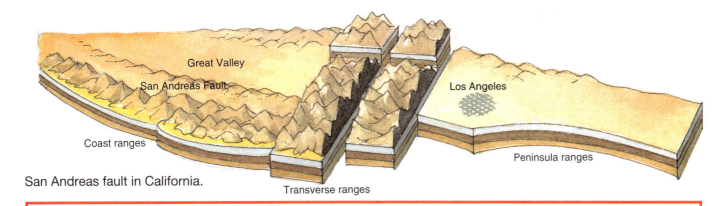

San Andreas fault in California.

Labels on diagram: Great Valley, San Andreas Fault, Coast ranges, Transverse ranges, Los Angeles, Peninsula ranges

Model the steps involved during a continental collision

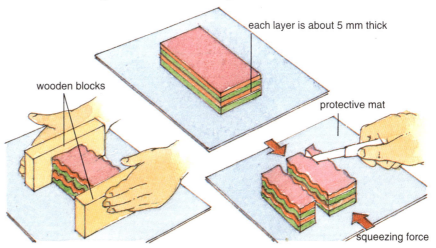

Labels: each layer is about 5 mm thick, wooden blocks, protective mat, squeezing force

1 Sandwich together the Plasticine squares in layers of alternate colours about 5 mm thick as shown in the diagram on the right.

2 Compress the Plasticine sandwich between two blocks. Note the direction of squeeze.

3 Now gently press the top of the Plasticine sandwich flat using one of the blocks.

4 Make two clean slices through the Plasticine sandwich in the direction of compression. Try not to press on the Plasticine during slicing.

5 Select the best of the three sections and examine the cut faces. Using your observations explain what happens when two plates collide. Illustrate your answer with diagrams of the Plasticine.

6 Model some of the geological features shown in the diagram below with Plasticine layers. Think of and explain the reasons why these features develop in the Earth.

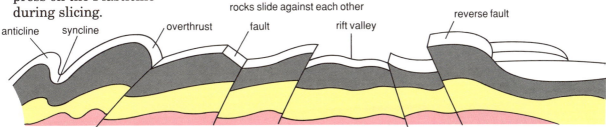

Labels: anticline, syncline, overthrust, fault, rocks slide against each other, rift valley, reverse fault

Formation of rocks

In 1943 a Mexican farmer Dionisio Pulido had firsthand experience of the birth of rocks — and lived to tell the tale. For some years he had been filling a hole which kept mysteriously reappearing in the middle of his corn field. On 20th February a column of smoke appeared in the hole. Next day a cone had grown to a height of 50 m and small explosions were throwing out hot fragments. One week later the cone had grown to a height of 140 m and the noise of the explosions could be heard as far as 350 km away. The volcano continued to grow until 1952. There have been no further eruptions.

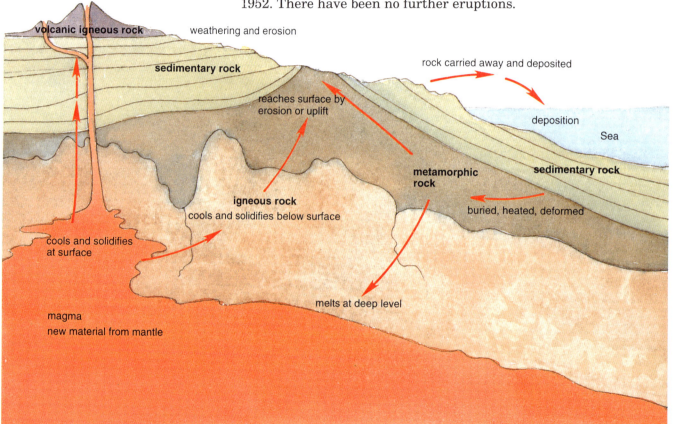

The rock cycle is a dynamic process where mountains and rocks are formed and destroyed.

Weathered granite rock, Dartmoor.

Igneous rocks

Igneous rocks originate from **magma** (hot molten rock) deep inside the Earth. Magma which cools on the surface of the Earth forms **extrusive** rock such as volcanic rock. This rock cools quickly and the minerals within it form tiny **crystals**. **Intrusive** rock has been compressed between other rocks and cooled deep underground. This slower cooling results in the formation of larger crystals.
Granite and **basalt** are very hard intrusive crystalline rocks formed deep below the surface of the Earth. Granite is one of the most common rocks in the parts of the Earth's crust that are under land, while crust under the ocean is largely made up of basalt.

Granite is very common in Britain. It is used to make road kerbstones, edging, pavings, shop fronts, building blocks and panels, ornamental concrete work and road chippings. Granite is made up of a mixture of **minerals**. As we learnt earlier slow cooling of hot molten rock leads to the formation of large crystals. These can be black shiny **mica**, glass-like **quartz**, or pink and white **feldspar**.

Sedimentary rock layers showing anticlinal folding (where strata slope down from the crest), Outer Hebrides, Scotland.

Metamorphic rocks

Metamorphic rocks can be formed from either igneous or sedimentary rocks. When molten magma passes close to either of these rock types they are changed by the intense heat and pressure.

Clay becomes **slate** largely as a result of enormous pressure. Limestone changes to **marble** mainly due to intense heat. Minerals containing copper, tin and gold sometimes concentrate in veins between the layers of rock. These metamorphic rocks have wide uses.

Clay pit in Cornwall.

Welsh-slate roofs on houses built of limestone, Dorset.

Sedimentary rocks

Sedimentary rocks are formed from silt or sediments laid down under the sea. These include **clay** formed from mud, **sandstone** from sand and **limestone** from the shells and skeletons of sea creatures and corals. As layers build up water is squeezed out and rock forms.

Sedimentary rocks usually:

- are found in layers which can be folded or tilted by movement of the Earth

- are made from grains (sometimes held together by a crystalline cement)

- contain fossils.

Q1 What properties help basalt to last longer than limestone?

Q2 Look up the meaning of the word metamorphosis in a dictionary. Explain how the meaning relates to metamorphic rocks.

Take notes

Make a simplified diagram of the rock cycle. Write about igneous, sedimentary and metamorphic rocks; mention how each rock type is formed, and give examples of their uses.

Weathering — an erosion process

The surface of the Earth is dynamic (constantly changing). The changes can stretch over millions of years or be very sudden, for example, when a volcano erupts.

The disintegration and decomposition of rocks caused by temperature, wind, rain and frost is called **weathering**. Weathering plays a part in **erosion**. This is the process by which the land surface is lowered by weathering, corrosion and transportation, under the influence of gravity, wind and running water. Rocks can be broken down by **physical**, **chemical**, **biological** and **mechanical** means.

Brimham Rocks in North Yorkshire.

Physical weathering of rock is caused by the interaction of wind and water. An example can be seen in the slopes above Wastwater in the Lake District. Steep slopes of pieces of rock, called **scree**, are formed by frost shattering. Rock expands during the heat of the day and contracts at night when it is cooler. Cracks form when the rocks expand. Water enters these cracks and in very cold weather it freezes. Water expands when it freezes forcing the cracks to become larger and eventually causing chunks of rock to break away from the surface.

Chemical weathering is mostly caused by chemical reactions between rainwater and rock. Rainwater often contains many dissolved chemicals like carbon dioxide and sulphur dioxide. These gases become acidic when dissolved in water and form so-called acid rain. Acid rain dissolves rocks such as limestone and marble which contain calcium carbonate. Plants such as **lichens** also produce acidic substances which contribute to chemical weathering.

Biological disintegration of rocks is caused by the actions of plants and animals. Animals that burrow expose and dislodge rock. The roots of plants can penetrate small cracks in the rock and make them larger, eventually causing a rock to split into fragments.

When heavy rain falls on to steep areas of land the fast moving water that results can carry large amounts of rock fragments, often depositing them at a great distance. This is an example of **mechanical** deposition.

This sculpture in Cracow, Poland has been badly damaged by acid rain.

Collect
- resource sheet
- safety glasses

Weathering effects
Collect a resource sheet if you need help.
1 Design an experiment to determine what happens when water in a closed plastic container is frozen. Remember to consider safety aspects. Can you calculate the percentage change in volume when water changes to ice?
2 Design an experiment to work out percentage loss of mass which occurs when acid is added to crushed limestone.
3 Check with your teacher before beginning the experiments. Produce a report and relate your results to actual weathering effects.

Q1 What are the differences between physical, chemical, biological and mechanical weathering?

Although plants may cause biological disintegration of rocks they also help to protect the upper surfaces of the land from erosion by binding the topsoil with their roots. When forests are cut down mechanical deposition and erosion speed up considerably and large amounts of soil are washed away.

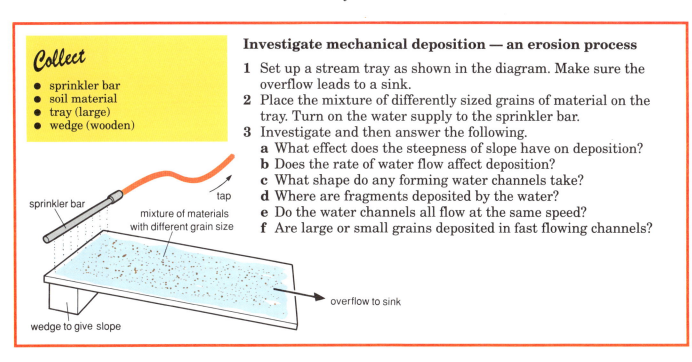

Collect

- sprinkler bar
- soil material
- tray (large)
- wedge (wooden)

sprinkler bar

tap

mixture of materials with different grain size

overflow to sink

wedge to give slope

Investigate mechanical deposition — an erosion process

1. Set up a stream tray as shown in the diagram. Make sure the overflow leads to a sink.
2. Place the mixture of differently sized grains of material on the tray. Turn on the water supply to the sprinkler bar.
3. Investigate and then answer the following.
   a. What effect does the steepness of slope have on deposition?
   b. Does the rate of water flow affect deposition?
   c. What shape do any forming water channels take?
   d. Where are fragments deposited by the water?
   e. Do the water channels all flow at the same speed?
   f. Are large or small grains deposited in fast flowing channels?

Soil formation

Sizes of rock can vary from large boulders of granite or basalt to fine particles of sand or clay. The only free substances in the Earth which are not considered to be rock are soil particles.

Soil is made from assorted particles mixed with air, water and **humus** (decaying plant or animal matter). The type of soil formed depends upon the parent rock, the size of particles or grains present and the humus content. There are also soluble minerals present which give alkalinity or acidity to soil.

A **soil profile** can be exposed reaching to the **bedrock** (underlying rock). The soil particles become smaller the nearer they are to the surface. Weathering of the rock has created the fragments. Decaying plants and animals produce humus. Living plants encourage the presence of animals which break up and add air to the soil.

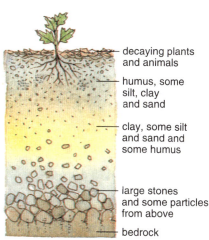

decaying plants and animals

humus, some silt, clay and sand

clay, some silt and sand and some humus

large stones and some particles from above

bedrock

A soil profile.

Take notes

Draw up a table to compare different processes of rock weathering.

Draw a flow diagram, including the words *erosion* and *weathering* to show how rocks may be altered.

Project

Investigate weathering effects on buildings in your local area. You may need to visit a local library and compare old photographs with buildings which are still standing.

A lot of hot air?

World winds

The Earth is cloaked in a mixture of gases which make up the atmosphere. These gases move around the Earth in great swirls carrying water vapour with them. The Earth is constantly bombarded with radiation. The atmosphere shields the Earth from dangerous rays such as ultraviolet (UV). Heat energy that is needed for life is trapped by the atmosphere (see pages 178 and 191 for a different look at our atmosphere). The gases in our atmosphere are held to Earth by the force of gravity.

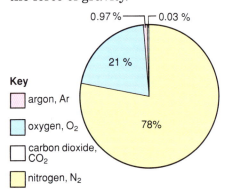

Key
- argon, Ar
- oxygen, O_2
- carbon dioxide, CO_2
- nitrogen, N_2

also water vapour in variable amounts

The composition of air.

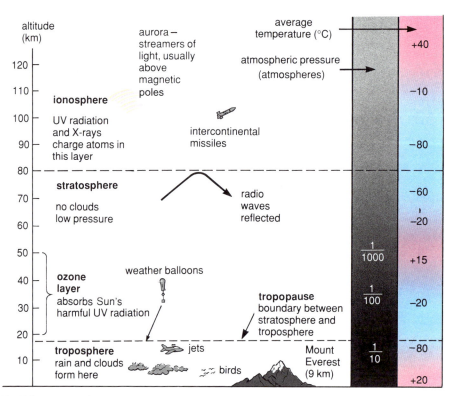

Earth's atmosphere.

Weather is the constant variation in atmospheric conditions. Climate is the average weather occurring over a period of years (usually 30 years). The **troposphere**, which is the most dense layer of the atmosphere, gives rise to effects collectively called weather. Heat radiation from the Sun causes gases to expand. The expanding gases move the air in the troposphere. This constant movement of air causes constant change in our weather.

Constant horizontal movement of air over the Earth's surface is called **wind**. Wind is directional and measured in units of metres per second, miles per hour or knots. Large-scale air movements are important factors in weather and climate.

Air movements are affected by:

- pressure gradients (differences)
- the Coriolis effect
- friction.

At the Equator the heat of the Sun warms the air at the surface of the Earth more than at the poles. The air over the Equator is then less dense so it rises causing a drop in local air pressure. Cold air over the poles is heavier and therefore sinks causing high pressure.

Convection currents move air from the Equator to the poles. In fact the warm tropical air and the colder polar air do not mix easily resulting in two separate convection currents either side of the Equator.

Jet streams

During the Second World War bombers flew at very great heights (to avoid radar) and they found a westerly wind blowing at speeds of 200 km/h. Meteorologists (weather scientists) realised that this was a westerly **jet stream** flowing from west to east at great speed approximately half way between the polar and tropical convection currents.

Jet streams are used by modern aeroplanes to save fuel on journeys to the east. They try to avoid the jet stream when flying to the west.

As air moves from the Equator to the poles it is deflected (bent) to the right in the Northern hemisphere and to the left in the Southern hemisphere. This is caused by the rotation of the Earth and is called the **Coriolis effect**. This deflection of wind means that air systems, of high or low pressure, are created with associated winds circulating at their centres.

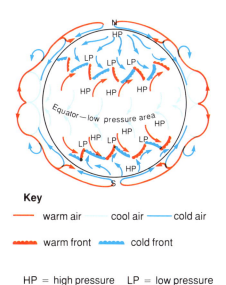

Key

— warm air — cool air — cold air

~ warm front ~ cold front

HP = high pressure   LP = low pressure

Wind patterns on Earth.

Surface features, such as mountains and hills, force moving air upwards leading to friction between the air and the land, causing **turbulence**. Turbulence can also occur around buildings.

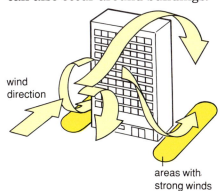

wind direction

areas with strong winds

Turbulence around a building.

Pressure

Pressure is the force acting on unit area. The unit of pressure is the Pascal (Pa).

$$\text{pressure (pascals)} = \frac{\text{force (newtons)}}{\text{area (metres squared)}}$$

You can push a drawing pin, but not your finger, into a piece of wood. This is because force acting over a small area gives a larger pressure than the same force acting over a larger area.

Pressure in liquids and gases

The two diagrams show that a volume of liquid exerts a pressure, and the pressure in a column of liquid is greatest at the bottom. An advantage to engineers is that pressure in a liquid can be **transmitted**. This feature is used in hydraulic disc brakes shown below.

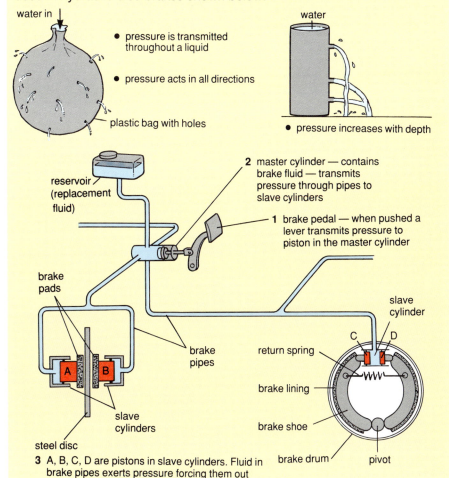

water in

● pressure is transmitted throughout a liquid

● pressure acts in all directions

plastic bag with holes

water

● pressure increases with depth

reservoir (replacement fluid)

2 master cylinder — contains brake fluid — transmits pressure through pipes to slave cylinders

1 brake pedal — when pushed a lever transmits pressure to piston in the master cylinder

brake pads

brake pipes

slave cylinder

return spring

C D

brake lining

brake shoe

A B

slave cylinders

steel disc

brake drum

pivot

3 A, B, C, D are pistons in slave cylinders. Fluid in brake pipes exerts pressure forcing them out

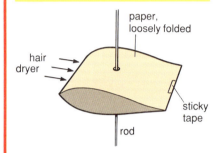

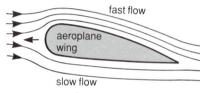

an aeroplane wing experiences the Bernoulli effect

We have seen how movements of air in the atmosphere set up winds. The faster the air flows, the lower its pressure. This was first explained by a Swiss mathematician called Daniel Bernoulli. The **Bernoulli effect** applies to any liquid or gas.

Investigate the Bernoulli effect

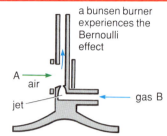

a bunsen burner experiences the Bernoulli effect

air is drawn in at A by the gas coming in at B and narrowing through the jet

1 You are going to investigate the effect of wind speed on high and low pressures.
   a Holding one of the pieces of paper at one end near your mouth, blow on it (or use a hair dryer).
   b Note what happens. Which surface has less air pressure?
   c Cut a small flap in the end of the piece of paper. Fold it down and blow again. Note what happens. Explain your results in terms of high and low pressure.
2 Carry out the experiment as shown in the diagram on the top left using the second piece of paper. What do you observe? Does it model the effect experienced by the aeroplane wing and the air around the bunsen burner shown in the diagrams?
3 The resource sheets show a copy of a shipping forecast, the **Beaufort wind scale,** and sea areas around Britain. For each of the areas shown put arrows on the map to show wind direction and mark the force by the side of each arrow.

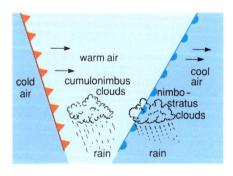

Weather fronts. An occluded front is where a cold front moves faster than a warm front, gradually squeezing out the warm air sector.

A column of air exerts a force on the surface of the Earth causing a pressure. This is called **atmospheric pressure**. It is an important factor involved in weather.

Lines are drawn on a weather map to link regions of equal pressure at a given time. These lines are called **isobars** (*iso* means the same). Wind direction is roughly parallel to the isobars. If the isobars are close together the wind will be strong.

Weather forecasters also look for **fronts** or **depressions**. These are very important because they bring about changes in the weather. A front is the forward edge of an advancing mass of cold or warm air. A depression is an area of low pressure that develops when tropical and polar air streams mix. Air trapped between the two air masses begins to turn, forming a mass of revolving air. The air caught in these swirls pulls outwards, lowering the pressure at the centre.

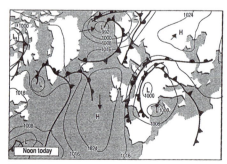

Key
H=high pressure
L=low pressure
cold front
warm front
occluded front

Q1 What is the difference between weather and climate?

Q2 Which layer of the atmosphere is responsible for the weather?

A model depression

Follow the instructions in the diagram.

1 Fold a sheet of paper like this.

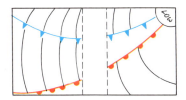

2 Draw a cold front and a warm front. Add lines of equal pressure. Label the area of low pressure.

3 Label the warm sector in a pink-coloured pen. Colour cold air blue.

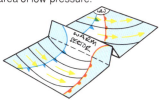

4 Add arrows to show wind direction.

Satellite image of Europe. A few dense clouds can be seen.

Water vapour

Precipitation (rainfall) is more likely to occur if air passes over water and then rises over a large land mass such as a mountain range. This is because evaporation takes place due to the Sun's heating effect and water is turned into water vapour. This water vapour is invisible. As the air rises over a land mass, the temperature drops, causing the water vapour to condense. The water molecules coat dust and ice particles that float in the air, forming water droplets. These water droplets aggregate (join) to form clouds. When the water content of a cloud reaches a certain level, it rains.

When water vapour in the atmosphere condenses, hail, frost, dew, fog, snow and ice can form in addition to clouds and rain. The nature of the condensate formed depends largely on the prevailing temperature. Weather satellites in space that orbit the Earth transmit signals of cloud patterns back to computers on Earth. These signals are interpreted to produce an image of air movement. These pictures help meteorologists to forecast weather.

Take notes

Make notes on the key ideas covered in this unit. Your headings could include: *The atmosphere, Wind, Pressure, Precipitation.*

Project

Design a method to work out from which direction the wind usually blows in your area. Over what period of time will you record your observations? How often will you take readings from your apparatus?

Earth beginnings

The snake and duck produce the cosmic egg.

The Egyptian sky goddess Nut whose supple body supports the arched roof of the heavens. Across her body travel the Sun and Moon producing the pattern of night and day. She is supported by Shu, the god of air. At his feet is Geb, Earth-god and husband of Nut.

The Egyptian sky goddess.

Early ideas

The Earth is one of nine planets that orbit the Sun. The planets, their moons and the Sun form a group called the **Solar System**. The Solar System was probably formed when dust and gases condensed about 400 to 600 million years ago. The Sun is one of the billions of stars which make up our **galaxy** known as the **Milky Way**. There are many other galaxies in the Universe. For thousands of years people have wondered how the Universe began and invented many theories to explain it. Some of these are shown on the left or discussed below.

The modern theory most widely accepted is **Big Bang**. This states that the Universe was born about 15 billion (15 000 000 000) years ago in a super-dense, super-hot fireball. This ejected matter in all directions and eventually stars formed from gases and then clustered together forming galaxies. If anything existed before Big Bang it must have been so different from the Universe as we know it that none of the laws of science would be true. This is the reason why astronomers say that nothing existed before Big Bang.

Collect

- resource sheet
- scissors
- glue
- paper (1 piece)

After Big Bang

1 Cut out the sections on the resource sheet and assemble them to give the chronological order of what happened after Big Bang.

Astronomers learnt in the 1920s that the Universe is expanding. They noticed that over a period of time the plotted position of stars viewed through a telescope seemed to have changed. The calculated rate of expansion suggests that all matter may have been in one place at the moment of Big Bang about 15 billion years ago.

In 1964 radiation from Big Bang was first detected by Arno Penzias and Robert Wilson. The two astronomers were working at the Bell Laboratories, New Jersey. They were trying to measure faint radio waves coming from the edges of the Milky Way. Instead they discovered a glow of radiation coming from all over the sky. They were awarded the Nobel Prize in 1978 for their work.

In April 1992 a NASA satellite found 'ripples' in radiation from Big Bang. Astronomers were very excited by the news because it added additional information that may confirm the Big Bang theory. These ripples also support another idea that most of the matter in the Universe is made of 'dark matter'. Dark matter is thought to consist of elementary particles (found in atoms, for example protons and neutrons) which clump together forming regions of powerful gravity. These regions then attract gas clouds that eventually form into stars and galaxies. Astronomers have yet to discover dark matter in laboratories but they are hopeful that further observations from the NASA satellite will aid them in their research.

Arno Penzias.

Q1 What evidence is there for the Big Bang theory?

Q2 What is dark matter?

Astronomy is one of the oldest sciences. Humans have dreamed about and worshipped the stars since their first awareness of them. Many religious beliefs centre around particular stars. The only star presently within reach is the Sun, which is far too hot to visit.

The Sun may have originated as a large gas cloud which began to implode (collapse inwards) due to its own gravitational pull. The collapse stopped when **nuclear fusion** reactions began in the Sun's centre. In these reactions two different types of hydrogen nuclei ($^2_1$H and $^3_1$H) fuse together to form a heavier nucleus of helium ($^4_2$He) and then other elements. This nuclear fusion gives out vast amounts of energy and new elements are created. It is predicted that the Sun's central hydrogen supply could fuel these reactions for up to 10 billion years. The Sun will then expand, cool and become a **red giant** (a star that has exhausted its hydrogen supply and emits red light).

During the next phase the Sun is expected to lose its outer layers and form a planetary nebula. Finally, the core will collapse under its own gravity effect to become a **white dwarf** star. This is a very small, dense body which emits white light.

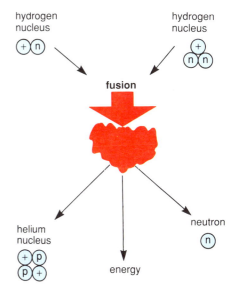

Nuclear fusion reaction in the Sun.

The planets

Scientists have gathered a great deal of information about the planets from recent **space probes**. The evidence gathered has largely confirmed a theory that the Solar System started as a giant, whirling dust cloud. Small globes developed from whirlpools in the cloud and these picked up more matter and eventually formed spinning planets. Planets were named from the Greek word meaning *wanderers*.

The four planets nearest to the Sun, including Earth, are small dense planets with a hard surface. This is because heat from the Sun's nuclear furnace has evaporated any surface gases. The intense heat makes Mercury and Venus searingly hot but gives Earth an energy level suitable to support life because it is not as close to the Sun.

The next four planets are less affected by the heat so the gases remain trapped, forming **gas giants**. These are giant planets with lower densities and thicker atmospheres than the inner planets. The last planet, Pluto, does not fit this pattern. One theory is that it may be a moon that has migrated away from another planet.

When the planets were formed many rocky icy chunks, known as **asteroids**, remained. Most of these orbit the Sun in a type of band or belt called the **asteroid belt** which is found beyond Mars. One theory is that the asteroid belt may have been formed from a planet which exploded, although no one has yet explained why a planet might explode. Another suggestion is that the asteroids never joined to form a planet because the effect of Jupiter's gravity was to keep shifting their orbits.

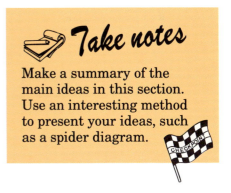

Take notes

Make a summary of the main ideas in this section. Use an interesting method to present your ideas, such as a spider diagram.

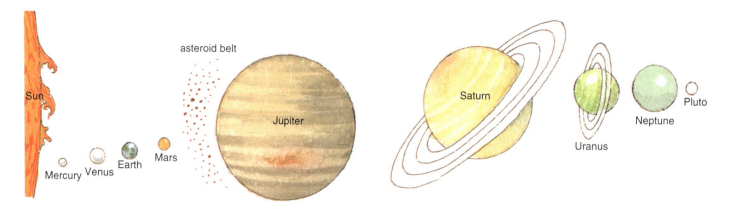

The Solar System, size to scale, distance not to scale.

Mercury.

Venus.

Earth.

Mars.

Jupiter.

Saturn.

Uranus.

Neptune.

Pluto.

Compare the planets

1 Name each planet on the resource sheet using the clues given.
2 Sketch a picture of each planet in the space given and complete the details.
3 Draw a graph to compare:
  a the mass of each planet with its distance from the Sun
  b the surface temperature of each planet with its distance from the Sun.
Comment on your graphs.

All the planets except Venus orbit the Sun in the same direction, anti-clockwise, but obviously at different distances. The orbits or paths are not circular but **elliptical** (oval) and they nearly all orbit in the same plane. Planets can be seen through a telescope because light from the Sun reflects off their surfaces.

Q1 List the planets in order of their distance from the Sun.

Q2 Why are the first four planets different from the rest?

Q3 What are asteroids?

Reaching to the stars

On a clear night there are over 5000 stars visible to the naked eye. The nearest star (other than the Sun) is **Proxima Centauri** which is 4.22 light years away.

The furthest object that can be seen without binoculars is the **Andromeda** galaxy which is the nearest galaxy to our Milky Way.

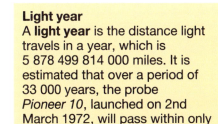

Light year
A **light year** is the distance light travels in a year, which is 5 878 499 814 000 miles. It is estimated that over a period of 33 000 years, the probe *Pioneer 10*, launched on 2nd March 1972, will pass within only 3.3 light years of its first star, Ross 248.

Edwin Hubble (1889–1953), an American astronomer, devised a system for classifying galaxies that is still in use. He grouped galaxies according to their shapes: (a) elliptical, (b) spiral and (c) irregular.

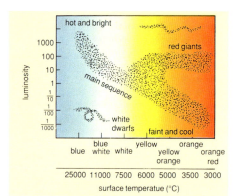

1 A young star born from gas and dust becomes hotter until nuclear fusion reactions begin within it and it moves on to the main sequence. The more massive the star the higher it will join the H–R sequence. It could stay for 10 000 million years.

2 The star continues to become hotter and brighter until its hydrogen supply is exhausted. The core then contracts and the temperature increases to approximately 100 million °C.

3 Helium begins a fusion reaction and the star suddenly increases in size, becoming a red giant.

4 Near to the end of its life as a red giant the outer layer of the star is expelled blowing particles of matter into space (a planetary nebula). The core shrinks forming a white dwarf. It has used up all its nuclear fuel and gradually becomes a dark and very dense corpse.

The Hertzsprung–Russell life cycle of a star.

The life and death of a star

When the temperature and luminosity (brightness) of stars are measured and compared, patterns are seen. These patterns give clues to the life cycle of a star. Ejnar Hertzsprung (1873–1967), a Danish astronomer, and an American astronomer Henry Norris Russell (1877–1957), worked together to devise a diagram comparing the luminosity of a star with its temperature. The **Hertzsprung–Russell (H–R)** diagram is shown on the left.

Spectral type (letters identify group type)	Colour	Temperature (°C)
O	blue	25 000–40 000
B	blue	11 000–25 000
A	blue/white	7500–11 000
F	white	6000–7500
G	yellow	5000–6000
K	orange	3500–5000
M	red	3000–3500

You will see there is a pattern in the diagram. Most stars fit into a linear area called the **main sequence**. Our Sun lies at about the centre of the main sequence. Not every star exhibits this life cycle. Small stars such as **brown dwarfs** are not large enough or hot enough to trigger nuclear fusion. They are 'failed' stars. Very large stars may blast themselves apart in a mighty **supernova** explosion which, for a short time, is nearly as bright as a galaxy.

Collect

● resource sheet

Life and death of a star

1 Collect a copy of the H–R diagram.
2 Mark the positions of stages **1** to **4** in the life cycle of a star on the diagram.
3 Join the positions **1** to **4** with an arrowed line to show the life cycle of a star.
4 Estimate the age and position of our Sun and draw it on the diagram.

Space travel

Over 20 years have passed since Neil Armstrong set foot on the moon in 1969 and made his famous statement 'one small step for man . . . one giant leap for mankind'. The earliest spacecraft were disposable but this changed when space shuttles were developed. These are reusable because the main vehicle is winged and can land like a glider on its return to Earth. The first shuttle, *Columbia*, was first launched by America on 12th April 1981. Unfortunately the 25th launch ended in tragedy because of a leak from a rocket booster which caused an explosion 73 seconds after take-off, killing the crew of seven.

The first shuttle, *Columbia*.

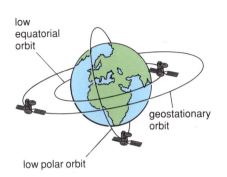

equatorial
orbit

geostationary
orbit

low polar orbit

Satellite orbits.

Since the 1980s several space stations have been launched by America and Russia. These are used for scientific, military and environmental research and also for testing the ability of humans to endure long periods of weightlessness.

There are many artificial satellites orbiting the Earth. These are often placed in **geostationary** orbits (moving in an orbit so that the satellite remains above the same point on the Earth's surface) or in **polar** orbits (orbiting the Poles).

Satellites provide better and faster communication, connect places which are far apart, monitor the Earth and observe the Universe. Communication satellites or **Comsats** are often placed in geostationary orbit. Weather satellites can be placed in either type of orbit depending upon the information required. There are also Earth Resource satellites which are able to prospect for minerals, check the spread of diseases in crops or monitor the spread of pollution.

The **Hubble space telescope** was launched in November 1989. This can detect much fainter objects than can be seen by telescopes on Earth which are handicapped by atmospheric distortions.

There are also, of course, **spy satellites**. The American Strategic Defence Initiative, known as 'Star Wars', aimed to provide a space-based laser defence system against nuclear attack.

Comets

About one light year from the Sun there is a region called the Oort Cloud. This is made up of billions of fragments of rocky ice, up to 8 km in diameter. Sometimes one of the fragments is disturbed and sent in the direction of the Sun. As the fragment enters the Solar System the heat from the Sun begins to melt the ice. Part of the nucleus vaporises to form a cloud around the fragment and a tail of ice and gas forms. This is called a **comet**.

Halley's Comet is the most famous but new comets appear quite frequently. In 1990 **Comet Austin** was seen.

A comet seen in night sky.

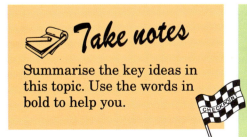

Take notes

Summarise the key ideas in this topic. Use the words in bold to help you.

Project

Find out more about a comet of your choice. For example, Halley's Comet approached Earth in 1986 and a great deal of data were collected by scientists. Does your comet have a period (a fixed orbit time)? If so, when will it next be seen?

Identifying rocks

Geologists sometimes have to act as detectives. They look for clues from rocks. A theory for the history of the Earth can be pieced together using evidence gleaned from rocks. To obtain this evidence geologists need to be able to recognise the many different rock types. There are many clues which geologists use to help them identify a rock. These include: colour, hardness, layering, reaction with acid, fossils present and relative density. Geologists also use evidence from geological features of the landscape and data from satellites to identify important minerals for mining and quarrying.

Welsh slate.

Chalk.

Granite from Shap Fell, Westmoreland.

Rock	Relative density
basalt	2.8–3.3
gneiss	2.6–2.8
granite	2.6–2.7
marble	2.6–2.8
sandstone	2.0–2.6
slate	2.8

Q1 Do your results agree with those shown in the table above?

Identify four types of rock

1 Follow the key on the resource sheet to identify your four rock types.

Calculate the density of rocks

2 One way to help identify a rock is to work out its density (mass per unit volume).

$$\text{density (kg/m}^3 \text{ or g/cm}^3) = \frac{\text{mass}}{\text{volume}}$$

3 Find the density of your four rock types. How will you find the volume of an irregular object such as a rock? Which units would be best?

4 Scientists have estimated the average relative density (density compared to that of water) of the Earth to be 5.5. This value is much higher than the average relative densities of most of the rock types found in the crust. What does this tell us about the relative density of the Earth's core?

5 You should now be able to use your results to compare the relative densities of your rock types.

$$\text{relative density} = \frac{\text{mass of the rock}}{\text{mass of equal volume of water}}$$

(1 cm^3 of water has a mass of 1 g)

6 Record your results in a suitable table. Include details about type of rock and its formation.

Spin-offs from space

The exploration of space has brought about nearly 30 000 technological advances which have improved our lives in many areas.

Benefits from space

1 Study the resource sheet thoroughly and then prepare a short talk about the benefits of each of the products shown on this page.
2 Do any of these products have problems or disadvantages?

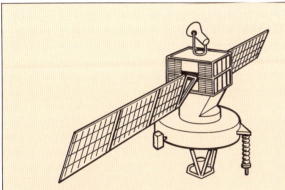

Meterological satellite.

Anticorrosion paint.

Scratch-resistant glass in sunglasses.

Breathing system for firefighters.

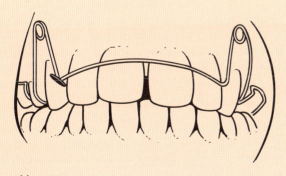

Dental braces.

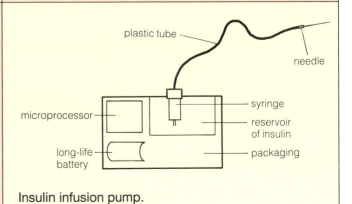

Insulin infusion pump.

plastic tube

needle

microprocessor

syringe

reservoir of insulin

long-life battery

packaging

1 The diagram shows how rocks are formed and changed over a long period of time.

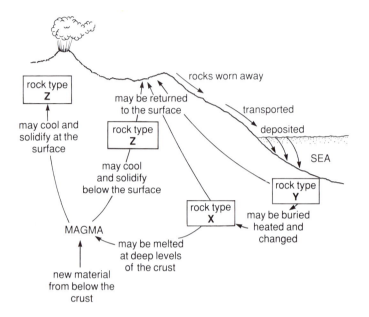

a The three main types of rock involved in the rock cycle are igneous, metamorphic and sedimentary.

Copy and complete this table using letters from the diagram.

Rock type	Rock type letter
igneous	
metamorphic	
sedimentary	

b A sample of solid rock at 1000 °C cooled to 20 °C (room temperature).

i Copy the axes on the right and draw a sketch graph to show how the temperature of the rock is likely to change during the time it takes to decrease from 1000 °C to 20 °C.

ii Suggest an explanation for the shape of the graph you have drawn in part i.

c A sample of a pure mineral from another rock is liquid at 1000 °C.

i Copy the same axes below and draw a sketch graph to show how the temperature of this sample is likely to change during the time it takes to decrease from 1000 °C to 20 °C, by which time it has become solid.

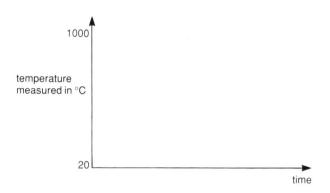

ii Suggest an explanation for the shape of the graph you have drawn in part i.

d By looking at a rock you can sometimes tell whether it has cooled and solidified slowly or quickly.

Explain how you could decide whether a rock had cooled slowly or quickly.

(SEG 1990 Integrated Science)

2 a A list of planets is given below.

Mercury, Pluto, Mars, Saturn, Venus

From this list choose which planet:

i has the most moons

ii is the smallest planet

iii has the longest year.

b If you attempted to live on Venus, describe two problems you might encounter other than those of getting there.

(MEG 1988 Science Syllabus)

5

Making materials

Petrochemicals

Oil refinery at Stanlow, Cheshire.

Black gold

A very mixed group of materials is shown above. Surprisingly, they are all made from chemical compounds called **hydrocarbons** found in crude oil. (Hydrocarbons contain hydrogen, H, and carbon, C, atoms only.) Crude oil is an extremely valuable natural resource and has earned itself the unusual name of black gold!

The mixture of hydrocarbons in crude oil is separated into useful substances. This separation process takes place at an oil refinery and is called **fractional distillation**.

Hydrocarbon families

Each family of hydrocarbons forms a **homologous series**, and each member of the series is called a **homologue**. Homologues from the same homologous series have similar physical and chemical properties but differ in their number of atoms. The **alkanes** form the simplest homologous series of hydrocarbons. Look at the first four homologues:

methane ethane propane butane

Collect
- resource sheet

1 Complete the resource sheet. (Use *US 3* to help you.)

Collect
- data sheet
- model-making kit

Look at the alkanes

1 Use the data to complete a table for the four alkanes shown above with the headings: *Name, Formula, Melting point (°C), Boiling point (°C), State at room temperature and pressure.*
2 Construct models of methane, ethane, propane and butane molecules.

Q1 For the same four alkanes can you find a pattern in:
a their formulae (fill in the gap in the formula (C_nH_{2n+})
b their melting and boiling points?

Q2 Which molecule will have the higher boiling point, heptane (7 carbon atoms) or octane (8 carbon atoms)? Give a reason for your answer.

Q3 Look at the shape of the methane molecule and discuss which word best describes its shape: *triangular, square, tetrahedral, pyramidal.*

Saturation

Look at the simple structural formulae for methane, ethane, propane and butane on page 92. In each structure the carbon atoms are linked by single covalent bonds; the alkanes are described as **saturated**.

Unsaturation

We will now consider another homologous series called the **alkenes**. Can you see how the structures of the first two homologues in the series differ from those of the alkanes?

The alkenes have a double covalent bond between two carbon atoms. The alkenes are **unsaturated**. Can you see a series pattern for the number of carbon and hydrogen atoms in alkenes?

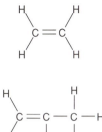

Ethene and propene.

ethene $+ Br_2$ (aq) $\xrightarrow{\text{addition reaction}}$ bromine

1,2-dibromoethane

Look at the alkenes

Collect
- data sheet
- model-making kit

1 Use the data to complete a table for the first three alkenes similar to the one you have for alkanes.
2 Construct models of ethene, propene and butene molecules.

Q1 Are there similar patterns in the chemical characteristics of the alkenes and alkanes?

Q2 Draw a structural formula for butene. Can you draw more than one structure for the hydrocarbon?

Polymers in nature

Polymers occur frequently in nature. Examples are protein molecules (many amino acid monomers joined) and cellulose (many glucose monomers joined). These polymers play a great number of different roles in nature, one of which is structural. Cellulose forms cotton, wood and paper. These polymers are used widely in our everyday lives.

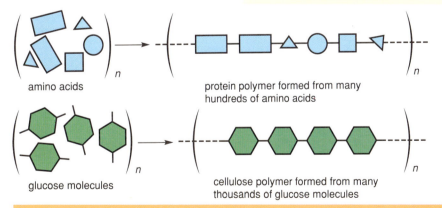

Polymers.

amino acids → protein polymer formed from many hundreds of amino acids

glucose molecules → cellulose polymer formed from many thousands of glucose molecules

Proteins are the building blocks of wool, hair, feathers, nails, claws and hooves.

Take notes

Write notes that include the following words: *hydrocarbon, homologous series, homologue, alkane, alkene, saturated, unsaturated*. Use examples where appropriate and draw structural formulae.

A synthetic polymer

In the 1930s Wallace Carothers made **nylon**, the first **synthetic polymer**. He used hydrocarbons extracted from crude oil. Nylon was used to make stockings and parachutes instead of the natural polymer, silk. Nylon is not as soft as silk and does not absorb water as well but it is tougher and more durable than silk.

Condensation polymers

Most polymers that occur naturally are formed during a reaction called **condensation polymerisation**. Condensation takes place when two molecules join with the loss of a water molecule.

An example of a synthetic polymer formed by condensation is nylon.

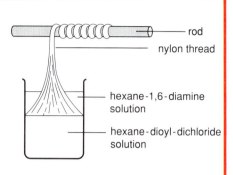
Condensation polymerisation.

Addition polymers

A molecule with one or more double bond, for example ethene, can undergo an **addition reaction**. When a large number of ethene molecules combine in this way a polymer called polyethene (polythene) is formed.

Two other examples of **addition polymers** are shown in the table.

Monomer	Polymer	Uses
vinyl chloride	polyvinylchloride	music records waterproof clothing
styrene	polystyrene	packaging disposable cups

Formation of polyethene.

94

Different plastics.

Q1 Which of the structures (a) and (b) on the right do you think represents a thermosetting plastic? Explain your reasoning.

Plastics in our environment

Although the introduction of plastics has improved our lives greatly, they can be harmful to the environment. They are usually non-biodegradable (do not decompose) and release toxic fumes when they are burnt.

Biodegradable plastics are now manufactured and recycling bins have been introduced into many public areas for the collection of non-biodegradable and biodegradable plastics.

 Project

Plastic washing-up bowls are made by injection moulding whereas plastic curtain rails are made by extrusion. Find out about injection moulding and extrusion techniques.

Plastics

Polymers such as wool, cellulose and polyester are tough and inelastic and are classed as **fibres**. Other polymers can be deformed easily and these are classed as **plastics**, for example polyethene. Plastics can be divided into two groups based on the way they behave on heating.

Thermoplastics These are also known as thermosoftening and can be softened repeatedly by heating and remoulded on cooling. Examples are polyethene, polyvinylchloride (PVC) and polystyrene.

Thermoset plastics These cannot be melted or remoulded. Examples are melamine and bakelite.

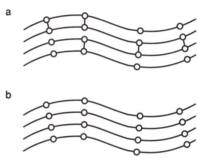

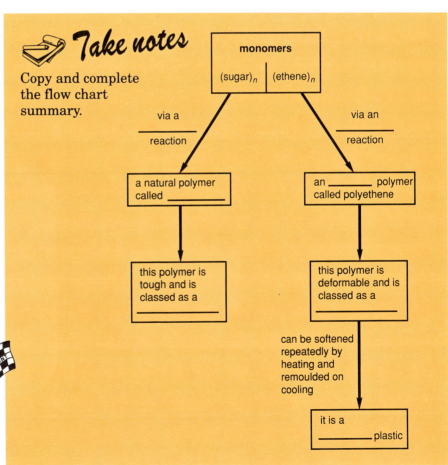

Take notes

Copy and complete the flow chart summary.

95

Farmer spreading nitrogen-rich manure to improve the soil.

At one time, guano, sea bird droppings was imported from Peru for fertiliser.

Nitrogen — its manufacture and importance to plants

For many centuries farmers used natural methods to maintain the nitrogen balance in the soil. They spread nitrogen-rich manure and practised crop rotation to avoid 'exhausting' the nitrogen in the soil. As the population increased, more food was required, putting increased demand on farmers to raise their yields. It became uneconomic to leave fields to lie fallow. At the end of the nineteenth century sodium nitrate was imported from Chile. Although the supply was large, sodium nitrate was needed for industrial processes, such as producing dyes and explosives, and farmers could not rely on a limitless supply.

Air contains 80% nitrogen gas, and scientists realised that if they could learn how to convert it to useful compounds, this would be an abundant source of nitrogen. A German called Fritz Haber devised a way of combining nitrogen gas in air with hydrogen to form ammonia.

The Haber process

The **Haber process** produces approximately 2 555 kilotonnes of ammonia each year. Ammonia is used in industrial processes and is an extremely important compound.

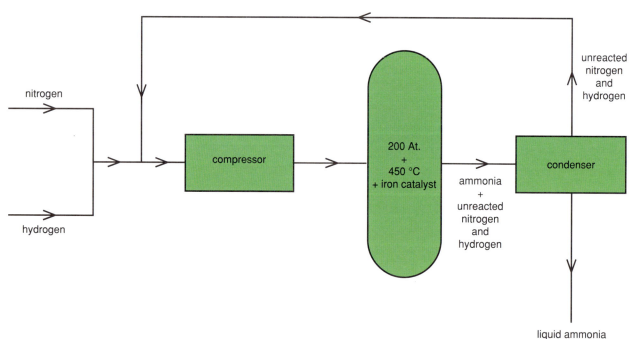

Production of ammonia.

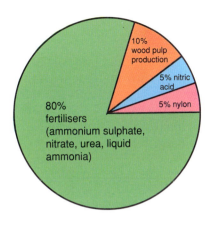

The main industrial uses of ammonia.

The raw materials of nitrogen and hydrogen form the reactants. Nitrogen is removed from air by fractional distillation. Hydrogen is produced when natural gas (methane) reacts with steam.

$$CH_{4(g)} + 2H_2O_{(g)} \rightarrow CO_{2(g)} + 4H_{2(g)}$$

methane   steam   carbon   hydrogen
dioxide

☞ 166

The reaction pathway
The overall reaction can be represented by the following equation.

$$N_{2(g)} + 3H_{2(g)} \rightleftharpoons 2NH_{3(g)} \qquad \Delta H = -92 \text{ kJ/mol}$$

nitrogen   hydrogen   ammonia
(reactant)   (reactant)   (product)

☞ 166

ΔH is the amount of heat released during a reaction (see *UAS 4*, page 88).

The reaction is reversible ($\rightleftharpoons$) which means that at any time during the reaction, a proportion of the ammonia formed splits to reform nitrogen and hydrogen. Therefore, conditions are chosen to make the nitrogen and hydrogen combine, forming ammonia, as quickly as possible compared to the reverse reaction.

The gases are compressed to approximately 200 atmospheres and heated to about 450 °C. They are then passed over an iron catalyst. This results in a mixture containing about 15% ammonia by volume. The ammonia is liquefied by cooling and can be removed for storage.

The unused nitrogen and hydrogen are recycled. The process is continuous, running day and night. Approximately 7000 tonnes of ammonia are produced each day in Britain. The pie chart above left shows the main industrial uses of ammonia.

Ammonia production plant.

Q1 What is meant by a continuous process?

Q2 What do you think is meant by working 'unsociable hours'?

Q3 How do you think running a continuous process would affect the cost of labour?

Q4 What mass of nitrogen (in tonnes) would be needed to produce 7000 tonnes of ammonia? ☞ 168

Q5 What volume of nitrogen at room temperature and pressure would be needed to produce 7000 tonnes of ammonia? ☞ 172

Prepare ammonia in the laboratory

1 Put two spatula-measures ammonium chloride and two spatula-measures calcium hydroxide in the boiling tube and stir with the rod.
2 Cover the ammonium chloride with ceramic wool.
3 Add several large lumps of calcium oxide to the boiling tube.
4 Set up the apparatus as shown in the diagram.

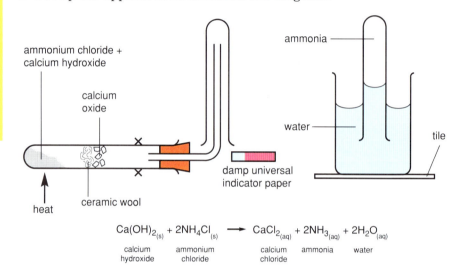

$$Ca(OH)_{2(s)} + 2NH_4Cl_{(s)} \longrightarrow CaCl_{2(aq)} + 2NH_{3(aq)} + 2H_2O_{(aq)}$$

calcium hydroxide · ammonium chloride · calcium chloride · ammonia · water

5 Heat the boiling tube.
6 Hold a damp strip of universal indicator paper at the mouth of the test tube; the colour of the indicator paper will change when the tube is full. Stopper the tube quickly.
7 Half-fill the beaker with water.
8 Open the test tube of ammonia under the water.

Q1 Write a clear account of your experiment and include a diagram. Record all the observations you made during the experiment, and include answers to the following:
a Is the gas coloured?
b What does the gas's smell remind you of?
c Is the gas acidic, alkaline or neutral?
d Is the gas soluble in water? Explain how you know.

Fertilisers

Ammonia can be used in factories to make fertilisers. The ammonia is first converted to nitric acid, which is used to make two main types of fertiliser:

- **nitrogen only fertiliser**   providing only nitrogen, for example ammonium nitrate, NH_4NO_3

- **compound fertiliser**   providing nitrogen, phosphate and potassium. These are known as NPK fertilisers

Making ammonium nitrate fertiliser

1 Ammonia is mixed with air and passed over a platinum-rhodium catalyst at 900°C. The process is called **catalytic oxidation**.

$$4NH_{3(g)} + 5O_{2(g)} \rightleftharpoons 4NO_{(g)} + 6H_2O_{(g)} \quad \Delta H = -950 \text{ kJ/mol}$$

ammonia   oxygen   nitrogen monoxide   steam

2 The nitrogen monoxide and steam are cooled and mixed with air. The nitrogen monoxide is oxidised to nitrogen dioxide.

$$2NO_{(g)} + O_{2(g)} \rightarrow 2NO_{2(g)} \quad \Delta H = -114 \text{ kJ/mol}$$

3 The nitrogen dioxide is dissolved in water to form nitric acid.
4 About 80% of the nitric acid produced is neutralised with excess ammonia solution to produce ammonium nitrate. This ammonium nitrate can be used as fertiliser.

Analysing a fertiliser

You may have made a fertiliser called ammonium sulphate (*UAS 4*). Commercially it is mixed with sand and sold as lawn fertiliser.

> 1 Plan an experiment to find the percentage by mass of ammonium sulphate in lawn fertiliser. (*Hint*: Which mass is easier to find accurately: the sand or the ammonium sulphate? Why?)
> 2 When your teacher has approved your plan carry out the experiment.

Q1 Write a report of your experiment and record your results.

 Q2 Calculate the percentage nitrogen in the following fertilisers.

Compound	Formula	Mass of 1 mole	Mass of N in 1 mole	Nitrogen percentage
ammonium sulphate	$(NH_4)_2SO_4$	132 g	28 g	$\frac{28}{132} \times 100\% = 21\%$
ammonium nitrate	NH_4NO_3			
urea	CH_4N_2O			

The amount of nitrogen, phosphorus and potassium is marked on the bag.

Take notes

Use a flow diagram to outline the stages of the Haber process.
Note the main uses of ammonia.

Project

Compare the contents of different plant fertilisers. The contents are listed on the label. Are some fertilisers more suited for particular plants than others?

Industrial electrolysis

Purifying copper

In its natural form, copper exists as ores. Two of the most important ores economically are copper pyrites, $CuFeS_2$, and malachite, $Cu_2(OH)_2CO_3$. When these ores are mined they contain sand and other rocks. To remove these impurities, the ores are powdered and made into a slurry using water. A frothing agent is then added to 'wet' the powders and an air jet is directed through the mixture to separate the ore from its impurities (**froth flotation**). Aluminium sulphate is used to aggregate (collect) the fine particles of ore.

The copper can then be extracted from the ore by heating strongly. Copper oxide is formed and this is heated in the presence of carbon.

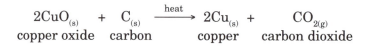

$$CuCO_{3(s)} \xrightarrow{\text{heat}} CuO_{(s)} + CO_{2(g)}$$
copper carbonate $\quad$ copper oxide $\quad$ carbon dioxide

166

$$2CuO_{(s)} + C_{(s)} \xrightarrow{\text{heat}} 2Cu_{(s)} + CO_{2(g)}$$
copper oxide $\quad$ carbon $\quad$ copper $\quad$ carbon dioxide

166

The copper obtained is approximately 98% pure. The impurities can adversely affect the electrical conductivity and mechanical properties of copper. Therefore, the metal must be refined further. This is done by electrolysis.

Copper is purified from ore for use in electrical wires.

Collect

- strips of copper foil (2)
- sandpaper
- power pack
- connecting wires
- beaker
- balance
- copper sulphate solution
- clock
- safety glasses

Purification of copper by electrolysis

1 Rub the two strips of copper foil with the sandpaper.
2 Scratch on one strip of foil 'A' and on the other 'C'.
3 Weigh each strip of copper foil. Make a note of the mass.
4 Set up the circuit as shown in the diagram and switch on the power supply for 15 minutes.
5 Remove and dry the copper electrodes in air.
6 Reweigh the copper electrodes.

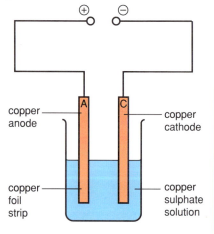

Q1 Describe your experiment, choosing a suitable method to present your results.

Q2 Draw a flow diagram to describe the steps used in the industrial refinement of copper ore. Include equations where appropriate.

Q3 Write ionic equations to describe how:
a the copper anode produces copper ions
b copper ions are discharged on the cathode.

The chlor-alkali industry

The **chlor-alkali industry** is one of the most important branches of chemical manufacturing. Sodium chloride solution is electrolysed to produce three products: *sodium hydroxide*, *chlorine* and *hydrogen*.

Products of the chlor-alkali industry.

Carry out the following experiment that models the stages involved during the chlor-alkali process.

Collect

- electrolysis cell
- power pack
- test tubes (2)
- phenolphthalein
- splint
- universal indicator paper
- sodium chloride solution
- potassium iodide
- beaker (100 cm³)
- spatula
- safety glasses

Electrolysis of sodium chloride solution

1 Set up the apparatus as shown in the diagram.
2 Add a few drops of phenolphthalein to the cell.
3 Switch on the power supply until the test tube over the cathode electrode is full of gas.
4 Test the gas collected at the cathode with a lighted splint.
5 Test the gas collected at the anode with a strip of damp universal indicator paper.
6 Wash out the cell and repeat steps (1) and (3).
7 Pour the contents of the cell into a small beaker.
8 Add a spatula-measure of potassium iodide to the beaker.

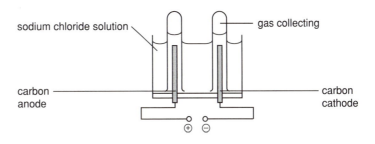

Q1 Write a report of the experiment. Include a diagram. Can you explain the colour changes of phenolphthalein and potassium iodide?

Q2 Write an ionic equation to explain each reaction taking place (use *UAS 4* to help you).

When sodium chloride is electrolysed on an industrial scale the products must be separated because sodium hydroxide reacts with chlorine and a mixture of hydrogen and chlorine is explosive. This can be done in industry in three different types of apparatus, called **cells**.

The mercury cell

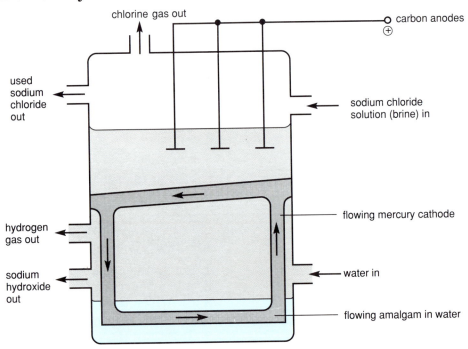

A mercury cell for the industrial production of very pure sodium hydroxide.

A large electric current of 400 000 amps is passed through the electrolyte, which contains the following ions.

$$NaCl \rightarrow Na^+ + Cl^-$$

$$H_2O \rightarrow H^+ + OH^-$$

Each sodium ion migrates to the flowing mercury cathode where it gains a single electron to become a sodium atom.

$$Na^+ + e^- \rightarrow Na$$

The sodium atoms then form an alloy with the mercury called an **amalgam**. As the amalgam flows, the sodium reacts with the water producing sodium hydroxide and hydrogen gas, which leave the cell along different channels.

$$2Na_{(s)} + 2H_2O_{(l)} \rightarrow 2NaOH_{(aq)} + H_{2(g)}$$

166

At the anodes each chloride ion loses a single electron to form a chlorine atom. Two chlorine atoms then combine to form a gaseous chlorine molecule.

$$Cl^- - e^- \rightarrow Cl \qquad Cl + Cl \rightarrow Cl_2$$

A mercury cell produces very pure sodium hydroxide. It is used widely in industry, for example the manufacture of other chemicals, and pulp and paper. However, mercury is expensive and highly toxic and leaks into the environment cause pollution.

The diaphragm cell

This cell uses a **diaphragm** (thin sheet) through which sodium ions and chloride ions pass freely but not chlorine or hydrogen molecules.

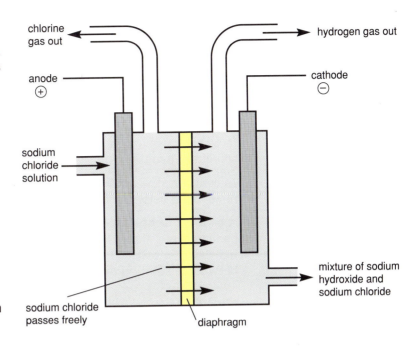

The diaphragm cell is used in the electrolysis of sodium chloride on an industrial scale.

The membrane cell

This is the most up-to-date cell. A plastic membrane separates the anode from the cathode. Only positive ions are able to pass through the membrane.

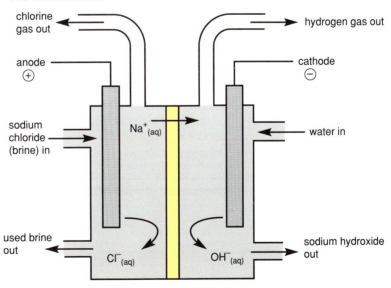

A membrane cell.

 **Take notes**

Write notes and diagrams to explain the stages in the production of sodium hydroxide, hydrogen and chlorine in three types of industrial cells.

Project

Find out what process is used to electroplate metal articles, for example silver-plated cutlery.

Examples of colloids.

What is a colloid?

The illustrations on the left show, in part or in total, **colloidal dispersions**. Can you pick out the colloidal dispersions that occur naturally and those that are produced industrially?

When a solute dissolves in a solvent a solution is formed. The solute particles are usually ions or molecules, and are extremely small, in fact they measure no more than 1 nm (10^{-9} m) in diameter. The solvent is usually a liquid.

In contrast, the particles in a colloid are considerably larger, measuring between 1 and 1000 nm in diameter.

A beam of light shone on a solution will pass straight through but a beam of light shone on a colloid will be scattered. This scattering of light rays is called the **Tyndall effect** and can be used to distinguish between a solution and a colloid.

Each colloid has at least two parts, one called the **continuous phase** and the other the **disperse phase**, which consists of scattered particles. For example, in mist (above), the air forms the continuous phase and the water droplets form the disperse phase. Eight types of colloid are shown in the table.

Continuous phase	Disperse phase	Type	Example
gas	gas	—	—
gas	liquid	aerosol	mist
gas	solid	aerosol	smoke
liquid	gas	foam	whipped cream
liquid	liquid	emulsion	mayonnaise
liquid	solid	sol*	paint
solid	gas	solid foam	pumice
solid	liquid	solid emulsion	butter
solid	solid	solid sol	pearl

* If the disperse phase becomes so sticky it stops flowing then it is known as a gel, not a sol.

Look at colloids

Carry out carefully the five experiments.

Q1 Describe each experiment and answer the questions.

Q2 Classify the following dispersions into their colloidal type:

meringue, clouds, salad dressing, custard.

Making and stabilising an emulsion

A colloidal dispersion of one liquid in another is called an **emulsion**. We often add emulsions to salads in the form of mayonnaise or salad dressing. They contain vinegar to give a sharp taste and oil for a rich texture. Both need to be spread evenly over the salad so an **emulsifying agent** is added to the emulsion to prevent it from separating.

Dressing-up

1 **a** Pour 1 cm³ vinegar into the test tube.
  b Add an equal volume of oil.
  c Stopper the tube, shake vigorously and then leave to stand in the rack. Note the time.
  d Repeat, but this time add a pinch of mustard powder to the vinegar before adding the oil. Note the time.

2 **a** Using the fork mix the egg-yolk, salt and mustard.
  b Add one drop of oil at a time, stirring thoroughly before adding the next drop.
  c Once the mixture starts to thicken add the oil faster.
  d When the mixture gets really thick add a teaspoonful of vinegar and keep stirring.

Q1 How long after the tube has been shaken does it take for the oil and vinegar to separate?

Q2 When mustard is added how long does it take for the oil and vinegar to separate?

Q3 Which is the most stable emulsion, mayonnaise or salad dressing?

 *Take notes*

Read the article on Seagel and then write a short summary, in note form, on colloids. Include the following words:

disperse phase, continuous phase, sol, gel, emulsion.

Mention the different types of colloids, their characteristics, their uses and the recent discovery of a solid that is lighter than air.

Seagel resting on air bubbles.

Incredible lightness of Seagel solid

AMERICAN scientists have invented a solid material that is lighter than air. They say it would float away if it were not weighed down by the air trapped in its microscopic pores and believe it is the lightest solid ever made.

Robert Morrison and his colleagues at the US government's Lawrence Livermore National Laboratory in California make the biodegradable material, called Seagel, from kelp. "After a storm, kelp washes up on the Pacific coast by the boxload, so there should be a plentiful supply," says Morrison.

He makes Seagel by processing agar, a component of kelp which is already widely used to thicken foods such as ice cream. He says that Seagel is safe enough to eat. When it burns, it leaves just carbon dioxide and water.

Morrison makes the product by first dissolving the agar in water. He then adds an organic solvent and an emulsifying agent which disperses the agar evenly throughout the liquid as tiny droplets.

The mixture then sets into a gel and Morrison hardens it into the final product by freeze-drying it. In this way, he can make materials with different properties to suit individual applications.

These range from insulation packaging to slow-release capsules for medicines.

"The light variety is more of a scientific curiosity," says Morrison. "The most useful grades of Seagel contain around 40 to 50 milligrams of material per cubic centilitre of volume."

This compares, for example, with 60 milligrams per cubic centilitre for balsa wood, which is widely used for insulation in supertankers and sound-damping in high-speed trains.

Morrison says the Seagel could also replace solid foam insulation materials such as polyurethane and polystyrene, but he stresses that the material would have to be hermetically sealed because it dissolves in water at temperatures of around 50°C. This property could, however, be put to good use in moulds which could simply be washed away to reveal the finished product.

(*New Scientist* 2/9/1992)

Paint

White gloss paint can be made by grinding titanium dioxide and mixing it with linseed oil. Alkyd resin, a polymer, is used to make the paint set hard. Titanium dioxide reflects light of all wavelengths and therefore appears white. This reflection of light is more efficient when the solid particles are of colloidal size. Emulsion paint is similar but is water based.

Collect

- plastic cup
- aluminium foil
- measuring cylinder (25 cm³)
- measuring cylinder (10 cm³)
- paint brush
- wood (2 pieces)
- commercial white paint
- titanium dioxide (15 g)
- white spirit
- alkyd resin solution
- spatula
- glass rod
- mat
- safety glasses

CARE!
The experiment should be carried out in a fume cupboard

Make white gloss paint

1 Line the plastic cup with aluminium foil.
2 Pour 25 cm³ alkyd resin solution into the cup.
3 Add 10 cm³ white spirit.
4 Add 15 g titanium dioxide and stir vigorously until mixed.
5 Test your paint on one piece of wood and the commercial brand on another. Remember to use a different brush.
6 Leave to dry for 24 hours.
7 Compare your paint with a commercial brand. How can you make sure that the comparison is fair?

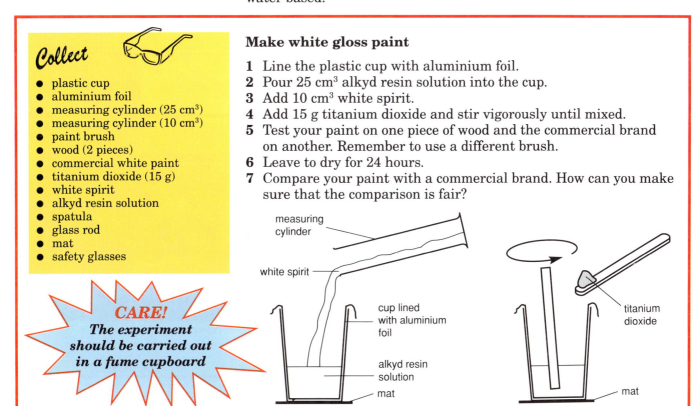

Q1 Describe how you made the paint. How did it compare with the commercial paint?

Q2 What is meant by the term polymer (see page 93)? Draw a diagram of how you imagine the polymer chains in paint to appear when it 'flows'.

Q3 As paint dries it sets. This happens because paint reacts with oxygen in the air. Draw a diagram of how you imagine polymer chains in paint to appear when it sets.

Q4 What is odd about the term 'emulsion paint'?

Project

Find out why sunsets are particularly attractive when seen in a region of volcanic activity.

Glasses and ceramics

Glass and pottery have been made for thousands of years. There are many types of glass that can be grouped depending on the raw materials used in their manufacture.

To make glass, a mixture of ground limestone ($CaCO_3$), sand (silica, SiO_2), and sodium carbonate (soda ash, Na_2CO_3) is melted by heating it to a high temperature in a furnace.

The reaction produces soda glass, made of sodium silicate and unchanged silica. The liquid glass is then cooled until it is thick enough to mould. Once shaped the glass is cooled again until it sets solid.

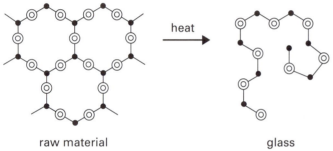

raw material   glass

Although glass behaves in a similar way to a solid it is not crystalline. The atoms in solid glass are arranged randomly but, unlike atoms in a liquid they cannot move freely. Instead they vibrate about fixed positions.

Soda glass.

Collect

- test tube and bung
- crucible and pipe-clay triangle
- bunsen burner, heat-proof mat, gauze, tripod
- tongs
- tile
- lead oxide (6.5 g)
- boric acid (3.5 g)
- zinc oxide (0.5 g)
- manganese(IV) oxide
- copper(II) oxide
- cobalt(II) carbonate
- safety glasses

Prepare a borate glass

1 Put the lead oxide, boric acid and zinc oxide into a test tube.
2 Stopper the test tube and shake vigorously.
3 Pour half the mixture into a crucible.
4 Heat with a hot flame until the mixture is molten.
5 Quickly pour the contents of the crucible onto a tile.
6 Repeat, adding manganese(IV) oxide or copper(II) oxide or cobalt(II) carbonate to the original mixture.

CARE!
*Hot molten mixtures
are dangerous*

Q1 Record your experiment and describe the product.

Q2 How did the compound you added in your repeat experiments alter the colour of the glass? (Share your results with other groups.)

Glass composites

Traditionally, glass items are blown into shape. Your teacher may let you try some glass blowing.

Glass has many uses in everyday life. It forms a valuable building material. Many people are seriously injured every day in glass-related accidents. A proportion of these accidents could be prevented by using **laminated glass,** for example in conservatories, door panels and car windscreens. Laminated glass is a **composite material**. Composites are made by combining two or more materials so that their properties are improved. Laminated glass is made by sandwiching a tough layer of plastic film between two layers of ordinary glass. The layers are then bound together at high temperature and pressure.

A glass blower at work.

Glass fibres used in some composites.

Another composite is **glass-reinforced plastic**. This is a plastic that contains glass fibres. The glass makes the plastic stronger so that it does not crack when bent or hit.

Glass-reinforced plastic is used in the construction of boats and aircraft because it is very strong and lightweight.

Q1 Laminated glass will break if it receives a sharp impact. Why do you think it is safer than ordinary glass?

Q2 Can you think of four other places where the use of laminated glass would be beneficial?

Ceramics

Ceramics are made from clay. Wet clay is malleable and can be moulded; while dry clay heated to 100 °C in a kiln becomes hard and brittle. During firing new minerals are formed as some of the substances in clay combine to form glass. The ceramic produced consists of minute crystals of silicate materials bound with glass.

Glass ceramic

Advantages	*Disadvantages*
● hard	● brittle
● strong under compression	● weak in tension
● chemically inert	● cracks with sudden
● heat resistant	temperature change
● electrical insulators	

Examples of ceramics.

Glasses and ceramics are very important in industry. They have high melting points, are chemically inert and unlike metals and polymers, they do not combine chemically with oxygen when heated. They are said to be **refractory**. Refractory ceramic materials are used to line furnaces used in metal extraction, ceramic and cement manufacture.

Glass or **ceramic insulators** are used to support the conducting cables over pylons because they do not conduct electricity. They are also resistant to corrosion and can be moulded easily.

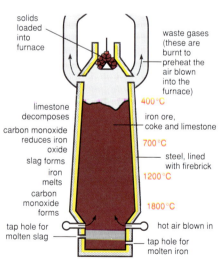

solids loaded into furnace

waste gases (these are burnt to preheat the air blown into the furnace)

limestone decomposes

carbon monoxide reduces iron oxide

slag forms

iron melts

carbon monoxide forms

tap hole for molten slag

400 °C

iron ore, coke and limestone

700 °C

steel, lined with firebrick

1200 °C

1800 °C

hot air blown in

tap hole for molten iron

Iron blast furnace showing a refractory ceramic lining.

Maintaining ceramic insulators at a hydroelectric power supply station.

Cement and concrete

Cement was first made by the Romans by mixing lime (calcium oxide) with volcanic ash. Today it is made by heating a mixture of limestone, clay and water at 1400 °C in a rotating kiln. The **clinker** that is produced is mixed with **gypsum** (calcium sulphate) and ground to a powder.

Concrete is a composite made by mixing gravel, sand, cement and water. It is stronger than cement because the crystals of cement bind the sand and gravel together.

Concrete has a high compressive strength but low tensile strength. If a beam of concrete is used to support a heavy load, the upper beam surface is strong in compression but the lower beam surface is weak in tension. The beam breaks.

To make the beam more resistant to bending, steel rods, which are strong in tension, are embedded in the concrete. This is called **reinforced concrete**.

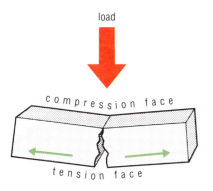

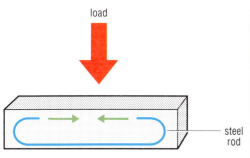

Steel rods make concrete more resistant to loads.

Collect

- test tubes and bungs (2)
- steel (2 pieces)
- concrete (broken pieces)

Investigate concrete

1 Half-fill each test tube with water.
2 Put a piece of steel in each of the two test tubes.
3 Add the concrete pieces to one of the tubes.
4 Leave for one week.

Q1 Describe the experiment. Which piece of steel corroded first? Try to explain your results.

 Take notes

Compare the different chemical and physical characteristics and uses of:

glass, ceramic, concrete.

Project

Tyres used on vehicles are not pure rubber. Find out about the composite material used to manufacture tyres of this type.

Black scab on apples can be treated with copper sulphate.

Profit and loss

Copper sulphate is a fungicide. A fungicide is used to control parasitic fungal infections in plants. Copper sulphate was used widely in Britain up until a few years ago. It kills the fungus *Phytophthora infestans*, which causes potato blight. It has also been used to control fungal growth in grape vines.

Copper sulphate is prepared from copper carbonate and sulphuric acid. Carbon dioxide is produced as a **by-product**. This reaction is a profitable one; both copper sulphate and carbon dioxide can be sold on a commercial scale.

Equipment

Equipment	Hire charge (£)
● small test tube	0.01
● boiling tube	0.03
● conical flask	0.15
● delivery tube and thistle funnel	0.10
● beaker (100 cm³)	0.08
● beaker (250 cm³)	0.25
● measuring cylinder (25 cm³)	0.30
● funnel	0.05
● bungs (10)	0.05
● evaporating basin	0.15

Material costs

The cost of 3.75 g copper carbonate and 15 cm³ sulphuric acid is £2.00.

Product values

1 boiling tube carbon dioxide 50p
1 g grade A crystals £2.40
1 g grade B crystals £1.20
1 g grade C crystals £1.00
(Ask your neighbour to 'grade' your crystals: grade A crystals are large and grade C crystals are small.)

The economics of a reaction

Imagine that you have £5.00 to buy equipment and chemicals. You will be able to sell the carbon dioxide that you collect and the crystals of copper sulphate that you produce.

Plan a production process making it as efficient as possible (so that your profits are high) and then carry out your experiment.

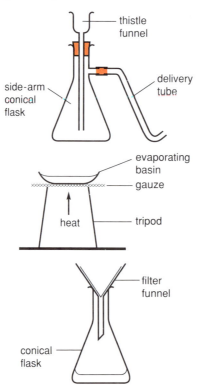

Q1 Write a balanced equation for the reaction taking place in the experiment and calculate the percentage yield if 3.75 g of copper carbonate are used as raw material. 〔166〕

Q2 Use the information on hire charge, material costs and product values to calculate whether you have made a profit or a loss.

Q3 Write a report including:

- a description of the way you did the experiment

- the cost of your process

- the income from the potential sale of your products

- your calculation for percentage yield and profit or loss.

Talkabout

Setting up a factory

A large chemical company is planning to open a new factory. The raw materials are not found in this country and will therefore have to be imported. A by-product of the process will be a useful gas which is poisonous and more dense than air.

Discuss in your group:

- a suitable place to site the factory
- all the things the manufacturers will have to pay for before they can begin to make a profit.

1 a What is the difference between a colloid and a solution?

b Name the type of colloid and give the continuous and disperse phase for each of the following:

- custard
- milk
- whipped egg-white
- paint.

c Explain why egg yolk is added to salad dressing. [3]

2 Many chemicals are made from crude oil. Four such groups of chemicals are polymers, fertilisers, weedkillers and soapless detergents.

a The figure shows the primary fractional distillation of crude oil.

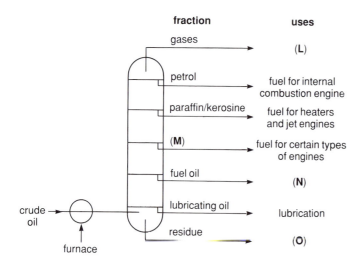

i Give the use (**L**). [1]
ii Name the fraction (**M**). [1]
iii Give the use (**N**). [1]
iv Name the product (**O**). [1]

b Crude oil is a mixture of alkanes. Alkanes can be gases or low boiling point liquids and are non-conductors of electricity.

Name the type of chemical bonding present in alkanes.

By showing all the outer energy level electrons draw a diagram to illustrate the chemical bonding in a molecule of ethane, C_2H_6. [3]

Total [7]

(NEA 1982 Chemistry II)

3 Read this passage about the elements in Group VII of the Periodic Table and answer the questions which follow.

'Chlorine, bromine and iodine are in Group VII of the Periodic Table of the elements.

Chlorine is manufactured by the electrolysis of sodium chloride. The sodium chloride must be molten or in the form of a concentrated aqueous solution. Chlorine is given off at the positive electrode.

Chlorine can also be produced from an acidic gas called hydrogen chloride. This gas is a waste product of many industrial processes. The hydrogen chloride is reacted with oxygen from the air at 400°C in the presence of a catalyst. Chlorine is used in the manufacture of both bromine and iodine.

Bromine is found in sea water as bromide ions. If the chlorine is bubbled through sea water, bromine is displaced and forms a solution in water. The maximum yield of bromine is obtained when the pH value of the sea water is made less than 3.5.

Iodine can be obtained from certain seaweeds which absorb the elements as iodide ions. The seaweed is dried and burnt to an ash.

The ash is treated with water and the solution formed is evaporated. On cooling, chlorides, carbonates and sulphates crystallise out. Iodine is then displaced from the remaining solution by adding chlorine.'

a Explain why electrolysis only occurs if the solution chloride is molten or in aqueous solution. [2]

b In each case name the substance formed at the negative electrode during the electrolysis of
i molten sodium chloride
ii sodium chloride solution. [2]

c i Suggest **one** reason why hydrogen chloride could be converted to chlorine instead of being allowed to escape into the atmosphere as a waste gas. [1]
ii Write a symbol equation for the reaction in which hydrogen chloride reacts with oxygen to form chlorine. [1]

Total [6]

(adapted from NEA 1990 Chemistry II)

6

The quality of life

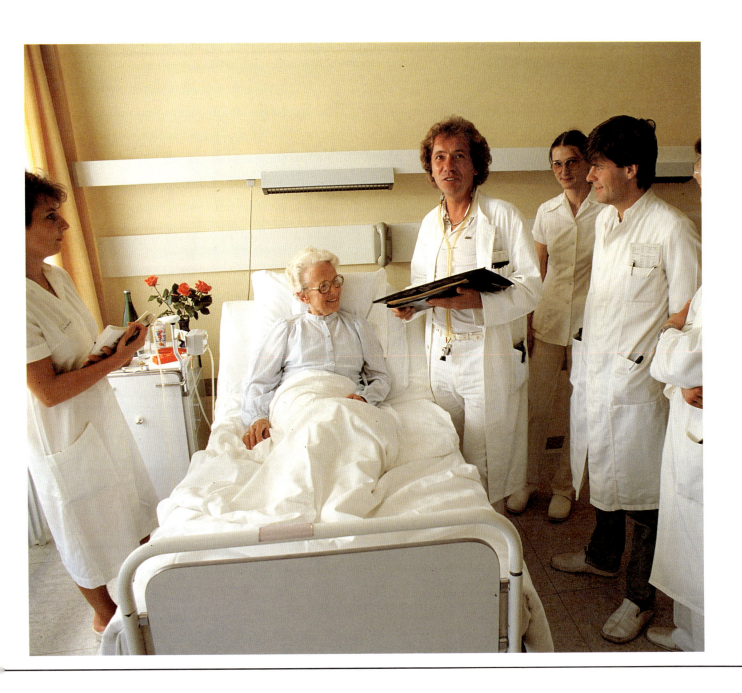

Head start

An organised body

To sustain life all organisms respire, are mobile, react to the environment, take in energy and excrete waste products. Reproduction allows a species to continue as long as disease or other factors do not wipe out the members able to breed.

The human body

The body can be divided into four levels of structural organisation.

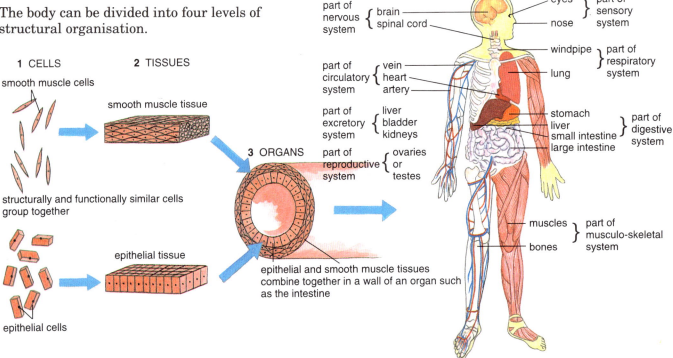

1 CELLS

smooth muscle cells

structurally and functionally similar cells group together

epithelial cells

2 TISSUES

smooth muscle tissue

epithelial tissue

3 ORGANS

epithelial and smooth muscle tissues combine together in a wall of an organ such as the intestine

4 SYSTEMS

part of nervous system { brain, spinal cord

part of circulatory system { vein, heart, artery

part of excretory system { liver, bladder, kidneys

part of reproductive system { ovaries or testes

eyes, nose } part of sensory system

windpipe } part of respiratory system

lung

stomach, liver, small intestine, large intestine } part of digestive system

muscles } part of musculo-skeletal system

bones

The body systems interact with each other and are controlled by various mechanisms, for example **positive** and **negative feedback** (see *UAS 4*, page 142). Some organs function in more than one system, for example the liver is often called the major organ of the body as it performs such a wide range of different functions.

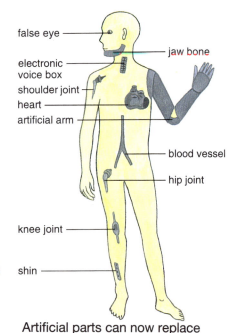

false eye

electronic voice box

shoulder joint

heart

artificial arm

jaw bone

blood vessel

hip joint

knee joint

shin

Artificial parts can now replace defective structures in the body.

Collect
● resource sheet

Functions of body systems

Label the human body diagram and complete the table by matching each system to its function.

Q1 Choose three of the artificial parts shown in the diagram on the right and say what materials you would choose to make them from and why.

Q2 Which body organs do not yet have artificial replacements?

Q3 Suggest three parts of the body which are unlikely to be artificially replaced in the future. Give reasons for your answer.

The brain

The brain controls the process of **homeostasis**. Homeostasis means 'stay the same'. It describes the process by which the composition of the tissue fluid in the body is kept constant. (Look up in *UAS 4*, page 142.) Enzymes control every chemical reaction taking place in our cells.

> Enzymes work best under a narrow range of conditions, called **optimum conditions**. A slight change in the concentration, pH or temperature of the cell can reduce an enzyme's activity. An enzyme will be **denatured** (structurally damaged) when the conditions fluctuate too far outside its optimum range, and will cease to function.

It is very important to keep conditions in the body as steady as possible. The brain checks the temperature and concentration of the blood as it flows through. If a change is needed then a hormone is released into the blood stream or electrical impulses carried by the nervous system prompt other organs to release a hormone.

Body coordination

Body systems are coordinated to enable the body to work efficiently. The nervous and endocrine systems (see page 203) act together to regulate the other body systems. The body must be ready to react quickly to any demands that are made on it. If a person runs to catch a bus their muscles will need extra glucose and oxygen as their respiration rate increases. Muscles send an electrical impulse to the brain, which responds by sending more electrical impulses to the lungs and liver. The electrical impulses reaching the liver instruct it to break down a proportion of the stored glycogen to glucose, which is released into the blood. The lungs inhale and exhale faster and more deeply to increase the uptake of oxygen in the blood and the excretion of carbon dioxide. The heart pumps more rapidly, therefore speeding up blood flow. The transport of oxygen and glucose to the muscles and carbon dioxide away from the muscles becomes more efficient.

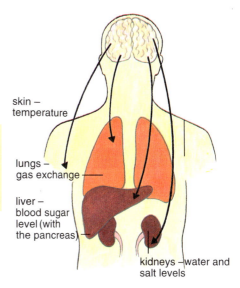

skin – temperature

lungs – gas exchange

liver – blood sugar level (with the pancreas)

kidneys – water and salt levels

The brain has overall control of organs involved in homeostasis.

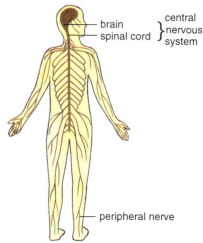

brain
spinal cord
} central nervous system

peripheral nerve

The nervous system.

Running to catch the bus.

The **nervous system** is made up of nerve cells called **neurones**. Each neurone has three main parts: a cell body, containing a nucleus, **dendrites** (long fibres), and an **axon** that transmits messages in the form of electrical impulses from one part of the body to another.

Reacting to a stimulus
The body has senses which enable it to detect and respond quickly to a wide range of stimuli. The senses are types of energy transformers. Sense organ receptors detect different kinds of external or internal stimuli. For example, the eye contains light-sensitive cells in the retina which detect light energy and convert it to electrical energy, which is sent along the neurones as electrical impulses.

Protection

The body is capable of protecting itself from harm by means of **reflex actions**. These are rapid 'automatic' responses to stimuli. For example, when dust gets in your eye you immediately blink. The stimulus causes a reaction to take place over which you have no control. It is an **involuntary reaction**.

Some reflex actions, such as a finger jerking away from a hot surface, or the knee jerk, are controlled by the spinal cord. Others, such as blinking and coughing, are controlled by the brain.

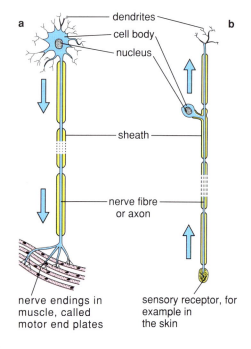

Three types of neurone (a) motor neurone, (b) sensory neurone and (c) multi-polar neurone.

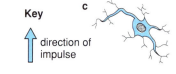

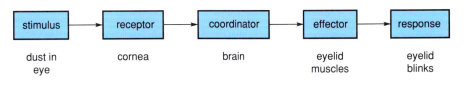

A simple reflex action.

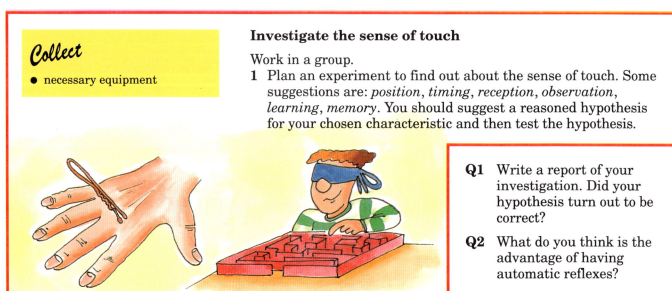

Investigate the sense of touch

Work in a group.
1 Plan an experiment to find out about the sense of touch. Some suggestions are: *position, timing, reception, observation, learning, memory*. You should suggest a reasoned hypothesis for your chosen characteristic and then test the hypothesis.

Q1 Write a report of your investigation. Did your hypothesis turn out to be correct?

Q2 What do you think is the advantage of having automatic reflexes?

Decision making

The brain is capable of storing a proportion of the information it receives as **memory**. Memory is a collection of past experiences, sensations and knowledge. Many actions are **voluntary** and are 'learnt' from past experience. Running for the bus is something that you decide to do. It is not automatic. You see the bus approaching and a message is sent from the retina along sensory neurones to the brain. Your brain 'decides' what action is appropriate and sends electrical impulses to your muscles and organs which act together to provide mobility and increased levels of oxygen and glucose in the blood.

Effects of alcohol

Alcohol depresses some of the functions of the brain. One of the most noticeable effects of drinking alcohol is that it slows down the time it takes to react to a stimulus. It also affects judgement so that the person is unaware that his or her reaction is slowed. Often sight is blurred and interference with hearing may also be experienced.

Research has shown that people who have drunk one to three pints of beer have more accidents compared to those people who have drunk less than one pint. Alcohol is a major cause of machine-related and road accidents.

REMEMBER, ALL THESE DRINKS ARE 1 UNIT EACH!

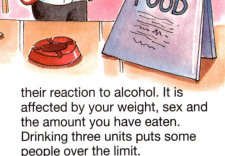

One in three drivers killed in road accidents is over the legal limit for alcohol consumption.

The facts

It is the amount of ethanol (pure alcohol) in a drink which is important. The strength of drinks can be compared by using units. The legal limit is 80 milligrams of alcohol in 100 millilitres of blood. It is difficult to know when you reach this limit because everyone varies in their reaction to alcohol. It is affected by your weight, sex and the amount you have eaten. Drinking three units puts some people over the limit.

Q1 What are the effects of alcohol on the body? Why is a person more likely to have an accident after drinking alcohol?

Take notes

Draw a flow diagram to link the levels of structural organisation in the body.

Outline the structure and function of the central and peripheral nervous systems. Pay particular attention to the role played by the brain.

Project

Multiple sclerosis, motor neurone disease, spina bifida, migraine, neuralgia, and epilepsy are all diseases that affect the nervous system. Pick one of the diseases and read about its symptoms and their possible alleviation. Some of the diseases can now be prevented. Find out if your chosen disease is one of these and if it is, give details. Prepare a short talk to give to the class.

Collect

● resource sheet

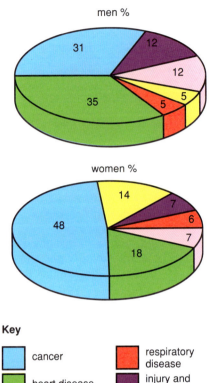

men %

women %

Key

- cancer
- heart disease
- stroke
- respiratory disease
- injury and poisoning
- other

Mortality statistics for England and Wales, 1989.

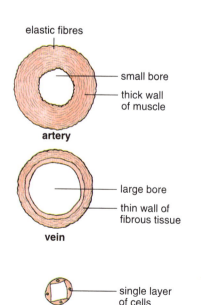

elastic fibres
- small bore
- thick wall of muscle

artery

- large bore
- thin wall of fibrous tissue

vein

- single layer of cells

capillary

Comparing an artery, a vein and a capillary.

Heart of the matter

There are many factors which can affect our health. In Britain such factors are income, the area we live in, occupation, age and our genetic make-up.

The health of people in different parts of the world also differs greatly. People in developing countries tend to die at an earlier age than people in the Western countries, and often of different illnesses. For every 100 000 people, 458 die of heart disease in Britain, 360 in the United States of America, 292 in Australia, but only 71 in Ecuador. However, in Ecuador 106 people in every 100 000 die from enteritis (inflammation of the intestines) and similar disorders. These diseases are usually curable in Britain.

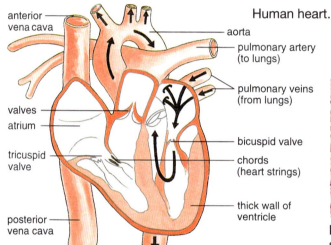

Human heart.

- anterior vena cava
- aorta
- pulmonary artery (to lungs)
- pulmonary veins (from lungs)
- valves
- atrium
- bicuspid valve
- tricuspid valve
- chords (heart strings)
- thick wall of ventricle
- posterior vena cava

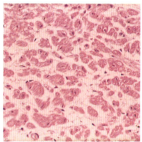

Pacemaker heart cells seen through a light microscope.

How the heart works

The **heart** pumps blood around the body. The heart is hollow with thick walls of muscle which contract and relax 60 to 200 times a minute depending upon how active the person is.

The heart is really a double pump. Each side has two chambers, an **atrium** above and a **ventricle** below. Blood flows through the heart in only one direction. Valves stop the blood from flowing backwards.

Everyone has a natural **pacemaker** which controls the beating of the heart by sending out little pulses of electricity. The natural pacemaker is a group of cells in the right atrium. Sometimes this goes wrong and an electronic pacemaker is fitted inside the chest.

Circulation

The blood flows around the body in blood vessels. Those carrying blood away from the heart are called **arteries** and those bringing blood to the heart are called **veins**. Arteries are connected to veins by narrow, thin-walled **capillaries**. Oxygen and other useful substances pass out of the blood through the walls of the capillaries into surrounding cells and waste products pass from the cells into the blood. Blood passes through the heart twice in each complete circuit; once to the body and once to the lungs.

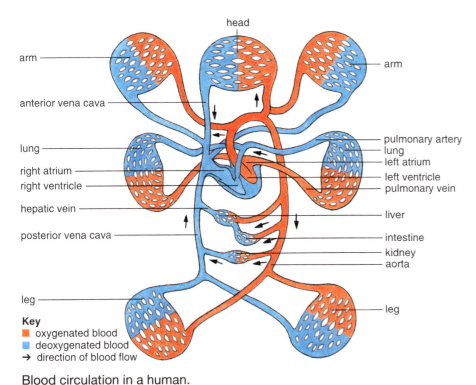

Key
■ oxygenated blood
■ deoxygenated blood
→ direction of blood flow

Blood circulation in a human.

Each beat of the heart sends a pressure wave along the main arteries called a **pulse wave**. You can feel the throb of the pulse by pressing on arteries in certain parts of the body.

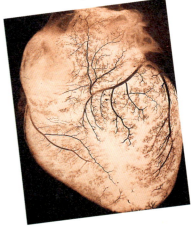

Human heart, showing the arteries and veins which serve the cardiac muscle.

Collect

- resource sheets (2)
- slides of an artery and a vein
- tubing pieces
- glue
- scissors
- clamp stands (2)
- masses and holder

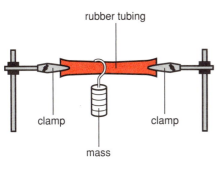

Investigate vessels

- From the human heart resource sheet, cut out and stick the labels on the diagram.

- [IT] Use a computer program to study the way the heart works.

- Look at the slides of the artery and the vein. Make an accurate drawing of each to compare their sizes and wall thicknesses. Label your diagrams.

- Select a different piece of tubing which best represents a vein, an artery and a capillary.

- Use each piece of tubing in turn to set up an experiment as shown in the diagram on the left. Before you begin suggest a hypothesis for your study. Write a report of your findings.

- On the second resource sheet, complete the tasks on the diagram of the human circulation.

 *Take notes*

Use a flow diagram to make notes on the heart.

Construct a table to compare the structure and function of the three types of blood vessel. Suggest why the structure of each suits its function.

Avoidable damage

There is a great deal of evidence to suggest that drugs, alcohol, smoking and stress can have a serious damaging effect on many of the body organs. These factors are thought to be instrumental in the development of heart disease, cancer, strokes and other diseases. Obviously if these damaging factors are avoided, the chances of developing disease will be significantly reduced.

Your heart needs food and oxygen to keep its muscle working continuously. A network of **coronary arteries** is spread over the surface of the heart bringing oxygen to the capillaries. Oxygen diffuses into the muscle cells of the heart and carbon dioxide diffuses from the cells into the blood. If one of these coronary arteries becomes wholly or partially blocked the heart muscle can be starved of oxygen, causing the heart to stop beating or to beat irregularly. This can cause a **heart attack** or **angina**. Sometimes surgeons can replace the damaged blood vessel with one taken from a patient's leg. It is, of course, much better if the damage could be avoided in the first place.

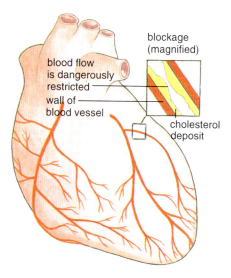

A blockage in a coronary artery.

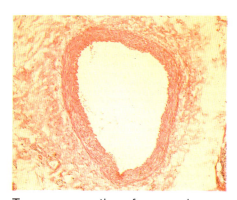

Transverse section of a normal human coronary artery, about × 20.

An artery can become blocked or hardened anywhere in the body. Blockages are caused by deposits of a fatty substance called **cholesterol** building up around the walls of blood vessels (rather like a domestic kettle 'furring' up with chalk deposits). Blood flow is slowed down as a result of the narrowed vessel and may eventually stop due to the formation of a **blood clot**. The blood clot may become dislodged and cause a blockage elsewhere in the body. Oxygen can then no longer reach the areas that are served by that artery.

One common problem found with the circulation of the blood is that of high blood pressure or **hypertension**. The pumping action of the heart through narrowed blood vessels results in a build-up of pressure in the arteries. Blood pressure needs to be fairly high to keep blood circulating around the whole body efficiently. Blood pressure can be raised by exercise, anger or excitement.

People who have continuously high blood pressure have extra strain placed on their heart which may eventually lead to heart failure. Raised blood pressure also pushes the sides of arteries out and may cause them to burst. If this happens in the brain the leaking blood kills some of the brain cells and results in a **stroke**. Strokes can kill or leave a person partially paralysed or unable to speak.

There are thought to be many causes of high blood pressure: over-eating, eating foods high in cholesterol, drinking too much alcohol, and stress all contribute. Scientists also think there may be a hereditary link to high blood pressure.

Other diseases of the circulatory system can be caused by bacteria and viruses, which produce toxins that poison the body. Antibiotics are drugs widely used to kill bacterial infections anywhere in the body. However, antibiotics do not kill viruses so viral infections are difficult to cure.

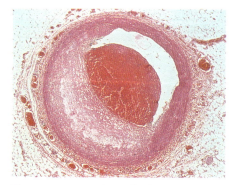

Transverse section of a human coronary artery showing almost total blockage due to a fatty deposit and a blood clot, about × 20.

Exercise

During exercise your brain senses the build-up of carbon dioxide in the blood produced by the muscles and sends electrical impulses to the heart making it pump faster. The arteries serving the muscles dilate (widen) and those serving other organs constrict (narrow) so that more blood and oxygen is diverted to the muscles where it is needed.

Exercise and heart rate

A With a partner design an experiment to investigate the effects of exercise on heart rate. Remember to suggest a hypothesis and to make a plan first. Check with your teacher then carry out the experiment.

The heart rate can be determined by taking the pulse as shown on the right.

B Repeat the experiment but measure the blood pressure before and after exercise. Continue recording after exercise until the blood pressure returns to normal. The shorter this time period is, the fitter you are.

CARE!
Check with your teacher that the exercise is safe

C Use a computer program to set up a database and compare your class results. (If this activity has been performed by younger pupils collect the data from your teacher and analyse their data.)

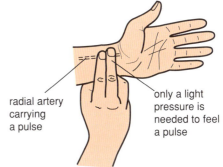

A sphygmomanometer used to measure blood pressure.

Collect

● necessary equipment

radial artery carrying a pulse

only a light pressure is needed to feel a pulse

Taking the pulse.

Q1 Draw a bar chart to show the number of deaths from heart disease in each country mentioned on page 120.

Q2 Construct a table listing the major diseases mentioned in this topic which affect the heart and circulation and the ways it is thought possible to avoid them.

Project

Find out what action you should take if somebody is bleeding badly. Use library books or perhaps guidelines published by the Red Cross or St John's Ambulance.

6.3 Diet, digestion and disease

Radiolabelling

To investigate the path of carbohydrate inside the body, scientists feed radioactively labelled glucose molecules to mice. The ^{14}C-glucose acts as a **radiotracer** inside the mice enabling the scientists to monitor the movement of glucose. It is found that the mice start to breathe out radioactive carbon dioxide after only a short time. Scientists conclude that this ^{14}C-carbon dioxide must come from the ^{14}C-glucose molecules ingested by the mice.

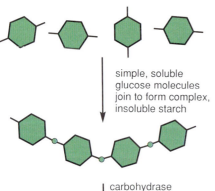

simple, soluble glucose molecules join to form complex, insoluble starch

carbohydrase enzymes break starch down to glucose

carbohydrase enzyme molecule

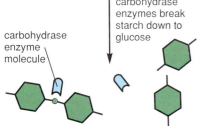

Formation of starch and its breakdown to glucose.

A balanced diet

To remain healthy we must eat a varied diet. A person on a poor diet may be suffering from **malnutrition**. This means the body is not getting enough of the nutrients and vitamins it needs.

A **balanced diet** consists of: carbohydrate, fat, protein, fibre, vitamins, minerals and fluid.

Over the last 20 years ideas about a properly balanced diet have changed considerably and will probably continue to change in the future! The table shows balanced diets recommended up until the present day.

Dietary component	Energy values per day (kJ)		
	1970s	1980s	1990s
fat	5956	1827	1155
carbohydrate	924	3087	3045
protein	1940	1386	1050
total	8820	6300	5250
dietary fibre	9.5 g	47.6 g	32 g

1970s

1980s

1990s

Q1 What are the differences between the 1970s and the 1990s in the recommended amounts of each type of food?

Q2 Use a computer program such as *Analyse Your Diet* to work out how much of each type of food you eat during a typical day. (Remember to include any snacks!) [IT]

Body fuel

Carbohydrates such as starch provide the main fuel of the body.

Starch is broken down to form glucose which is oxidised in most living cells to give carbon dioxide and water during the process of respiration (see page 132). Cellulose is also a type of carbohydrate. Cellulose cannot be digested by humans but it provides fibre in the diet which helps digestion. It is found in foods of plant origin.

Fats as an energy store

saturated (animal) fats

unsaturated (vegetable) fats — less likely to cause deposits in the arteries

FAT ● is a useful store of energy ● provides a protective layer around the heart and kidneys ● provides a store for some vitamins

Proteins as building materials

Proteins are used by the body for repairing and building new cells, transporting substances around the body and in fighting infection as antibodies. There are many different kinds of protein, each of which is built up from a pool of 20 monomers called amino acids.

We can synthesise about half of these 20 different amino acids; the others we have to obtain from our diet, and are called **essential amino acids**.

Meat, fish, milk, cheese and eggs are all good sources of protein. However, food manufacturers are always looking for new types of food products.

Good sources of protein.

Vitamins and minerals

Food also contains vitamins and minerals which are essential for health. **Vitamins** are chemicals which are needed in very small amounts for many chemical reactions within the body. There are many different kinds of vitamin and lack of one of them may cause a **deficiency disease**. For example lack of vitamin D causes rickets and lack of vitamin C causes scurvy.

Minerals are substances which are also needed for chemical reactions. For example, sodium ions (Na^+) in the extracellular fluid (liquid that bathes cells) regulate the cell's internal environment. Sodium is found naturally in many foods and in table salt. Too much sodium is linked to high blood pressure.

Scurvy

A ship's doctor called James Lind published an article about scurvy in 1753. He said that sailors did not develop the disease when they ate fresh fruit which is rich in vitamin C. In 1804 an Admiralty order made sure that all sailors received a regular issue of lime juice, hence the old nickname for British people, *Limeys*.

A child suffering from rickets.

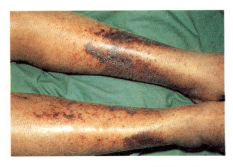

The shins of a person suffering from scurvy.

Biotechnology

In the 1960s many food manufacturers were researching methods to enable them to turn cheap carbohydrate into high-protein food. Many problems were encountered but one of the most successful processes developed uses a fungus grown on the waste left over from milling flour. The fungus is grown in cultures and later harvested, then processed to make fibres. The fibres are compressed to produce a material called **myco-protein** (*myco* is Greek for fungus). The myco-protein can be flavoured as desired. It is often used in beef and chicken flavour pies under the trade name Quorn. It is high in protein and fibre and low in cholesterol.

Tofu is another meat substitute. It is made by curdling the milk made from soya beans (by adding calcium sulphate). The smooth, cheesy-tasting tofu is widely used in Asia. In Britain it is added to many pre-prepared meals and is also used in desserts.

The manufacture of Quorn and tofu are examples of **biotechnology**.

Biotechnology is the scaling up of biological processes combined with the use of technology to provide improved goods and services. Bread, beer, wine, vinegar, cheese and yoghurt are examples of products which have been made by biotechnology for many years. More recent developments using fermentation technology include biological fuels and drugs for medical use.

Food as an energy source

The amount of energy an individual needs over a period of time is dictated by the **metabolic rate** of the person. **Metabolism** describes the energy release and usage in a person's body.

The total amount of energy needed depends on a person's metabolic rate which is dependent on age, sex and how active the person is. The table on the right gives an average energy requirement for males and females at various ages.

Food labels

By law, the label on food must show the following:
- a correct description of the contents
- all the ingredients in descending order of mass
- the volume or mass present
- the name and address of the packer.

Pre-packed foods must also have:
- a date stamp which shows the date by which food must be eaten or thrown away
- the total mass and the unit price (for example, price per pound).

Age (years)	Daily energy requirements (kJ)	
	male	female
0–1	3 500	3 500
4–6	7 600	7 600
10–12	10 800	9 000
13–15	12 000	9 500
16–19	13 000	10 000
adult	12 000	9 000
very active adult	15 200	12 600

Marrowfat Processed Peas in Water – sugar and salt added

INGREDIENTS (greatest first): Processed Peas, Water, Sugar, Salt, Colours (E102, 133), Mint Flavouring.

NUTRITION INFORMATION
Typical values per 100g of peas

Energy	340kJ/80kcal
Protein	6.5g
Carbohydrate	13.4g
Fat	0.4g

BEST BEFORE END–See end of can

STORE IN A COOL DRY PLACE

Part of a typical food label.

Collect
- calorimeter resource sheet

Collect
- resource sheet
- food samples
- food test kits

Food tests
Your task is to find out which foods contain fat, protein, starch and sugar. Compare Quorn, beef, bread and cheese. Draw up a table of your results.

Q1 What are the advantages of using Quorn instead of beef?

Q2 Why are vitamins and minerals an essential part of the diet?

Q3 Why is too much fat thought to be bad for us?

An unbalanced diet

Eating either too little or too much food can result in **malnutrition** (bad nutrition). When insufficient food is eaten the body uses up its stores of fat and when these are exhausted the muscles and flesh are used to keep us alive. It is also possible to eat too much fat and carbohydrate and not enough protein. Protein deficiency is common in many developing countries and a severe disease called kwashiorkor can result. Kwashiorkor is common in tropical Africa. Children with this disease become listless, miserable and weak. Protein and vitamin deficiency can also occur in heavy alcohol drinkers, as these people tend to substitute alcohol for food intake.

Obesity

Obesity can be due to too much fat in the diet. If a person is more than 20% overweight, that person is more likely to suffer from heart disease, high blood pressure and diabetes.

In the developed world we tend to eat foods which contain too little fibre. This is linked with diseases of the gut such as bowel cancer, appendicitis, diverticular disease and constipation.

Digestion

When we eat a meal it stops us feeling hungry immediately but its energy value is not released until after digestion.

In digestion large complex molecules are broken down into smaller and soluble simple molecules. Food is chewed in the mouth, moistened with saliva and rolled by the tongue into a loose ball called a **bolus**. Different **enzymes** break down the food molecules as they pass through the digestive system. Enzymes are biological catalysts which speed up chemical reactions. In this case the reactions break down the **substrates** (specific substance each enzyme works on) into simple molecules which are small enough to be absorbed into the blood.

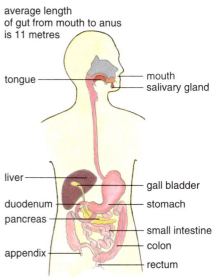

average length of gut from mouth to anus is 11 metres

The human digestive tract.

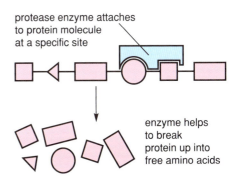

protease enzyme attaches to protein molecule at a specific site

enzyme helps to break protein up into free amino acids

Proteins are broken down by enzymes to amino acids.

Digestive enzymes

Collect
- resource sheet
- necessary equipment

1 Using the information on the resource sheet, construct a table with the headings: *Enzyme, Where from, Substrate, Products.*

2 Pepsin is an enzyme found in the stomach which breaks down specific proteins in the stomach. Design an experiment to determine the optimum pH for pepsin. You could use egg white as your protein sample. Read the following suggestions before you finish your plan.

- Only small amounts of acid or alkali are needed (about 3 drops).

- What temperature do you think would be best? Why?

- Do you need a control? Show your design to your teacher before carrying out the experiment.

Take notes

Write down the main constituents of a balanced diet. You may wish to include how each is processed by the body, the function of each and the effects of deficiencies.

Project

Find out about food substitutes other than tofu. An example is textured vegetable protein (TVP).

Human reproduction

Reproduction is necessary to maintain the population of a species. The environment is often unfavourable to the survival of young, so a large number of offspring may be produced, increasing the probability that a few will survive to maturity and reproduce. Other organisms, such as human beings, produce fewer offspring but look after them for longer, increasing their chance of survival.

In sexual reproduction a male gamete joins with a female gamete. In humans, gametes start to be produced when puberty is reached at about 11 to 14 years. **Hormones** control the onset of sexual maturity. They are chemicals released by the **endocrine glands** which control many different functions in the body.

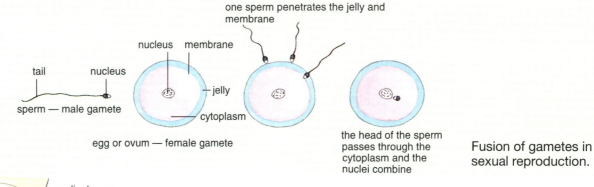

Fusion of gametes in sexual reproduction.

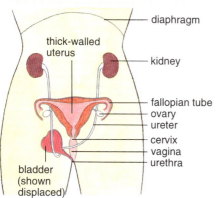

The female reproductive system.

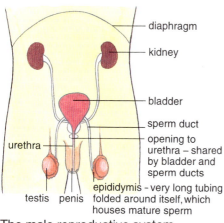

The male reproductive system.

• female sex hormones stimulate body changes such as body hair, breast development and the onset of menstruation

• male sex hormones stimulate body changes such as body hair, penis growth and muscle development

Key
only in female
only in male
FSH follicle stimulating hormone
LH luteinising hormone

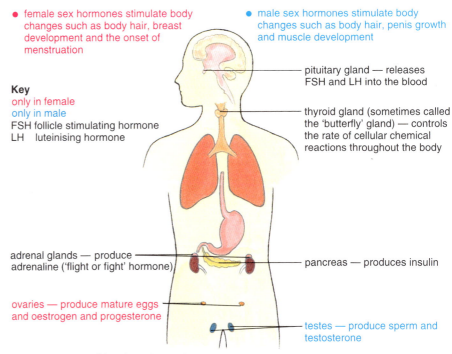

Glands release hormones which are carried in the blood to specific sites called **target organs**, stimulating the organs to perform specific tasks.

Pregnancy

When human sexual intercourse takes place up to 400 million sperms are released but only one can fertilise an egg. This can only take place in one of the fallopian tubes. When the sperm enters the egg it loses its tail and its head swells up as it travels to the nucleus of the egg. **Fertilisation** has taken place once the nuclei fuse together. The fertilised egg or **zygote** then continues its journey, dividing continuously. The walls of the fallopian tube push the ball of cells to the uterus where it embeds in the lining. This is called **implantation** and the woman is now pregnant. For the next two months the dividing clump of cells is called an **embryo**.

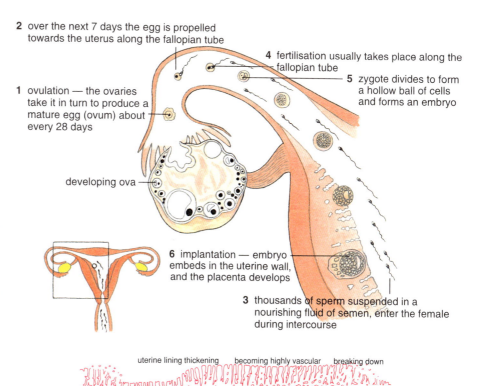

2 over the next 7 days the egg is propelled towards the uterus along the fallopian tube

1 ovulation — the ovaries take it in turn to produce a mature egg (ovum) about every 28 days

4 fertilisation usually takes place along the fallopian tube

5 zygote divides to form a hollow ball of cells and forms an embryo

developing ova

6 implantation — embryo embeds in the uterine wall, and the placenta develops

3 thousands of sperm suspended in a nourishing fluid of semen, enter the female during intercourse

uterine lining thickening becoming highly vascular breaking down

Graafian follicle maturing ovulation corpus luteum developing corpus luteum degenerating

oestrogens

progesterone

menstruation

copulation could result in fertilisation

menstruation

days 1 2 3 4 5 6 7 8 9 10 11 12 13 14 15 16 17 18 19 20 21 22 23 24 25 26 27 28 1 2 3 4 5

beginning of menstruation

end of menstruation

The menstrual cycle in a female. If the egg is not fertilised, the uterine lining breaks down and a period of bleeding begins, normally lasting 3 to 5 days.

Human reproduction

Collect
- resource sheet

A
- List the order of tissues through which the sperm pass after being made in the testes.
- List the order of tissues through which the egg passes after release from the ovary.
- List the order of tissues through which the sperm passes after reaching the vagina.

B
- On the resource sheet, match the descriptions to the stages of development of the embryo and fetus.

Q1 What are hormones?

Q2 Construct a table of the hormones mentioned in this topic to show where each hormone is produced and its function.

Take notes

Summarise the stages in human reproduction from egg to fetus.

Health of the fetus

The fetus obtains oxygen and food for growth through a highly specialised organ called the **placenta**. Waste products from the fetus pass across the placenta to be excreted by the mother. The placenta protects the baby from most diseases but some bacteria and viruses, such as rubella and HIV, pass through the placenta to the baby.

It is important that the mother has been vaccinated against rubella (German measles) because the virus can damage the fetus, especially during the first three months of pregnancy. The baby can be born with hearing or sight problems or deformed limbs.

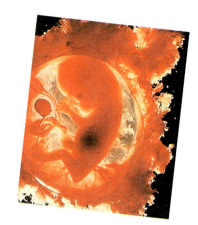

A human fetus.

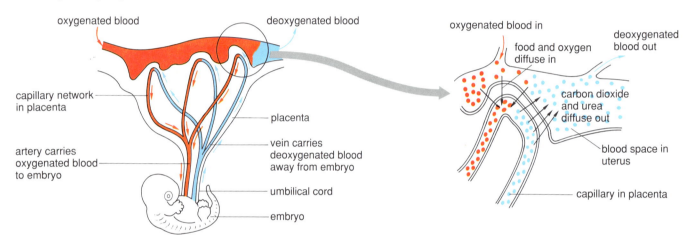

The part played by the placenta during pregnancy.

There are some things that a mother can do to ensure a healthy baby even before she becomes pregnant. Giving up smoking is essential because smoking is known to affect the fetus by reducing its birth weight, affecting the development of its intelligence or even increasing the mother's chance of miscarriage. Mothers who smoke have carbon monoxide and nicotine in their blood and these pass through the placenta. Nicotine makes the fetal heart beat faster and carbon monoxide restricts the oxygen supply to the fetus.

It is very useful for doctors and nurses to know how a fetus is developing in the mother's womb. They can listen to the baby's heart using a stethoscope or monitor it electronically.

Recently it has become routine for mothers to go for an ultrasound 'scan' during pregnancy. The ultrasound monitor produces an image of the fetus on the screen, enabling the doctor to check that the fetus is developing normally.

Illnesses can be treated at birth or even in the womb before birth if necessary. In Britain, fetal surgery is usually only used where some kind of defect will hinder development of the fetus. An example of such an operation is when a tube called a catheter is passed into the ureter to bypass a urinary blockage, which prevents damage to the kidneys. Rhesus disease can also be treated by transfusing red blood cells into the blood of a susceptible fetus.

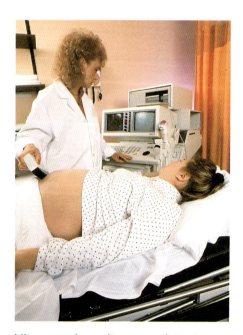

Ultrasound monitors can detect illnesses that cause physical change to the fetus. This has revolutionised fetal medicine.

From birth to maturity

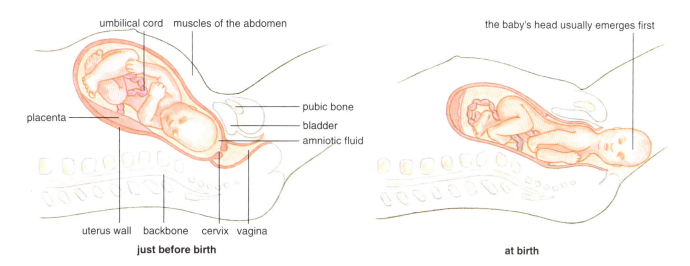

umbilical cord   muscles of the abdomen

placenta

pubic bone
bladder
amniotic fluid

uterus wall   backbone   cervix   vagina

just before birth

the baby's head usually emerges first

at birth

The first thing the baby does is controlled by a reflex action — it breathes. A combination of the cold air outside the mother's body and air entering the baby's lungs stimulates breathing and gaseous exchange. The baby is now able to breathe, feed and excrete on its own so the **umbilical cord**, which connects the baby to the mother's placenta can be cut. The baby is left with a 'tummy button' or navel.

In the early months a baby relies on milk either from breast feeding or bottle feeding to provide all the nutrients necessary for its growth. Many mothers choose to breast feed because human milk is the perfect mix for the baby and it also provides antibodies which protect the baby from disease in its first few vulnerable months. It is also produced at the correct temperature.

Childhood

Parental care is very important at this stage. Love and attention are essential if a child is to thrive and develop normally. Correct diet is especially important whilst the child is still growing and developing rapidly.

Adolescence

This is the part of growing up which includes **puberty**. Hormones are released which affect the whole body both physically and mentally.

Boys tend to enter puberty later than girls so that girls' growth outstrips that of boys for a short time, but not in the long term.

Puberty may take years to complete and during this time growth may occur unevenly. Hormones have a very important part to play over these years and quite often cause problems because they can become unbalanced. These problems include skin disturbances, heavy sweating, behavioural and mood changes. It is little consolation to be told you will grow out of it!

After a **gestation period** of approximately nine months birth takes place. The fetus usually moves into the birth position a few weeks before birth with its head close to the cervix. Birth begins when hormones are released in the mother's body. These cause regular contractions of the uterine wall to begin, and the mother goes into 'labour'. After some time, which can be from a few hours to over a day, the cervix has opened wide enough for the baby to be born.

Project

Find out what tests are performed on a newborn baby.

Sport and fitness

Sport and exercise help us to keep fit, make us feel good and help to keep the heart in good working order. However, too much exercise can put a strain on the heart muscles, especially if we are not very fit in the first place.

Most people start taking part in sporting activities while they are at school. The benefits of sport are shown below.

- **health and fitness**
  jogging

- **aesthetic reasons**
  gymnastics

- **excitement**
  rock climbing

- **'safety valve'**
  karate

- **company**
  sitting in the sports centre changing room

Collect

- resource sheet

 *Take notes*

Use a flow diagram to summarise the steps involved when a molecule of glucose is respired in the body.

Respiration

The process of **respiration** should not be confused with that of 'breathing', which is the movement of air into and out of the lungs.

There are two types of respiration.

In **aerobic respiration**, oxygen is needed for energy-releasing chemical reactions to take place. Glucose molecules are combined with oxygen; they are **oxidised**. All the products of digestion contain carbon, hydrogen and oxygen atoms so the reaction can be summarised as:

$$C_6H_{12}O_{6(s)} + 6O_{2(g)} \xrightarrow{\text{enzymes}} 6CO_{2(g)} + 6H_2O_{(1)} \qquad \Delta H = -2830 \text{ kJ}$$

glucose   oxygen   carbon dioxide   water

166

When 180 g glucose are completely oxidised to carbon dioxide and water, 2830 kJ of energy are released. The energy is not released all at once because the reaction takes place in a series of small steps each of which is controlled by a specific enzyme.

Anaerobic respiration is a reaction which takes place in cells under conditions of limited oxygen. Like aerobic respiration it takes place in small steps each controlled by a specific enzyme.

$$C_6H_{12}O_6 \xrightarrow{\text{enzymes}} 2CH_3CH(OH)COOH \qquad \Delta H = -150 \text{ kJ}$$

glucose   lactic acid

166

During strenuous exercise the demand made by the muscles for more oxygen is often not met. In the absence of oxygen, anaerobic respiration takes place. This produces lactic acid. Anaerobic respiration is a much less efficient way of producing energy than aerobic respiration. (Compare 2830 kJ produced by aerobic respiration with 150 kJ produced by anaerobic respiration.)

Lactic acid is a mild poison. It makes the muscles ache and can cause a 'stitch' at the side of the stomach or muscle cramps. When lactic acid is formed after strenuous exercise it is removed when it combines with oxygen forming carbon dioxide and water. A person 'pants' immediately after strenuous exercise to provide the oxygen for this.

Produce lactic acid

Raise your hand in the air. Clench your fist frequently. Comment on what happens.

Q1 Explain what happened when you clenched your fist in terms of energy supply to your muscles.

Bones and muscles

Human **locomotion** is possible because of a skeleton, muscles and nerves.

The skeleton

Functions of the skeleton include:

- protection — for example the pelvic girdle protects the kidneys, and the ribs form a cage around the lungs

- support — the skeleton gives shape to the body and also suspends some organs

- movement — a jointed skeleton makes a wide range of movements possible. **Ligaments** hold the bones together at a joint and **tendons** join muscle to bone. Contraction of muscles causes the bones to move

- blood production — red blood cells and some white cells are made in the **bone marrow** of the larger bones, for example the femur (thigh bone).

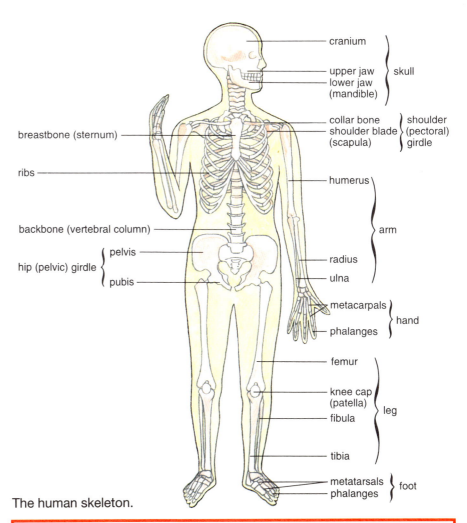

The human skeleton.

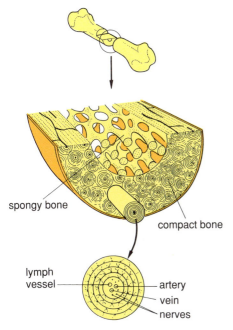

The structure of bone.

Demonstration — the properties of bone

Collect

- necessary equipment

Bone is a living tissue. It is a **composite tissue** made of a network of fibres of a protein called collagen. Calcium salts, such as calcium phosphate ($Ca_3(PO_4)_2$) and calcium carbonate ($CaCO_3$), are deposited among the fibres.

1. Design an experiment to find out some of the properties of collagen and a calcium salt.
- Try to predict the properties of these two substances in bone. Make your ideas act as your hypothesis.
- To remove the calcium salts from bone you could try dissolving them. You would need to leave the bone soaking for a few days. What solution would you use as your solvent?

Show your plan to your teacher. Together decide which of the class plans should be carried out. Your teacher will demonstrate some of them. Record the results and comment on your findings.

The muscles

Movement is possible because muscles move the bones. The nervous system coordinates muscle movements.

About 50% of the body is muscle. Muscle tissue is made from fibres.

The different types of muscle are illustrated below:

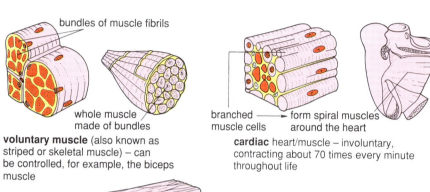

voluntary muscle (also known as striped or skeletal muscle) – can be controlled, for example, the biceps muscle

single muscle cells

cardiac heart/muscle – involuntary, contracting about 70 times every minute throughout life

involuntary (also known as smooth or autonomic) – cannot be consciously controlled, for example, the iris muscle in the eye

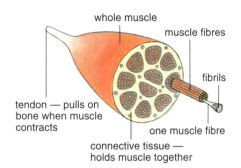

Transverse section through a muscle.

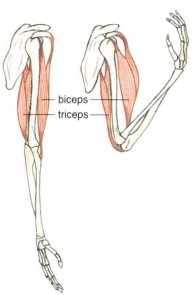

as one muscle contracts, the other relaxes, producing movement

Antagonistic muscles.

Movement — the arm

The forearm is moved by two main muscles: the biceps and the triceps.

The biceps and triceps move the arm up and down. Muscles which work in pairs to produce opposite effects are called **antagonistic muscles**. There are other muscles which are used to move the arm from side to side.

The **joints** help the muscles to do their job properly. They help the bones **articulate** (move easily against each other).

Some joints are freely moveable or **synovial joints**, whilst others have limited or no movement at all. See below for examples.

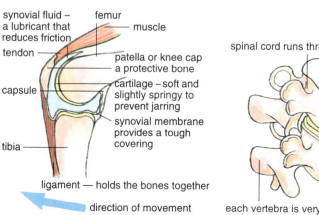

The hinge joint of the human knee has movement in two planes.

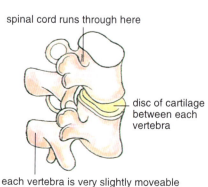

The human spine has limited movement.

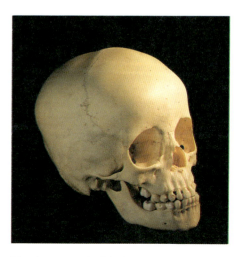

The human skull is immoveable.

Look at the structure of muscle

1 Put the small piece of muscle on a microscope slide.
2 Use two needles to *gently* spread the muscle fibres out on the slide.
3 Add a drop of salt solution and place the coverslip over the top.
4 Observe under the microscope.

Q1 Note the appearance of individual muscle fibres and make a drawing of what you see. Label your drawing.

Q2 How many fibres do you think the muscle is made from? (A rough guess.)

Sometimes the mechanisms responsible for motion become diseased. **Arthritis** is one of the diseases which attacks the joints. Arthritis is a very painful and crippling disease.

There are two kinds of arthritis as shown in the diagram.

Modern technology has brought about replacement joints which can give much improved movement to arthritic patients.

Two kinds of arthritis.

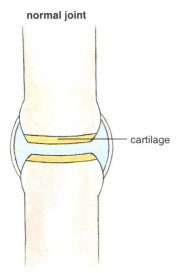

normal joint

cartilage

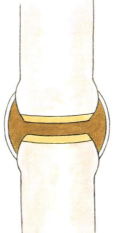

rheumatoid arthritis

bones are fused together by invading connective tissue which hardens

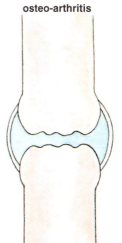

osteo-arthritis

cartilage breaks down
bony knobs develop on articulating surfaces

Preventing tooth decay

Are your teeth in a perfect state of health? If so, you are in the minority. A statistic shows that over half of the 15-year-old people in Britain have actively decaying teeth.

Tooth decay and gum disease

A build-up of **plaque** is the main cause of both tooth decay and gum disease. Plaque is a sticky layer of germs that coats teeth. It reacts with sugary and starchy food that we eat converting it to acids. The acids can attack the tooth enamel causing holes. If the holes are not treated the tooth is slowly, and eventually painfully, destroyed. Plaque also produces toxins (poisons) which can cause the gums to become inflamed.

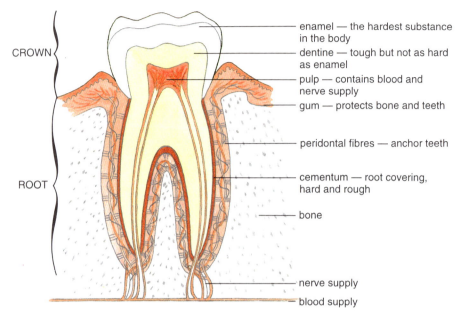

enamel — the hardest substance in the body

dentine — tough but not as hard as enamel

pulp — contains blood and nerve supply

gum — protects bone and teeth

peridontal fibres — anchor teeth

cementum — root covering, hard and rough

bone

nerve supply

blood supply

CROWN

ROOT

Longitudinal section of a human molar tooth.

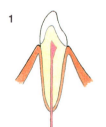
1
healthy gums surround the neck of the tooth tightly

2
plaque builds–up round the edge of the gum and bacteria cause inflammation and swelling, so gums bleed easily

3
the seal between the tooth and gums is broken and bacteria invade the spaces which the toothbrush cannot reach

4
the bacteria attack and wear away the bone supporting the teeth, which gradually become loose and may eventually be lost

Stages in gum disease and tooth decay.

How gum disease happens

Does the statistic mentioned above apply to your school? If so, what measures do you think should be taken to decrease the number of pupils experiencing tooth decay?

1 Design and carry out a survey in your school to find how many pupils have fillings and how many fillings each pupil has. You could find out how many pupils have had toothache, and how often they visit the dentist. You might prefer to ask people to fill in a form anonymously.

2 Collect information about how to keep teeth healthy. Design a poster or booklet for young people which will help them to learn how to look after their teeth properly from an early age.

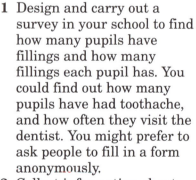

Talkabout

Drug abuse

Any chemical substance which affects the way the body works can be called a **drug**. Medicines contain drugs and so do many foods and drinks.

Some drugs are prescribed by a doctor, while others can be bought at a chemist.

Drugs can also be obtained illegally.

Being prescribed medicine.

Buying non-prescription medicine over the counter.

HOW TO ESCAPE DRUG DEATH

EXCLUSIVE

A DRUGS education leaflet which tells ravers they can take ecstasy without killing themselves is being distributed in Manchester.

The guide, Too Damn Hot, says most deaths related to the acid house ''love drug'' could be avoided.

And information in the five-page pamphlet is supported by doctors at the National Poisons Unit.

Researchers say young ravers who collapsed and died after taking the Class A drug were killed by heatstroke.

But by keeping cool and replacing the pints of fluid lost during dancing at hot, sweaty raves, most would have survived.

The startling evidence, which was used by the Manchester drugs agency Lifeline to prepare Too Damn Hot, is contained in a medical report soon to be published.

Research leader Dr John Henry, based at London's Guys Hospital, says the seven ecstasy-linked deaths he has investigated could "almost certainly" have been avoided if victims had followed advice being given in the new ''users' guide''.

Previously, it was thought ecstasy was solely responsible for the death of victims like Claire Leighton after she took the drug at Manchester's Hacienda night club and teenage student Robert Parsonage, from Denton, who died after downing five ecstasy ''love doves'' at a sports centre rave.

Dr Henry said: "In at least seven ecstasy-related tragedies there have been a number of problems that have led to death. The drug is not responsible on its own. Raves are hot, dancing makes you hot and ecstasy makes you hot. In all the cases I have studied, the victims died from heatstroke.''

The Lifeline leaflet, which is being marketed nationally, urges ravers to ''chill-out'' and regularly replace lost fluid by downing pints of water and other soft drinks.

Dr Henry said: "These people keep going for a long, long time and way beyond normal body restraints. They are hyped-up and high and can dance non-stop for anything up to six hours. That's twice the length of time it takes to run a marathon."

Ian Wardle at Lifeline said: "It is exceptionally important to get these matters across to young people as quickly and to as many as possible so we can go some way to preventing the kind of tragedies that have been reported."

(*Manchester Evening News* 16.4.1992)

Discussion

- Discuss legal and illegal drug use.
- Why do people smoke when the dangers are well known?
- Why do some people still drink and drive?
- What does addiction mean? Which of the drugs represented below are addictive?

1 The figure shows four types of human cell. *(Not to scale.)*

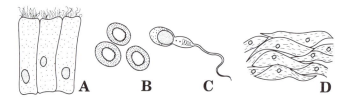

Which type of cell, **A** to **D**:

- has its cilia damaged by smoking? [1]
- lines the breathing passages? [1]
- carries oxygen? [1]
- contains half the number of chromosomes? [1]

Total [4]

(NEA 1990 Biology)

2 The figure shows sections of arteries from a healthy person and from a person suffering from circulatory disease.

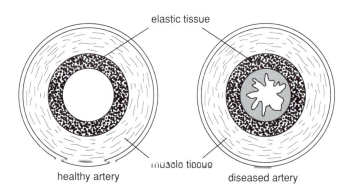

a i Give *one* difference between the two arteries. [1]
 ii What effect might this difference have on the pressure of blood in the diseased artery? [1]
 iii Explain the reason for your answer to part (ii). [1]
 iv Why might this change of blood pressure be dangerous to the health of the person? [1]

b Give *one* way in which we can prevent our arteries becoming diseased in this way. [1]

Total [5]

(NEA 1990 Human and Social Biology)

3 a The figure shows the heart, the stomach and a kidney.

Carefully copy the outline of the human body below, and draw diagrams of these three organs in the correct position and the right way up. [4]

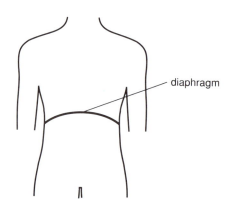

b The table gives a record of how much urine a healthy man produced each day during one week. The man's diet included the same amount of water each day.

Day	Volume of urine produced (cm^3)
Monday	1540
Tuesday	1470
Wednesday	1510
Thursday	1240
Friday	1450
Saturday	1770
Sunday	1520

One day was much hotter than the others.

i Which day was this? [1]
ii Give the reason for your answer. [1]

Total [6]

(NEA 1992 Biology)

7

The Periodic Table

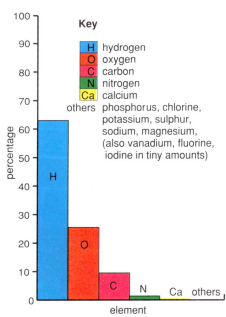

The main substances found in the body.

Purifying materials

Glance around the classroom and name as many different materials as you can. You will see wood, paper, glass, plaster, different kinds of metal, rubber and leather. What are humans made of? The more obvious substances are skin, bone, nails, hair, muscle, blood . . . you can probably continue the list. Other animals, such as insects, are made from different materials. Plants are made from yet more varieties of materials. There are hundreds of thousands of different substances, many of them man-made but most of them naturally occurring.

To investigate an unknown material, scientists often separate and identify its parts. Very few materials are pure substances. Most are mixtures or composites (page 109). Some materials, especially those from living things, are made from many different substances; others from just a few. It can be quite a complicated procedure to separate the different substances in composites. Material from living things can also be difficult to purify. However, there are some basic techniques which are used with many substances. More complicated mixtures need specially devised methods.

Method	Type of mixtures that can be separated	Example
filtration centrifugation	suspension — mixture of a pure liquid and an insoluble solid, or a solution and an insoluble solid	sand (insoluble) from water, or sand from salt solution
simple distillation	solutions	pure water from salt solution
fractional distillation	mixture of liquids which dissolve completely in one another (miscible liquids)	ethanol (b.p. 78 °C) and water (b.p.100 °C). Crude oil can be partially separated. Each fraction boils over a range of temperatures and is still a mixture.
separating funnel	mixture of liquids that do not dissolve in each other (immiscible liquids)	oil and water
paper chromatography	mixture of different substances (often coloured) which all dissolve in the same solvent	mixture of dyes in ink or food colouring
dialysis	mixture of differently sized soluble solids	protein solutions can be purified

Collect • resource sheets

Separation techniques

Study the separation methods carefully.

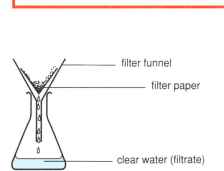

Filtration.

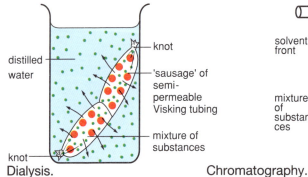

Dialysis.

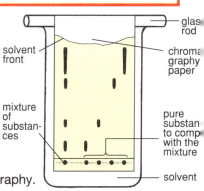

Chromatography.

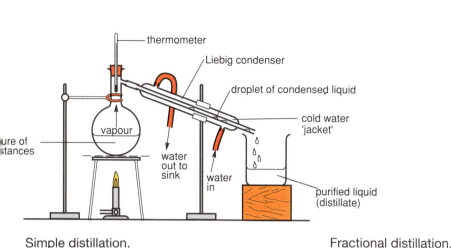

Simple distillation.

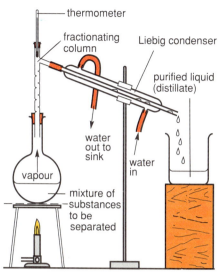

Fractional distillation.

Gas–liquid chromatography (GLC)

A **gas chromatograph** consists of a long tube, the inside of which is coated with charcoal. An extremely small sample of a mixture is injected into one end of the tube and is carried the length of the tube by a **carrier gas**, usually nitrogen. Each of the substances leaves the end of the tube at a different time. A detector and chart recorder produce a **chromatogram** (a graph of the amount of each substance present in the mixture, against time). The chromatograph is calibrated beforehand with known substances. The chromatogram of the known substances is compared to that produced by the substances in the mixture. In this way the substances can be identified. It is also possible to analyse the relative amount of each substance in the mixture.

A simple gas chromatograph and a chromatogram of human breath are shown here.

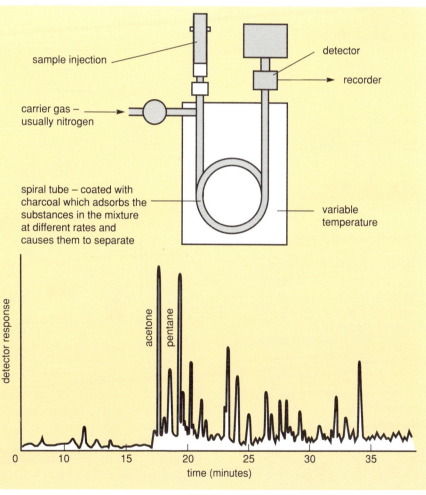

How do we know if we have a **pure substance** or a **mixture**? Firstly, pure substances cannot be separated by any of the procedures mentioned on page 140. Unfortunately, some mixtures are very difficult to separate and it may look as if a substance is pure when that is not the case. A pure substance, however, has definite, sharp melting and boiling points. So we can check the purity of some substances by testing melting and boiling points.

Collect

1
- jelly (small piece)
- hexadecan-1-ol (2cm³)
- beaker
- large test tubes (2)
- thermometers (2)
- bunsen burner and heat-proof mat
- tripod and gauze
- clock
- safety glasses

2
- seaweed ash
- beaker (100 cm³)
- stirring rod
- hydrogen peroxide solution
- 1,1,1-trichloroethane
- sulphuric acid (1M)
- filter funnel and paper
- evaporating dish
- measuring cylinder
- separating funnel
- spatula
- balance
- safety glasses

2 Iodine from seaweed

Seaweed needs iodine in order to grow properly. It takes up iodine, which is present in tiny amounts in sea water and concentrates it in its cells. In order to extract iodine it is first necessary to burn large quantities of seaweed.

a Put 3–5 spatula measures seaweed ash in a beaker.

b Add 50 cm³ water and shake.

CARE!
Hydrogen peroxide solution is highly corrosive
Steps e–g must be carried out in a fume cupboard

1 Melting points

a Half-fill the beaker with water and boil.

b Put the two test tubes in the beaker of boiling water and place a thermometer in each of the tubes. Add jelly to one test tube and hexadecan-1-ol to the other and at the same time start the clock.

c Take the temperature every 30 seconds until both substances have completely melted.

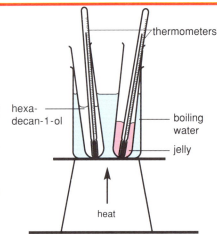

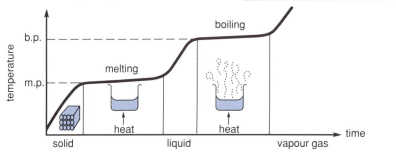

Graph of temperature against time for a *pure substance*.

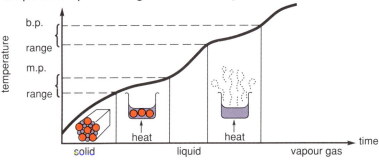

Graph of temperature against time for a *mixture*.

c Filter the mixture.

d Add 10 cm³ hydrogen peroxide solution.

e Pour into a separating funnel.

f Add 3 cm³ 1,1,1-trichlorethane and 2 cm³ sulphuric acid, shake and then allow to settle.

g Run off the layer containing the iodine into an evaporating dish and leave in the fume cupboard until all the solvent has evaporated.

Q1 Write a short report of both experiments.

Q2 For the melting point experiment draw two graphs of your results. Use the graphs to find the melting point or range of temperature over which each substance melted. Label each substance as *a mixture* or *pure*.

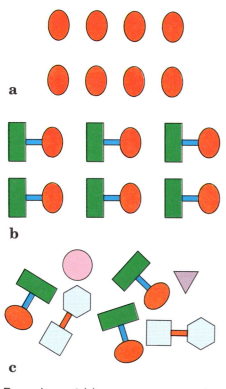

a

b

c

Pure element (a), a pure compound (b) and a mixture (c).

What are substances?

All substances are made up of very small particles — **atoms**, **molecules** or **ions**. The simplest kind of particle that can take part in a chemical reaction is an atom. There are 103 different kinds of atom listed in the Periodic Table. Atoms can combine covalently or form electrically charged ions that form into lattices, as shown below.

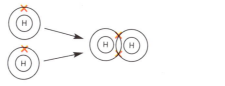

A covalent hydrogen molecule.

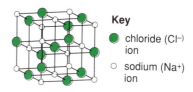

Key

● chloride (Cl⁻) ion

○ sodium (Na⁺) ion

An ionic lattice.

Classifying the elements

There are several ways of classifying the elements. One way is to divide them into **metals** and **non-metals**. Metals only form compounds with non-metals. Non-metals can form compounds with metals and non-metals.

Some elements do not fit comfortably into either category. These are called the **semi-metals** or **metalloids**. There are 17 non-metals, 85 metals and 5 metalloids. Metals have the following properties.

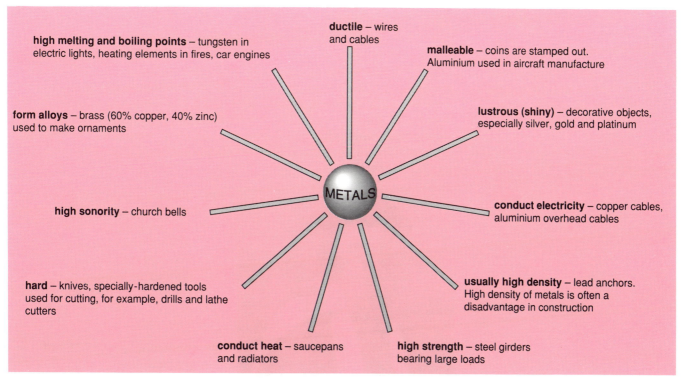

ductile – wires and cables

malleable – coins are stamped out. Aluminium used in aircraft manufacture

high melting and boiling points – tungsten in electric lights, heating elements in fires, car engines

lustrous (shiny) – decorative objects, especially silver, gold and platinum

form alloys – brass (60% copper, 40% zinc) used to make ornaments

METALS

conduct electricity – copper cables, aluminium overhead cables

high sonority – church bells

usually high density – lead anchors. High density of metals is often a disadvantage in construction

hard – knives, specially-hardened tools used for cutting, for example, drills and lathe cutters

conduct heat – saucepans and radiators

high strength – steel girders bearing large loads

The properties and uses of metals.

Another way to group substances is to classify them according to their physical and chemical properties. This helps our understanding by emphasising any similarities.

Sort the elements

Each card shows the name and symbol of an element and outlines its physical and chemical properties. Use the instructions to sort out the elements according to the information given on each card.

List in order of atomic number:

- metals that form ions with one positive charge
- metals that form ions with two positive charges
- metals that have coloured compounds
- gaseous elements that form very few gaseous compounds
- elements that are gases at room temperature
- elements that are liquids at room temperature
- elements that form ions with a single negative charge
- elements that form ions with just two negative charges
- elements that combine with sodium to form compounds with formula NaX
- elements that can combine with chlorine to form compounds with formula MCl.

Q1 Compare your lists. Can you work out two or three families of elements?

Q2 Find the card for chlorine. Select cards from the pack to find other elements with similar properties.

Families of elements and the Periodic Table

In 1869 in St Petersburg, a Russian chemist called Dimitri Mendeleev (1834 –1907) proposed the first detailed Periodic Table by which to classify the elements. There were scientists in Germany and Britain studying the same classification problem and Mendeleev owed much to their work. It had been noticed that when the elements were arranged in order of atomic weight those with similar properties occurred at regular intervals. This was called **periodicity**. Mendeleev devised a table with rows and columns. The columns showed elements with similar properties.

Q3 Make a list of the properties of lithium. Arrange the first 20 elements in order of atomic weight and look for two elements that are similar to lithium. Use information from the activity at the top of this page to help you.

Q4 Repeat question (3), but for helium.

Dimitri Mendeleev, who proposed the Periodic Table of elements.

The modern form of the Periodic Table orders the elements according to atomic number. The columns are called **groups** and the rows are called **periods**. The groups contain families of elements. Sometimes the family resemblances are very strong but in others they are harder to see. Four element groups of the eight prominent families are:

- Group I – the alkali metals
- Group II – the alkaline earth metals
- Group VII – the halogens
- Group O – the noble gases.

Q1 Find the families in the Periodic Table. You should recognise these elements from your work with the element cards.

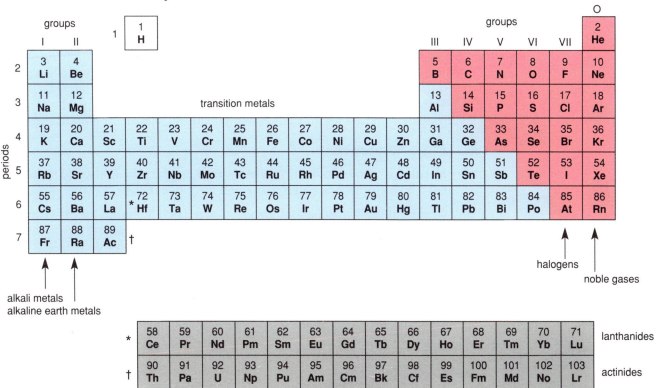

Take notes

Collect

- Periodic Table resource sheet

Explain, using examples, what is meant by periodicity. On the Periodic Table, label the names of the groups, the numbers of the periods and the alkaline earth metals.

Project

Aluminium is used to make cheap, useful objects such as jugs for use in the kitchen. These objects are often coloured. Find out how aluminium can be coloured. (*Hint:* anodising.)

Element groups

Compounds of lithium, sodium and potassium are widely used.

sodium hydrogencarbonate, $NaHCO_3$

sodium carbonate, Na_2CO_3

sodium hydroxide, $NaOH$

sodium hypochlorite, $NaOCl$

potassium nitrate, KNO_3

The alkali metals

The alkali metals make up Group I of the Periodic Table.

Group I	Symbol	Atomic number	Relative atomic mass
lithium	Li	3	6.9
sodium	Na	11	2.3
potassium	K	19	39.1
rubidium	Rb	37	85.5
caesium	Cs	55	132.9
francium	Fr	87	223.0

Francium is a rare radioactive metal. Its properties are not known for certain because it has not been isolated in large enough quantities to be investigated thoroughly. Rubidium and caesium occur in very small quantities in some salt deposits and are very hazardous elements. Your teacher may show you some of the physical and chemical properties of the alkali metals using lithium, sodium and potassium.

Physical properties

Metals are good conductors of heat; good conductors of electricity; and have a shiny surface (lustrous) when freshly cut.

Group I metals also have unusual properties not shared by the Group II metals. Group I metals are soft; are easily cut; have low strength; have low melting and boiling points; and have very low densities compared with other metals.

Lithium, sodium and potassium float on water while rubidium and caesium sink.

Chemical properties

Group I metals all have similar chemical properties. These properties are different to metals we are used to. Your teacher may demonstrate some of the following properties.

Group I metals:

- lose their shine in air (tarnish) as they react readily with oxygen, producing metal oxide.

- react readily with water vapour in the air. They are stored in mineral oil which protects them from the air.

- react violently with water. As they react they effervesce (fizz) and hydrogen gas is evolved. The water is alkaline (it has a pH greater than 7), because hydroxide ions ($OH^-_{(aq)}$) are also produced. This is why Group I metals are also called alkali metals. Sometimes the reaction takes place so quickly that the heat produced causes the hydrogen to catch fire. The colour of the flame is different for each alkali metal (see data sheet).

Group I metal + water → metal hydroxide + hydrogen gas

$$Na_{(s)} + 2H_2O_{(l)} \rightarrow 2NaOH_{(aq)} + H_{2(g)}$$

166

continued

- react when heated with chlorine to form a metal chloride.
  Group I metal + chlorine → metal chloride
  $$2Li_{(s)} + Cl_{2(g)} → 2LiCl_{(s)}$$
- burn in oxygen with a coloured flame and form metal oxides. Notice the different formulae of the oxides.
  lithium + oxygen → lithium oxide   sodium + oxygen → sodium oxide potassium + oxygen → potassium oxide

  $$4Li_{(s)} + O_{2(g)} → 2Li_2O_{(s)} \qquad 2Na_{(s)} + O_{2(g)} → Na_2O_{2(s)} \qquad K_{(s)} + O_2 → KO_{2(s)}$$
- burn in oxygen to form metal oxides which react readily with water.

166

Study this page from Katie's laboratory notebook.

Alkali metal oxides – reaction with water   2nd June 19–

Add metal oxide to water

Method

1. Add a spatula-full of lithium, sodium or potassium oxide to water.

   BE CAREFUL!

2. Over a period of 3 minutes monitor the temperature change, the gas produced and the pH of the water in the beaker.

spatula-full of oxides of lithium or sodium or potassium added to water → thermometer, distilled water

Electrolysis

Method

1. Set up the apparatus as in the diagram.

2. Try to predict what gases will be formed and test any that do form. (Remember that oxygen relights a glowing splint and hydrogen causes a squeaky pop.)

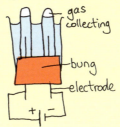

gas collecting, bung, electrode, + –

Group I metal oxides and water

Collect

- resource sheet
- beaker (100 cm³)
- oxides of sodium and potassium
- spatula
- indicator solution /pH paper
- thermometer
- wooden splint
- electrolysis apparatus
- safety glasses

1 Carry out the same two experiments shown in Katie's notebook using lithium, sodium and potassium oxides.

2 Copy Katie's table and add your results. Are your results for lithium the same as Katie's?

CARE!
Be sure not to let the oxides or solutions come into contact with your skin

Q1 Write reports of your two experiments. Write out a general (word) equation for the reaction of a Group I metal oxide with water.

Q2 Explain the results of the electrolysis experiments.

Trends in the properties of Group I metals

Trend setting

Look up the three constants: boiling point, melting point and density for Group I metals in a data book or on data sheets. Draw line graphs to show the trends of these constants. Use the trends shown by your graphs to predict the boiling and melting points and density of francium (Fr).

Although the Group I alkali metals form a group or 'family' of elements with clear resemblances there are differences in their individual properties. A gradual change in some property as you move from element to element down a group is called a **trend**. When cut, Group I metals become softer down the group from lithium to caesium. This is an example of a simple trend. The chemical reactions of Group I metals get more vigorous as you progress down the group. The general trend is an increase in chemical reactivity.

There is also a trend in the way melting points of the metals change down the group. If the position of an element in the Periodic Table is known, trends can often be used to predict the element's properties.

[IT] Think back to the typical chemical reactions of Group I metals. (These may have been demonstrated by your teacher.) You may also have seen a video showing several of the chemical reactions of Group I metals including rubidium and caesium. Make a list of any trends that you have observed. Be sure to state the direction of each of the trends in the Periodic Table.

 *Take notes*

Describe the ways in which Group I metals are similar to each other. A table may be a good way of organising this information.

What differences are there in the properties of Group I metals? Give examples wherever possible, and show how these differences form trends. You should incorporate the graphs you drew earlier into your notes.

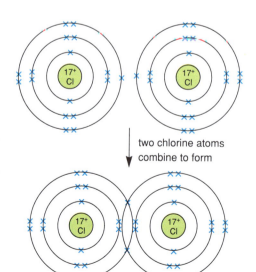

two chlorine atoms combine to form

a diatomic chlorine molecule

Chlorine exists as a covalently bonded diatomic molecule.

The halogens

We saw earlier (page 145) that halogens make up Group VII of the Periodic Table. All halogens exist as covalently bonded, diatomic molecules under normal laboratory conditions.

The halogens are all non-metals. Astatine is radioactive with a very short half-life and little is known about it. It is very rare. Fluorine is very hazardous.

Group VII	Symbol	Atomic number	Relative atomic mass
fluorine	F	9	18.9
chlorine	Cl	17	35.4
bromine	Br	35	79.9
iodine	I	53	126.9
astatine	At	85	–

When a halogen reacts with a metal the ionic compound formed is a **metal halide**. Metal halides are **salts** (see *UAS 4*, page 54). The metal always forms a cation (positive ion) and the halogen an anion (negative halide ion). (See *UAS 4*, page 162 to remind yourself of ionic compounds). Examples of metal halides are magnesium chloride ($MgCl_2$), lead iodide (PbI_2), sodium chloride (NaCl), potassium fluoride (KF), and iron bromide ($FeBr_3$). Some halides are found in the ground. Can you think of an obvious example? (The word halogen means *salt former*.)

Group I metal + halogen → metal halide

lithium + bromine → lithium bromide

$$2Li_{(s)} + Br_{2(g)} → 2LiBr_{(s)}$$

Metal halides are also formed when a halogen combines with a Group III metal.

aluminium + iodine → aluminium iodide

$$2Al_{(s)} + 3I_{2(s)} → 2AlI_{3(s)}$$

A halogen reacts with iron to produce an iron halide with three halide ions ($3I^-$) to one iron ion (Fe^{3+}) to balance the charges. There is a trend of decreasing chemical reactivity down the halogen group:

F > Cl > Br > I

Iron wool reacts most readily with fluorine; no extra heat is needed and the iron glows brightly. Iron wool must be heated to start a reaction with chlorine. The reaction continues by means of the heat it produces itself. A reaction in which heat is evolved is described as **exothermic**. Iron wool needs constant heat to react with bromine. Iodine reacts only very slowly with iron wool under conditions of constant heat.

Group O

Group O	Symbol	Atmospheric proportion (%)	Boiling point (°C)
helium	He	1.0005	−269
neon	Ne	0.0018	−246
argon	Ar	0.93	−186
krypton	Kr	0.0001	−152
xenon	Xe	0.00001	−107
radon	Ra	variable	−62

The noble gases are a very unreactive group. They are found in the air in tiny quantities. Helium is also found in larger quantities in some North American oil wells. Radon is a radioactive gas produced by the breakdown of radioactive elements in the Earth's crust (page 209). Because the noble gases are unreactive they exist as single atoms. A few noble gas compounds, notably of xenon, have been made but special conditions are needed.

The trend in chemical reactivity of the halogens can be demonstrated by a **displacement** reaction. When a more reactive halogen is mixed with a solution of a halide salt containing ions of a less reactive halogen, the more reactive halogen forms ions which displace the less reactive halide ions from the halide salt.

Uses of halogens

- **fluorine** toothpastes, non-stick cooking pans, CFCs in aerosol cans, as coolants in refrigerators and in cleaning fluids

- **chlorine** bleaches, antiseptics, disinfectants, pesticides, CFCs

- **bromine** petrol additive, flame retardant, coating on photographic film as silver salt

- **iodine** antiseptics, coating on photographic film as silver salt

Take notes

Write down the main properties, trends and uses of Group VII halogens and Group O noble gases.

Project

Find out if there are fluoride ions (F^-) in your local water supply. Are they added by the Local Water Authority or present naturally? Find out about possible effects of fluoride ions on the human body. What is your opinion about adding chemicals to the water supply? Should we be allowed to choose?

7.3 Periodicity

Properties across a period

As well as showing family trends down the groups the properties of the elements in the Periodic Table show regular patterns across rows that are called **periods**. This repetition or regularity of element properties is an example of periodicity.

Properties of elements in Periods 2 and 3

Collect

- resource sheets (2)
- data sheet

Either copy the resource sheet tables yourself or collect copies from your teacher. Complete both tables using information in this unit.

Elements of Period 2	Lithium Li	Be	Boron	Carbon (graphite) C	N	O	Fluorine	Ne
Atomic number	3							
Melting point (°C)	180							
Physical state and appearance at 25°C	silvery white solid						yellow gas	
Electrical conductivity at 25°C	good		intermediate					
Structure (giant/molecular)	giant atomic lattice (metallic)						poor	
Classification (metal/semi-metal/non-metal)	metal							non-metal

Elements of Period 3	Sodium	Mg	Al	Silicon	P	S	Cl	Ar
Atomic number								
Melting point (°C)								
Physical state and appearance at 25°C								
Electrical conductivity at 25°C								
Structure/bonding (giant/molecular covalent/metallic)								
Classification (metal/semi-metal/non-metal)								

Q1 How are the elements in Periods 2 and 3 ordered in the Periodic Table?

Q2 How do melting points and boiling points change across each period? Are there any sudden changes?

Q3 How does the classification of elements change across Period 2?

Q4 Is this change repeated in Period 3?

Q5 Describe how the atomic structure of the elements changes across each period.

Properties of Period 3 oxides

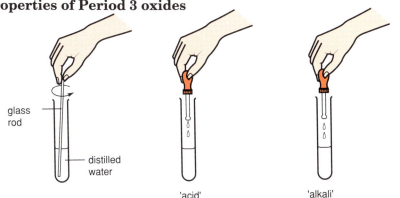

glass rod

distilled water

'acid'

'alkali'

The resource sheet shows some properties of the oxides and chlorine halides of some of the elements in Period 3 (sodium to argon).

1 Put a small amount of oxide in a test tube, add a few drops of water, stir, and test the pH of the solution with pH paper. Record your result.
2 If the oxide does not dissolve, set up another test tube of the same oxide with water. Add dilute acid to one and alkali to the other. Label the test tubes 'acid' or 'alkali'. Note what happens.
3 Copy and complete both tables, using data sheets to help you. Answer the questions that follow the tables.

Oxides

An oxide that reacts with an acid or produces an alkaline solution is a **basic** oxide. An oxide that reacts with an alkali or produces an acidic solution is an **acidic** oxide. An oxide that reacts with both acids and alkalis is an **amphoteric** oxide.

Q1 State which of the Period 3 oxides are basic, acidic or amphoteric.

Electron arrangement and reactivity

Elements 1 to 11

The arrangement of electrons in an atom is called the **electron configuration**. (*UAS 4*, page 152.) Electrons arranged in shells orbit the nucleus of an atom. The stable number of electrons in each shell is 2, 8, 8, 8 for the first four shells.

When an atom of an element reacts chemically one or more electrons in the outer shell are either lost forming an ion, or shared forming a covalently bonded molecule. An atom is stable when its outer shell of electrons is complete.

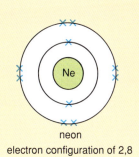

neon
electron configuration of 2,8

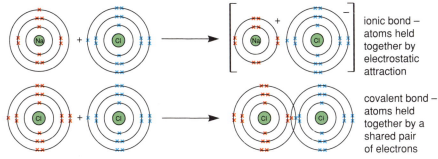

ionic bond – atoms held together by electrostatic attraction

covalent bond – atoms held together by a shared pair of electrons

Comparing ionic bonding and covalent bonding.

We have seen that the noble gases are very unreactive; they form very few compounds. This can be explained by their complete outer electron shell. Look at the electron configuration for neon on a data sheet.

Elements in Period 1 have electrons in the first shell only, for example hydrogen (H) and helium (He), whereas atoms in Period 2 have outer electrons in a second shell. Period 3 atoms have outer electrons in a third shell and so on for Periods 4 to 7.

Collect
- resource sheet
- Periodic Table sheet

Electron configurations

1 Complete the resource sheet up to calcium (Ca).
2 Calcium is in Period 4. List the noble gases in the first four periods and for each, work out the maximum and therefore stable number of electrons for the element in each period.

There is a similarity about the arrangement of electrons in every group of elements in the Periodic Table. Each of the elements in a group has a different number of electrons but always has the same number of electrons in the outer shell. This helps to explain why elements in the same group have similar chemical properties. Group I metals have one outer electron. Each metal takes part in vigorous chemical reactions in which it donates its outer electron and forms a cation with a positive charge of one. It then achieves the same number of outer electrons as a noble gas and is stable.

Group II elements all form cations with a positive charge of two and each one achieves a stable, noble gas electron configuration. The halogens all gain one electron when they undergo chemical reactions. They form anions with a negative charge of one. Each halogen element is one electron short of a stable noble gas electron configuration. Each halogen ion has the same arrangement of electrons as a noble gas and is stable.

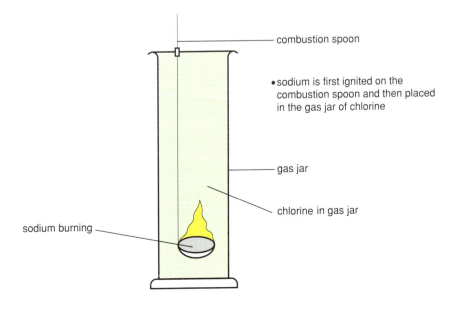

— combustion spoon

• sodium is first ignited on the combustion spoon and then placed in the gas jar of chlorine

— gas jar

— chlorine in gas jar

sodium burning

Reaction of a Group I metal with chlorine.

Elements of Group IV have four outer electrons which they share when they combine with other elements. Cations with a positive charge of four are not usually formed because there is too much repulsion between four 'like' charges.

Electron arrangement can also explain changes in reactivity. Atoms increase in diameter down a group. This is because each shell of electrons takes up more space. In Group I, the outer electron of lithium is quite near the nucleus but the outer electron of sodium is further away. The distance from the nucleus gets larger for each element down the group. As the distance increases, the **electrostatic force of attraction** between the positively charged nucleus and the negatively charged outer electron decreases. This means that the outer electron is more easily lost from an atom going down the group. So, for Group I metals, reactivity increases with increasing size. When the halogens react they gain electrons. It is easier for a small atom like fluorine to gain an electron than it is for a large atom like iodine because the extra electron in the fluoride ion is nearer to the nucleus. Thus reactivity increases up Group VII.

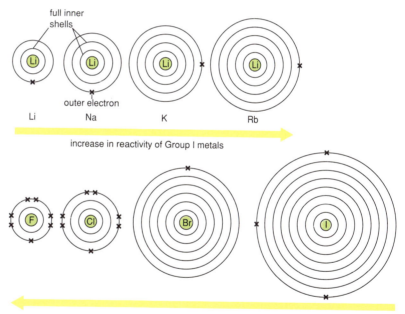

Increase in diameter of atoms down Group I and Group VII.

Take notes

Use notes and diagrams to summarise how the arrangement of electrons in the atom explains trends in periods and groups in the Periodic Table.

Project

The transition metals are a series of 31 elements that occupy a central block in the Periodic Table. Use books from the library to research characteristics that this group of elements have in common.

Radioactivity

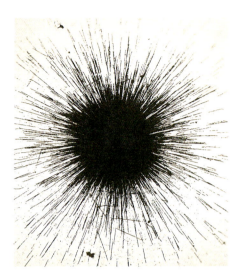

Dark traces of α-particles emitted by radium on a photographic plate.

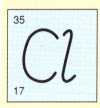 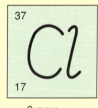

Isotopes

Isotopes are atoms of an element which have the same atomic number, and therefore similar chemical properties, but different numbers of neutrons in their nucleus.

Most isotopes occur naturally, for example $^{37}_{17}Cl$, and some can be made artificially.

2 more neutrons than $^{35}_{17}Cl$

Detecting radioactivity

Radioactivity was discovered in 1896 by a French scientist called Henri Becquerel (1852–1908). He found by chance that some crystals of a uranium (Ur) compound blackened a piece of photographic film. (The film was wrapped up in black paper so no light could get to it.)

Marie Curie (1867–1934), a Polish woman and Pierre Curie (1859–1906), her French husband, showed that all uranium and thorium compounds behaved in a similar way. They also showed that the compounds could affect the air around them. Air is normally a poor conductor of electricity but these substances enabled an electric current to pass through it. The Curies described these elements as being **radioactive**. They also discovered two other radioactive elements that appear in the radioactive decay pathways of uranium (see page 209) and thorium, called radium and polonium. They first identified them in the remains of some radioactively decayed uranium ore.

There are radioactive substances all around us emitting ionising radiation. The air, the ground, building materials and food are amongst the sources. Radiation also reaches us from space. This constant radiation is called **background radiation** — it is usually at a very low level and is not considered to be significant in terms of damage to health.

Since the work of the Curies many more radioactive elements have been discovered. In fact, many of the elements have isotopes that are radioactive, for example $^{14}_{6}C$, $^{2}_{1}H$ and $^{131}_{53}I$.

Radioactive elements and isotopes have unstable nuclei. In order to become more stable, the nuclei emit (push out) particles. There are two types: **alpha (α) particles** and **beta (β) particles**. Atoms often send out at the same time a pulse of energy called **gamma (γ) radiation**. This is a form of electromagnetic radiation of very high energy (*UAS 4*, page 36). Radioactive elements increase the electrical conductivity of air by displacing outer shell electrons from nitrogen and oxygen molecules, turning them into positively charged ions.

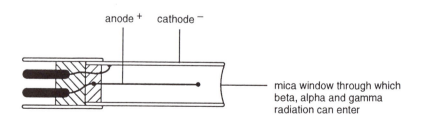

anode $^+$ cathode $^-$

mica window through which beta, alpha and gamma radiation can enter

A Geiger-Müller tube used to detect radiation.

Teacher demonstration

Your teacher will demonstrate some typical features of radiation. Alpha particles are made of two neutrons and two protons. (They are helium ($^4_2$He) nuclei.) Beta particles are fast moving electrons emitted from inside the nucleus. They are created inside the nucleus when neutrons decay. When an unstable nucleus splits up, an atom of a different element with a different number of protons is formed.

Alpha particles will only travel a few centimetres through air before they are stopped. A sheet of paper will stop them. Beta particles will pass through paper but are stopped by a light metal, such as aluminium. Gamma rays are stopped by thick concrete or lead and their energy is absorbed.

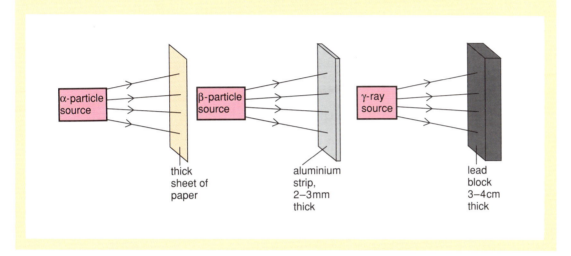

thick sheet of paper

aluminium strip, 2–3mm thick

lead block 3–4cm thick

People working in an atomic laboratory have their radiation level checked regularly.

The dangers of ionising radiation

Radioactivity is also known as **ionising radiation**. Living cells are very easily damaged by ionising radiation. Even alpha radiation which does not penetrate very far is dangerous. Radiation can trigger chemical reactions which cause molecules such as enzymes and other proteins in the cell to cease functioning properly. If the cells in a body are damaged in high numbers **radiation sickness** may result. Radiation can also damage the genetic material within the cells. The chromosomes may be damaged and the DNA altered causing mutations (see page 57). Mutated cells may progress to form cancers which can be fatal. (However, carefully controlled doses of radiation are now used to cure some forms of cancer.) Damage to the genetic material in the gametes may increase the probability of offspring being born with physical or mental handicaps. The body can often repair small amounts of damage caused by radiation but large doses are much more likely to cause irreparable damage to the cells which may also lead to cancer. The risk of developing cancer increases with the degree of exposure to radiation. People who work with radioactivity must undergo regular checks to see how much radiation they have been exposed to. They can then take steps to make sure they do not exceed the recommended upper limit.

The decay of a radioactive isotope

The uranium atoms in a small amount of a uranium compound are radioactive. The uranium nuclei continually **decay** or disintegrate (separate into smaller parts) and emit alpha particles. Eventually, nearly all the uranium atoms will have disintegrated to form different elements. The amount of radioactivity produced is proportional to the amount of uranium present at the start. Radioactive decay does not take place in a linear pattern, instead the rate becomes slower and slower. Radioactive decay is described as **exponential** which means the rate at which the uranium atoms decay is related to the number of atoms still left to decay at any instant. We can work out how long it takes for half the atoms in a sample to decay. This is called the **half-life** of an isotope. It is the time taken for the radiation emitted by a sample of radioactive element to drop by half.

Decay of protactinium-234

[IT] Your teacher may show you the following experiment, or you may be able to follow a computer simulation of the radioactive decay of an isotope.

The uranium atoms in a sample of uranium nitrate decay eventually to protactinium. Protactinium atoms can be separated from the rest of the radioactive isotope and its radioactivity measured at regular intervals.

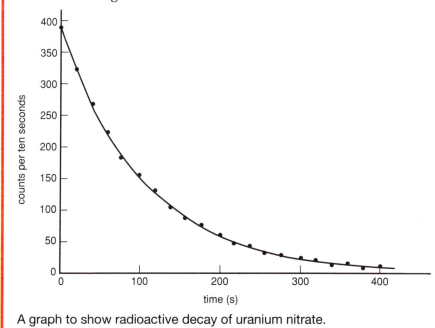

A graph to show radioactive decay of uranium nitrate.

Q1 Plot a graph of the results and work out the half-life for uranium nitrate from your graph.

Uses of radioactivity

Nuclear reactors and atom bombs

If neutrons are fired at certain isotopes of uranium something quite remarkable happens which is different from radioactive decay. The nucleus of the uranium atom splits up into the nuclei of other atoms. This is called **nuclear fission**. When the nucleus splits some of its mass is converted directly into **energy**. More neutrons are produced as the uranium nucleus splits. These can be captured by more uranium atoms which in turn release more energy and neutrons. The result is a **chain reaction**. In a nuclear chain reaction, a great deal of energy is released in a very short time. Chain reactions have been put to use in nuclear reactors and of course in nuclear weapons. A certain mass of uranium is needed to make sure that there are enough uranium atoms to absorb the neutrons that are released every time a nucleus splits, otherwise the reaction would cease. This mass of uranium is called the **critical mass**. The first atom bomb to be exploded (in a trial on July 16th 1945 in New Mexico, USA) used about 6 kilograms of plutonium — another element that undergoes nuclear fission. It had the explosive force of 20 000 tonnes of TNT (a conventional explosive)! A nuclear reactor controls the rate of fission by slowing down neutrons. The purpose of a nuclear power station is to provide heat energy used to heat water which produces steam to drive turbines as in coal- or oil-fired power stations. The temperature in a nuclear reactor is strictly controlled. It never reaches that of the heat released by an atom bomb. If a nuclear reactor were allowed to over-heat, the reactor core could be subject to 'melt-down', a very dangerous situation.

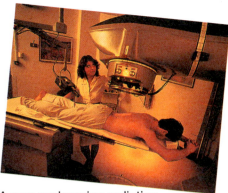

A man undergoing radiation treatment for cancer of the spine.

The power to heal

Radioactivity has many uses in medicine. It is used in **radiotherapy** to kill cancerous cells. For this, an isotope called **cobalt-60** is used which is a powerful gamma ray emitter. A special machine is used which targets a high dose of **cytotoxic** (toxic to cells) gamma rays to cancerous cells but a much smaller dose to the surrounding tissue.

A second major use of radioactivity is providing images of organs and glands in the body. These can help doctors to diagnose illness. An example of this is the use of radioactive iodine to produce images of the thyroid gland. The thyroid gland produces a hormone which affects metabolism and behaviour (see page 203). Radioactive iodine has a short half-life and is a gamma and beta emitter.

View of the top of the reactor at Dungeness B nuclear power station, Kent.

Take notes

Draw a table to compare the main features of alpha and beta particles and gamma radiation. Give examples of the main uses of each type of radioactivity.

Project

Radon gas is produced in the Earth's crust by radioactive decay. Find out in which areas of Britain radon gas is found and what kinds of rock are present in these areas. What kinds of problems can be caused by radon?

Investigating an element

Collect

- element X (small amount)
- conductivity apparatus
- test tubes and rack
- filter funnel and paper
- beaker (25 cm³)
- bunsen burner and heat-proof mat
- universal indicator / pH paper
- hollow glass tube
- safety glasses

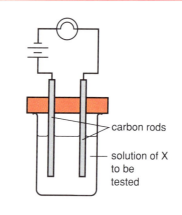

carbon rods

solution of X to be tested

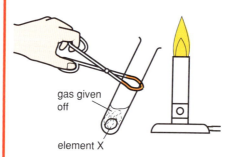

gas given off

element X

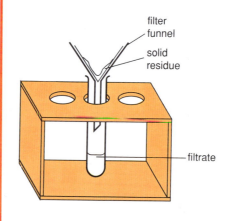

filter funnel

solid residue

filtrate

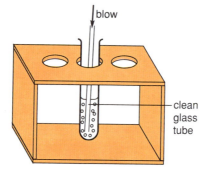

blow

clean glass tube

Element X

Investigate element X using the instructions below to help you. Keep a careful record of your observations at each stage of the investigation.

1. Describe the appearance of element X.
2. Test the conductivity of a solution of X as shown in the diagram.
3. Half-fill a test tube with water and add to it two or three small pieces of element X.
4. Test any gas evolved by holding the test tube near to a bunsen flame as shown in the diagram.
5. Filter the solution as shown in the diagram and collect the filtrate.
6. Measure the pH of the filtrate.
7. Blow through the filtrate using a clean hollow glass tube until a definite change occurs.
8. Measure the pH again.

Q1 Write a full report of your investigation. Include answers to the following questions.

a Is element X a metal or a non-metal?

b What gas is produced when element X is added to water?

c What can you say about the solubility of the solid from your experiment in step 3?

d Suggest a chemical name (or more common name) for element X and the filtrate it forms.

e Explain why the filtrate changes pH when you blow through it.

f In a separate experiment element X was found to form an oxide in which 0.4 g of element X combined with 1.6 g of oxygen. What is the molecular formula of this oxide? [165]

g In which group of the Periodic Table does element X belong?

h Try to write an equation for the reaction of the chemical you named in **d** with water. [166]

The nuclear industry

Nuclear power plants were designed and built to provide sources of cheap heat energy at a time when oil reserves are running out. The most efficient isotope of uranium to use is uranium-235 but supplies of this could run out in 50 to 100 years and coal reserves are fairly high. A fast breeder reactor (FBR) gets round this problem. As well as generating heat it produces enough neutrons to convert uranium-238 into plutonium-239 which can also be used in nuclear reactors. This seems a good way of converting a less useful material (uranium-238) into a more useful material (plutonium-239) but plutonium is one of the most poisonous substances known. As little as one millionth of a gram may be enough, if breathed in, to cause lung cancer.

Britain will pull plug on fast breeder programme

Fast breeders can extract about 60 times the amount of energy from uranium that existing thermal reactors do. During the 1950s, when projections suggested that uranium stocks would run out within decades, fast reactors were seen as a godsend.

Today, however, dwindling uranium supplies are not the principal concern; new reserves have been found, and neither the nuclear power industry nor energy demand has increased as quickly as expected. Added to this, fast breeders are expected to cost 20 per cent more to build than pressurised water reactors. The industry counters that the next phase of the European fast reactor (EFR) programme is aimed at reducing these costs and that if a fast reactor ran for more than 35 years it would prove cheaper than a pressurised water reactor (PWR).

In 1990, the House of Commons energy select committee recommended that Britain should pull out of the EFR programme in "1997 at the latest" if there was no new evidence of fast reactors becoming "viable" before 2030. The government agreed with that advice and, this week, a Department of Trade and Industry (DTI) spokesman said no new evidence had emerged to change its view.

Hartmut Mayer of Siemens Power Generation, one of the German partners in the EFR, said that if Britain withdrew, the project would miss the country's experience and technology.

"This is not a minor point," he said. It would also weaken the political position of the programme. In Germany, nuclear energy already suffers a bad image and the government is trying to cut whatever spending it can to pay for improved conditions in its eastern states. With federal funds uncertain, German companies are reluctant to invest.

Electricité de France, the national power generator, spends more than £30 million a year on fast breeder research. Pierre Bacher of EDF and a member of the EFR's steering committee says that in France support for the technology remains strong. "France would not wish to carry on work on fast breeders alone," he says. "We would look for other partners." According to Bacher, the obvious partner is Japan, which could have a marketable reactor by 2010.

Ian Fells, professor of energy conversion at the University of Newcastle, says the short-term arguments employed by the government against fast reactors could also be used against research into fusion. Britain still spends more than £16 million a year on fusion. "The government just doesn't seem to understand technology," he says. "I would put my money in the fast reactor rather than fusion because fast reactors have been proven."

(New Scientist 14.11.92)

Nuclear reactors are generally designed with very strict safety features. Loss of coolant can lead to serious over-heating and melt down of the reactor core and the release of radioactive particles into the atmosphere.

Coal-fired and oil-fired power plants burn fossil fuels to produce heat but this releases carbon dioxide into the atmosphere. The increased levels of atmospheric carbon dioxide, amongst other gases, are thought to add to global warming. These power plants also release sulphur dioxide which causes acid rain. Nuclear power plants do not produce carbon dioxide or sulphur dioxide but there is a problem with the disposal of nuclear waste. Plutonium has a half-life of 24 000 years and uranium-235 a half-life of 700 000 000 years!

Q1 List the reasons in favour of developing nuclear power plants and those against. Do you think the British Government are right in pulling out of the FBR development programme? Think of the long-term future of Britain's fuel reserves when you discuss this.

1 Use a copy of the Periodic Table to help you to answer the following questions.

The list below shows the symbols of some elements.

C Mg Cu O F Na Sr I Xe

From the list, give the symbol for:

a the element in Group 0 of the Periodic Table. [1]

b the element with only *one* electron in its outer electron energy level. [1]

c the *two* metals you would expect to be most alike in their chemical properties. [1]

d the *two* non-metals that you would expect to be most alike in their chemical properties. [1]

Total [4]

(NEA 1992 The Sciences)

2 Use a copy of the Periodic Table to answer the following questions.

a Sodium, symbol Na, is an element in Group I of the Periodic Table.

Name *two* other elements in this group. [2]

b Chlorine, symbol Cl, is an element in Group VII and can form chloride ions, symbol Cl^-.

Write the symbol for a fluoride ion. [1]

c The burning of sodium in chlorine produces the ionic compound sodium chloride which can be represented by the formula Na^+Cl^-. It has a high melting point and dissolves easily in water to give a solution that conducts electricity.

   i Give *one* property of *either* sodium *or* chlorine which makes it dangerous. [1]
   ii Suggest *two* precautions a teacher should take if burning sodium in chlorine. [2]
   iii Suggest *one* property of the ionic compound sodium bromide, formula Na^+Br^-. [1]

Total [7]

(MEG 1988 Science)

3 **a** The table contains information about alpha, beta and gamma radiation.

Name of radiation	Nature of radiation	Charge	Penetrating power
alpha	helium nuclei	positive	very low
beta			moderate
gamma	electromagnetic radiation		very high

   i Copy and complete the table. [3]
   ii The figure shows the passage of radiation from three sources **A**, **B** and **C**.

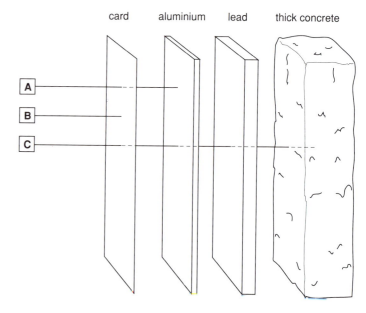

card   aluminium   lead   thick concrete

Which source, **A**, **B** or **C** produces:
   ● alpha radiation?
   ● beta radiation?
   ● gamma radiation? [3]
   iii A nuclear fall-out shelter is to be designed to enable a family of four to survive an atomic explosion. It is important to protect the family from the explosion and the effects of radiation.
Describe how you would build this shelter. [2]

Total [8]

(adapted from MEG 1992 Science)

8

Chemical calculations

Mass and number

Mass and number

Mass of atoms

Atoms are tiny so it would be impossible to weigh them on a balance. Instead, scientists have developed a method to find the mass of atoms called **mass spectrometry**. You can find out more by reading *UAS 4*, page 202.

Hydrogen is the smallest atom, with mass 1.7×10^{-24} g, which is

0.000 000 000 000 000 000 000 0017 g

Numbers like this are too small to use easily. Therefore scientists measure the masses of atoms relative to each other. This is known as the **relative atomic mass** scale. All atoms are weighed relative to a specified isotope of carbon which is given a mass of exactly 12.

Q1 Use the diagrams to work out the relative atomic mass for the atoms hydrogen, magnesium and helium.

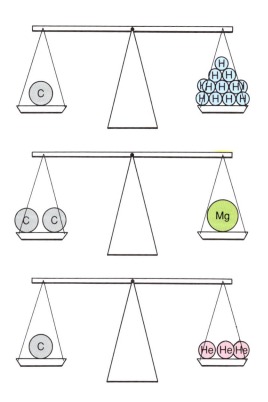

Q2 How can you find out the relative atomic mass of an atom using the Periodic Table?

Mass of molecules

You can use the formula of a molecule to calculate the **relative formula mass**. Simply add up the relative atomic masses of all the atoms in the formula.

> **Example**
> Water, H_2O
> relative atomic mass of 2 hydrogen atoms = $2 \times 1 = 2$
> relative atomic mass of 1 oxygen atom = 16
> *relative formula mass of water = 18*
> Carbon dioxide, CO_2
> relative atomic mass of 1 carbon atom = 12
> relative atomic mass of 2 oxygen atoms = $2 \times 16 = 32$
> *relative formula mass of carbon dioxide = 44*

Q3 Calculate the relative formula mass of nitrogen gas, N_2; methane, CH_4; hydrogen chloride, HCl; and ammonia gas, NH_3.

How many atoms?

When a shopkeeper takes a bag of £1 coins to the bank, the cashier will not count them out, instead they will be weighed. If the cashier knows the mass of one £1 coin, the value of the coins in the bag can be calculated.

> **Example**
> £1 coin = 10 g
> mass of a bag of £1 coins = 300 g
> *value of the bag of coins = 300 / 10 = £30*

The mass of atoms is calculated in packets of 6×10^{23} atoms. This is the number of atoms of any element that has a mass equal to the relative atomic mass of the element in grams.

Example
6×10^{23} hydrogen atoms have mass 1 g
6×10^{23} carbon atoms have mass 12 g
6×10^{23} magnesium atoms have mass 24 g

The number 6×10^{23} is called the **Avogadro constant,** named after the Italian scientist Amadeo Avogadro. This number of any kind of particle (atom, molecule) is called **1 mole** of particles.

One mole of atoms contains 6×10^{23} atoms. It has a mass equal to the relative atomic mass in grams.

Example
1 mole of calcium atoms has mass 40 g
40 g calcium contains 6×10^{23} calcium atoms

0.5 moles calcium atoms have mass 20 g

20 g calcium contain 3×10^{23} calcium atoms

(You can find the relative atomic mass of an atom from the Periodic Table or data sheet.)

Q1 Calculate the mass of:

1 mole lithium atoms, Li
10 moles sodium atoms, Na
0.2 moles iron atoms, Fe.

One mole of molecules contains 6×10^{23} molecules. It has a mass equal to the relative formula mass in grams.

Example
1 mole water molecules has mass 18 g
18 g water contains 6×10^{23} water molecules

0.5 moles water molecules has mass 9 g

9 g water contain 3×10^{23} water molecules

Q2 Calculate the mass of:

1 mole carbon dioxide, CO_2
0.1 moles oxygen, O_2
0.5 moles sodium chloride, NaCl.

If you know the mass of a substance you can find out the number of moles it contains by dividing its mass by the mass of 1 mole. The mass in 1 mole is equal to the relative atomic mass or relative formula mass and can be found on a data sheet or from the Periodic Table.

$$\text{number of moles} = \frac{\text{mass in grams}}{\text{mass of one mole}}$$

Example
How many moles magnesium are in 48 g magnesium, Mg?

From the Periodic Table or data sheet we find the relative atomic mass of Mg to be 24. This is the mass of one mole.

$$number\ of\ moles = \frac{48}{24} = 2\ moles$$

How many moles of water are in 36 g water, H_2O?

From the Periodic Table or data sheet we find the relative atomic mass of hydrogen is 1 and the relative atomic mass of oxygen is 16; so the relative formula mass for water is $(1 \times 2) + 16 = 18$. This is the mass of one mole. Therefore

$$number\ of\ moles = \frac{36}{18} = 2\ moles$$

Q3 Calculate how many moles, atoms or molecules are present in:
14 g nitrogen atoms, N
16 g copper atoms, Cu
132 g carbon dioxide, CO_2
8 g methane, CH_4.

Formulae

Empirical formulae

Chemical formulae were first found by experiment. This involves measuring the actual masses of the elements that combine to form a compound. This information is used to calculate the **empirical formula** giving the relative number of each atom in a compound.

Find the empirical formula of magnesium oxide

Collect

- resource sheet
- crucible and lid
- tongs
- tripod
- pipe-clay triangle
- bunsen burner and heat-proof mat
- magnesium ribbon (20 cm in length)
- emery paper
- balance
- safety glasses

1 Read the instructions on the resource sheet.
2 Write down possible sources of error in collecting the data used to work out the formula.
3 Carefully carry out the instructions on the sheet.
4 Were there any other sources of error which you noticed while you did the experiment?

Q1 Write an account of the experiment. Include the following results:
   a mass of magnesium used
   b mass of magnesium oxide produced
   c mass of oxygen combined with magnesium.

Example

If 0.24 g magnesium combined with 0.16 g oxygen:

	Mg	O
mass (g)	0.24	0.16
relative atomic mass	24	16
number moles	0.24/24	0.16/16
ratio number moles	0.01	0.01
whole number ratio number moles	1	1

empirical formula of magnesium oxide is MgO

Method

1 Note the mass of each element combined.

2 Use the relative atomic mass to write down the mass of 1 mole of each element combined.

3 Calculate number moles of each element combined.

4 Work out the simplest whole number ratio of number moles.

5 Write out the empirical formula.

Q2 In an experiment, 1.44 g copper oxide were reduced to 1.28 g copper. Calculate the mass of oxygen combined with the copper in copper oxide and then the empirical formula of the copper oxide.

Molecular formulae

A **molecular formula** indicates how many atoms of each type there are in a molecule. A molecular formula is a simple multiple of an empirical formula.

Example

CH_2 (empirical) C_4H_8 (molecular)

It can be found by using the relative formula mass of the compound.

Example

From experimental data it is found that a compound has the empirical formula CH_2O and relative formula mass 180.
Using the Periodic Table or data sheet it is found that:
the empirical formula mass is
$12 + (2 \times 1) + 16 = 30$

the relative formula mass is
$$\frac{180}{30} = 6 \text{ times the mass of } CH_2O$$

therefore the molecular formula is
$(CH_2O)_6 = C_6H_{12}O_6$

Q1 The empirical formula of ethanoic acid (vinegar) is CH_2O. The relative formula mass of ethanoic acid is 60. Calculate the molecular formula.

Finding formulae

Many compounds are made up of electrically charged ions — negatively charged anions and positively charged cations. The size of the charge depends on the elements making up the ion, though some elements can have more than one ion. For example iron has ions Fe^{2+} and Fe^{3+}. When writing the name of the compound in words you can show which ion is involved by using roman numerals, Iron(II) iodide or iron(III) oxide. Compounds formed from ions are electrically neutral so the total negative charge must be the same as the total positive charge.

Formulae of ionic compounds

Collect
- resource cards and sheet

The cards give the symbols for different ions. Make sure you know the name of the ion for each symbol. Pink cards represent positive ions and yellow cards negative ions. The size of the card depends on the size of the charge.

1 Use the cards to find the formulae given in List 1 on the resource sheet. To make sure the charge is balanced make sure there is one pink card and one yellow card and that the cards are the same size.

K^+
$Cl^- = KCl$ potassium chloride

Ca^{2+}
$SO_4^{2-} = CaSO_4$ calcium sulphate

2 You can also make sure the compounds are neutral by using more than one pink card or more than one yellow card, so long as the total sizes remain equal.

Al^{3+}
$Br^-\ Br^-\ Br^- = AlBr_3$ aluminium bromide

If an ion is made up of more than one element you must use brackets to show that the whole group occurs more than once.

Fe^{3+}
$OH^-\ OH^-\ OH^- = Fe(OH)_3$ iron(III) hydroxide

Use the cards to find the formulae given in List 2 on the resource sheet.

3 Write the formulae in List 3 without using the cards.

Q2 Write the following formulae without using the cards. (You can use the data sheet.)

ammonium nitrate   magnesium hydroxide
iron(II) oxide   aluminium hydroxide
aluminium iodide   ammonium sulphate
tin(II) chloride   magnesium hydrogen-
silver sulphate   carbonate.
aluminium oxide

Chemical equations

Balancing equations

An equation is a useful shorthand way of representing the amounts of materials in a reaction. In order to write a symbol equation you must first note down the word equation.

> **Example**
> sodium + hydrochloric → sodium + water
> hydroxide   acid   chloride

Then write the chemical formula for each of the substances.

> **Example**
> $NaOH + HCl \rightarrow NaCl + H_2O$

As matter cannot be created or destroyed the numbers of atoms present on each side of the equation must be the same. If we count the atoms we find:

Left-hand side	Right-hand side
Na = 1	Na = 1
O = 1	O = 1
H = 2	H = 2
Cl = 1	Cl = 1

The left-hand side equals the right-hand side. This means that the equation is balanced.

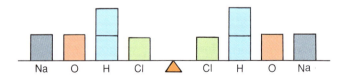

The numbers of atoms on each side are balanced.

Sometimes an equation is not balanced when the formulae are written.

> **Example**
> $Mg + HCl \rightarrow MgCl_2 + H_2$

Left-hand side	Right-hand side
Mg = 1	Mg = 1
H = 1	H = 2
Cl = 1	Cl = 2

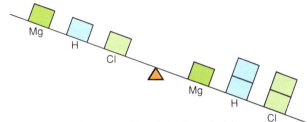

There are more atoms on the right-hand side, so the balance tips.

An equation can be balanced by placing a number in front of any of the substances. The number multiplies all the atoms in the substance by itself. 2 HCl means 2 hydrogen chloride molecules (2 hydrogen atoms and 2 chlorine atoms). 3 HCl means 3 hydrogen chloride molecules (3 hydrogen atoms and 3 chlorine atoms). The formula of any substance must never be altered when an equation is to be balanced.

The equation above can be balanced as follows:

Left-hand side	Right-hand side
Mg = 1	Mg = 1
H = 2	H = 2
Cl = 2	Cl = 2

> **Example**
> $Mg + 2HCl \rightarrow MgCl_2 + H_2$

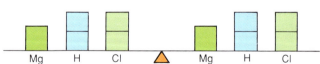

The numbers of atoms on each side are now balanced.

The final stage in writing equations is to add the state symbols, (s), (l), (g) or (aq), after each substance. These show whether the substance is solid, liquid, gaseous or aqueous (dissolved in water).

> **Example**
> $Mg_{(s)} + 2HCl_{(aq)} \rightarrow MgCl_{2(aq)} + H_{2(g)}$

Q1 Copy and balance the following equations (if necessary):

$$Zn_{(s)} + O_{2(g)} \rightarrow ZnO_{(s)}$$
$$Ca_{(s)} + H_2O_{(l)} \rightarrow Ca(OH)_{2(aq)} + H_{2(g)}$$
$$CaCO_{3(s)} \rightarrow CaO_{(s)} + CO_{2(g)}$$
$$CuCO_{3(s)} + 2HCl_{(aq)} \rightarrow CuCl_{2(aq)} + H_2O_{(l)} + CO_{2(g)}$$
$$Na_{(s)} + H_2O_{(l)} \rightarrow NaOH_{(aq)} + H_{2(g)}$$
$$Fe_2O_{3(s)} + CO_{(g)} \rightarrow Fe_{(s)} + CO_{2(g)}$$

Find the ratios in which substances react

Collect

- burettes and stands (2)
- test tubes (6) and rack
- pipette and filler
- ruler
- potassium iodide, KI, solution
- lead nitrate, $(PbNO_3)_2$, solution
- marker pen
- safety glasses

CARE!
Be careful not to spill any of the solutions

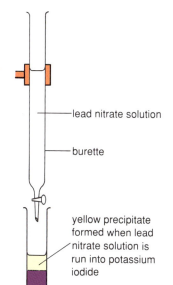

lead nitrate solution

burette

yellow precipitate formed when lead nitrate solution is run into potassium iodide

test tube 1

1 Fill one burette with potassium iodide solution and the other with lead nitrate solution.
2 Run 4 cm³ potassium iodide solution into each test tube.
3 Set up the apparatus as shown in the diagram.
4 Add lead nitrate solution in the quantities shown in the table below to each test tube and number the tubes as in the table.
5 Shake each test tube.
6 Allow the precipitate to settle and measure its height in each of the tubes.
7 After 15 minutes measure the height of each precipitate again.

 **Take notes**

Write a report of your experiment and copy and complete the table.

Test tube	Volume 0.5 M KI (cm³)	Volume 0.5 M Pb(NO₃)₂ (cm³)	Number moles KI	Number moles Pb(NO₃)₂	Height of precipitate	
					$t = 0$ min	$t = 15$ min
1	4.0	0.5	2.0×10^{-3}	2.5×10^{-4}		
2	4.0	1.0				
3	4.0	1.5				
4	4.0	2.0				
5	4.0	3.0				
6	4.0	4.0				

Q1 Plot precipitate height (on vertical axis) against the volume of lead nitrate solution (on horizontal axis) after $t = 0$ and $t = 15$ on the same graph.

Q2 From the graph find the minimum volume of lead nitrate solution that gives the maximum height of precipitate. Which test tube gave this result? Look in your table of results and find the number of moles lead nitrate solution and the number of moles potassium iodide solution for the same test tube. What is the simplest whole number ratio of these two numbers? This shows the number of molecules of lead nitrate and potassium iodide that react together.

Q3 Write a balanced equation for the reaction.

Working out how much product to expect from a reaction

Chemical manufacturers need to know how much raw material is required to make their product.

Example
Haber process (see page 96)

$$N_{2(g)} + 3H_{2(g)} \rightleftharpoons 2NH_{3(g)}$$

The balanced equation shows how many moles of reactants are used in the reaction and how many moles of products are formed during the reaction.

1 mole nitrogen gas reacts with 3 moles hydrogen gas to produce 2 moles ammonia. By looking up the relative atomic masses and calculating the relative formula masses we find that:

   28 g nitrogen react with (3×2) g hydrogen to produce (2×17) g ammonia

   28 g nitrogen react with 6 g hydrogen to produce 34 g ammonia

1 tonne is equal to 1000 kg (or 1000 000 g) so by multiplying all the numbers by 1000 000 we can say that:

   28 tonnes nitrogen react with 6 tonnes hydrogen to produce 34 tonnes ammonia.

Suppose the manufacturer needs to know how much nitrogen and hydrogen is required to produce 680 tonnes ammonia.

   28 tonnes nitrogen → 34 tonnes ammonia

   $\dfrac{28}{34}$ tonnes nitrogen → 1 tonne ammonia

   $\dfrac{28}{34} \times 680$ tonnes nitrogen → 680 tonnes ammonia

   = 560 tonnes nitrogen are needed to prepare 680 tonnes ammonia

   6 tonnes hydrogen → 34 tonnes ammonia

   $\dfrac{6}{34}$ tonnes hydrogen → 1 tonne ammonia

   $\dfrac{6}{34} \times 680$ tonnes hydrogen → 680 tonnes ammonia

   120 tonnes hydrogen are needed to prepare 680 tonnes ammonia

Q1 The following reaction takes place in a lime kiln:

$$CaCO_{3(s)} \rightarrow CaO_{(s)} + CO_{2(g)}$$

a What is the relative formula mass of calcium carbonate?

b What is the relative formula mass of calcium oxide?

c What mass of calcium carbonate is needed to produce 168 tonnes of calcium oxide?

Percentage yield

The amount of product that is produced is usually less than expected. This is due to:

a impurities in the reactants

b incomplete reaction

c loss of material due to spillage.

The percentage yield can be worked out as follows:

$$\text{percentage yield} = \frac{\text{mass of product obtained}}{\text{mass of product expected}} \times 100$$

Find the percentage yield for a reaction

Collect

- boiling tube and rack
- spatula
- bunsen burner and heat-proof mat
- mineral wool
- balance
- copper carbonate
- safety glasses

1 Weigh the boiling tube and mineral wool.
2 Weigh accurately about 2 g copper carbonate in the boiling tube.
3 Heat gently until all the copper carbonate has turned black.
4 Allow to cool.

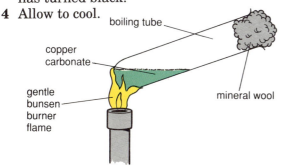

boiling tube

copper carbonate

gentle bunsen burner flame

mineral wool

 *Take notes*

Write a report of the experiment and complete a results table as follows:

mass boiling tube + mineral wool	=	g
mass boiling tube + mineral wool + copper carbonate	=	g
mass copper carbonate	=	g
mass boiling tube + mineral wool + copper oxide	=	g
mass copper oxide	=	g

Using the equation

$$CuCO_{3(s)} \rightarrow CuO_{(s)} + CO_{2(g)}$$

and the example below to help you, calculate the theoretical yield of copper oxide and the percentage yield of copper oxide obtained.

Example

50 g calcium carbonate should produce 28 g calcium oxide when heated. Only 20 g were obtained. Calculate the percentage yield.

$$\text{percentage yield} = \frac{\text{mass obtained}}{\text{mass expected}} \times 100$$

$$= \frac{20}{28} \times 100 = 71\%$$

Q2 When magnesium was burned in air, 10.2 g magnesium oxide were produced. 12.8 g were expected. Calculate the percentage yield.

Moles in a solution

When reactants or products are in solution the concentration of the solution is a measure of the amount of solute which is dissolved in a known volume of solution. The concentration may be given as the mass (in grams) dissolved in 1 dm³ (1000 cm³) solution so the units would be g/dm³ (g dm⁻³). It is more useful to measure the concentration in moles of the substance dissolved in 1 dm³ (mol dm⁻³). This is because chemical reactions involve definite numbers of particles reacting with each other. One mole of *any* substance contains 6×10^{23} particles of that substance. For different substances there will be different numbers of particles in one gram depending on the relative atomic masses of the elements in the substance.

A home wine-making kit. Various grape juice concentrates are shown. It is important to use the correct concentrations to achieve good results.

The concentration of the saline drip being administered to this patient must be carefully calculated.

A solution which contains 1 mole of the solute in 1 dm³ of solution has a concentration of 1 mol/dm³ (1 mol dm⁻³). Scientists often call this a molar solution and abbreviate it as 1 M.

A baby's sterilised bottle. The amount of milk powder added to water is carefully measured.

Example

a 1 M solution contains 1 mole of solute in 1 dm³ solution
a 2 M solution contains 2 moles of solute in 1 dm³ solution
a 3 M solution contains 3 moles of solute in 1 dm³ solution

Calculating the number of moles in a solution

Question How many moles sodium hydroxide are there in 500 cm³ of a 5 M solution (a solution that contains 5 moles/dm³)?

1 dm³ of a 1 M solution contains 1 mole NaOH
1000 cm³ of a 1 M solution contain 1 mole NaOH

500 cm³ of a 1 M solution contain $\dfrac{1}{1000} \times 500$ moles
$= 0.5$ moles NaOH

500 cm³ of a 5 M solution contain (0.5×5) moles NaOH
$= 2.5$ moles NaOH

Question How many moles potassium chloride are there in 2 dm³ of a 0.1 M solution (a solution that contains 0.1 moles/dm³)?

1 dm³ of a 1 M solution contains 1 mole of KCl
1000 cm³ of a 1 M solution contain 1 mole of KCl
1000 cm³ of a 0.1 M solution contain 0.1 mole of KCl
2000 cm³ of a 0.1 M solution contain $(0.1/1000 \times 2000)$ moles
$= 0.2$ moles KCl

number of moles of solute in solution:

$$\dfrac{\text{molarity (no. moles/dm}^3)}{1000} \times \text{volume of solution (cm}^3)$$

The triangle shows you:
number of moles = molarity × volume (dm³)

or $\text{molarity} = \dfrac{\text{number of moles}}{\text{volume (number of dm}^3)}$

or $\text{volume (number of dm}^3) = \dfrac{\text{number of moles}}{\text{molarity}}$

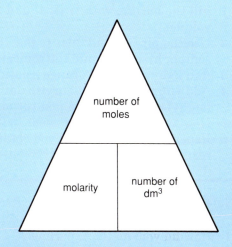

Q1 Calculate:
  a how many moles of sodium carbonate are present in 50 cm³ of 0.2 M solution (0.2 moles/dm³)
  b how many moles of copper chloride are present in 100 cm³ of 0.15 M solution (0.15 moles/dm³).

Vinegar contains ethanoic acid. It reacts with alkaline sodium hydroxide to produce sodium ethanoate and water. When all the acid has reacted with the alkali, the indicator changes colour.

Find the concentration of acid in vinegar

Collect

- burette
- pipette and filler
- conical flask (100 cm³)
- white tile and clamp stand
- sodium hydroxide solution 0.1 mol/dm³
- wine vinegar
- methyl orange solution
- safety glasses

1. Fill the burette with vinegar and note the volume.
2. Use the pipette and filler to put 10 cm³ sodium hydroxide into the conical flask.
3. Add 2 drops methyl orange solution.
4. Add vinegar from the burette until the methyl orange solution just turns pink.
5. Note the volume of acid used.
6. Repeat steps 1 to 5 until you obtain two results the same.

$$NaOH_{(aq)} + CH_3COOH_{(aq)} \rightarrow CH_3COONa_{(aq)} + H_2O_{(l)}$$

Q1 How did you do the experiment? Construct a suitable results table.

Q2 Calculate how many moles of ethanoic acid react with 1 mole sodium hydroxide.

Q3 Use the *collect* box to find out how many moles of sodium hydroxide are in 1 dm³ (1000 cm³).

Q4 What volume of sodium hydroxide was put in the conical flask?

Q5 How many moles of sodium hydroxide was that?

Q6 What volume of vinegar was used?

Q7 Use your answer to (2) to say how many moles of ethanoic acid are in that volume of vinegar.

Q8 How many moles of ethanoic acid are in 1 dm³ vinegar?

Moles of a gas

The **molar volume** of a gas is the volume occupied by 1 mole of the gas.

At room temperature and pressure the molar volume of any gas is about 24 dm³.

$$\frac{\text{number}}{\text{moles of gas}} = \frac{\text{volume of gas (dm}^3)}{\text{volume of 1 mole gas (dm}^3)}$$

$$\frac{\text{volume gas}}{\text{(dm}^3)} = \text{volume 1 mole (dm}^3) \times \text{number moles}$$

$$\text{number moles} = \frac{\text{volume (dm}^3)}{\text{volume 1 mole (dm}^3)}$$

$$\text{volume 1 mole (dm}^3) = \frac{\text{volume (dm}^3)}{\text{number moles}}$$

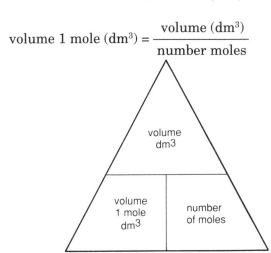

The triangle shows the described relationships above.

Q1 How many moles of helium are in the balloons at room temperature and pressure?

Q2 What volume of helium is in each of the following airships at room temperature and pressure?

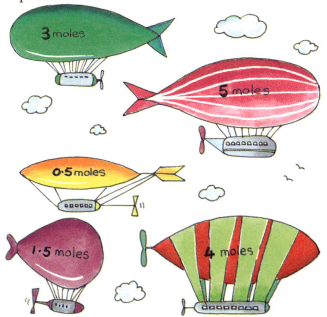

Take notes

Write an account of how you did the experiment.

What volume of hydrogen was collected?

$$Mg_{(s)} + 2HCl_{(aq)} \rightarrow MgCl_{2(aq)} + H_{2(g)}$$

How many moles of hydrogen are made from 1 mole magnesium?

What mass is 1 mole of magnesium?

0.024 g magnesium produced   cm³ hydrogen

1 mole magnesium produced   cm³ hydrogen

1 mole magnesium produced   dm³ hydrogen

The volume of 1 mole of hydrogen at room temperature and pressure was

(*Copy the method and fill in the gaps.*)

Find the molar volume of a gas

Collect

- clamp stand
- syringe (50 cm³)
- boiling tube and rack
- ignition tube
- delivery tube
- thermometer and barometer
- balance
- hydrochloric acid (2 M)
- magnesium ribbon
- emery paper
- safety glasses

1 Pour the hydrochloric acid into the boiling tube.
2 Weigh the magnesium ribbon. Cut or rub with emery paper until it weighs exactly 0.024 g.
3 Connect up the apparatus as directed by your teacher, and check the syringe reading.
4 Tilt the boiling tube and allow the magnesium to react with the acid.
5 Record the maximum reading on the syringe.
6 Record the room temperature and pressure.

Extensions

Chlorophyll and light

Why do leaves look green?

Collect

- spinach leaves (fresh)
- scissors
- pestle and mortar
- sand
- measuring cylinder
- ethanol
- test tubes (large) and rack
- filter funnel and paper
- conical flask
- spectroscope
- mat
- safety glasses

CARE!
Ethanol is flammable

Extract chlorophyll from spinach leaves

1 Grind a small handful of cut leaves in the mortar with about 15 cm³ of ethanol and a pinch of sand until you have a dark green solution as shown in the diagram. Do not over-fill the mortar. If necessary, use smaller amounts of leaf and ethanol and extract the chlorophyll in several batches.

ETHANOL · SAND · ethanol CARE!

2 Filter the solution into a large test tube.
3 Point the spectroscope at a window and examine the spectrum of sunlight.
4 Hold the test tube of chlorophyll solution in the path of the light and compare sunlight with the spectrum of light that has passed through the chlorophyll solution.

Absorption spectrum for sunlight seen through a spectroscope.

Q1 Write your own report, including answers to the following questions.
  a What colours are present in the spectrum of white light?
  b What colours are present in light that has passed through a solution of chlorophyll?
  c What colours have been absorbed by the chlorophyll solution?

Q2 Suppose you extracted a red solution from a plant. What would its spectrum seen through a spectroscope look like?

Q3 What colour(s) of light are necessary for photosynthesis?

Transport in phloem and xylem

Read the following accounts of experiments to investigate xylem and phloem and then answer the questions.

Ringing experiment

Phloem in woody plants (such as Privet) is found just inside the bark layer. It can be removed easily by cutting a ring round the stem. This leaves the xylem intact.

Radiolabelled glucose

Glucose is made up of carbon, hydrogen and oxygen atoms. Some of the carbon atoms (^{12}C) can be replaced by radioactive carbon atoms (^{14}C). This 'labels' the glucose molecules. Photographic film is darkened by radioactivity and can be used to record the movement of radiolabelled glucose molecules through a plant.

^{14}C-glucose injected into plant phloem here

Aphids (greenfly)

Aphids are small insects that feed on the solution being transported in phloem cells. They feed by piercing a plant stem with a sharp, pointed mouth part, called a stylet, which they use for sucking. An aphid can be anaesthetised and its body cut from its stylet. The stylet continues to ooze the phloem cell solution. When this solution is analysed chemically, it is found to be rich in sugars and amino acids.

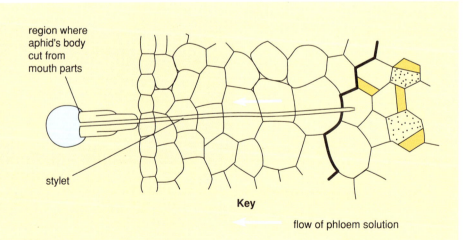

region where aphid's body cut from mouth parts

stylet

Key

→ flow of phloem solution

Q1 Which observations from the above experiments support the following:
  a Phloem cells can transport substances down a stem.
  b Phloem cells can transport substances made in the leaves.
  c Glucose is transported both up and down a plant by phloem cells.
  d Xylem cells transport water.
  e Phloem cells, not xylem cells, are responsible for transporting products of photosynthesis.

Improving plant growth

When plants are analysed chemically carbon, oxygen, nitrogen, phosphorus, calcium, sulphur and potassium are found. A plant obtains carbon and oxygen from air, but if nitrogen, phosphorus, calcium, sulphur or potassium are absent from or limited in the soil, then plants will not thrive and in some cases will not grow at all. Magnesium and iron are also needed by plants but in smaller amounts. Manganese and zinc are needed in very small amounts and are called **trace elements**.

Elements are present in the soil as chemical compounds called mineral salts. The table lists the uses of mineral salts in a plant.

Main mineral salts	Use in plants
nitrate	provides nitrogen to make proteins
sulphate	provides sulphur for healthy root growth
magnesium and iron	to make chlorophyll
phosphorus	to make ATP (used in respiration) and DNA (genetic material)
calcium	to make cell walls
potassium	varied uses within cells

Mineral nutrition

Plants can be grown in a solution of certain mineral salts in water. This method is called **hydroponics**. A typical culture solution is shown in the activity box.

Tomato plants being grown hydroponically.

Culture solution

Make up to 1 dm³ with distilled water:
  calcium nitrate 0.8 g
  potassium nitrate 0.2 g
  potassium dihydrogen phosphate 0.2 g
  magnesium sulphate 0.2 g
  iron(III) sulphate trace

1 Look up the formula of each of the chemicals and write down the ions that are provided by each one.
2 Write down the elements that are present.
3 Suggest how to make up a solution that had no nitrogen and left the amounts of calcium and potassium unchanged.
4 Compare the growth of broad bean or pea seedlings when grown in distilled water and in culture solution.
5 Plan an experiment to show the effect of growing a seedling in a solution which is deficient in one important element.

Q1 Write a full report of your experiment.

Global warming—can our planet cope?

There is no doubt that the concentration of carbon dioxide in the air is increasing. Should we assume that the situation is rapidly worsening and may become out of control? The atmosphere and the surface layers of the Earth seem to be capable, mostly, of maintaining an ecological balance, despite our repeated acts of destruction of the Earth's resources and our tampering with its natural balances. Carbon dioxide in the air is in **dynamic equilibrium** (balance) with carbon dioxide dissolved in the oceans. In water, carbon dioxide forms carbonate ions and hydrogencarbonate ions. To some extent the sea acts as a 'sink' for the carbon dioxide, mopping up any surplus. Will the sea become saturated and then unable to absorb carbon dioxide? Extensive land cultivation also causes an increase in carbon dioxide levels by stimulating microorganisms that break down organic matter in soil. Perhaps carbon dioxide levels will stabilise at a new point of equilibrium or even slowly decline. Sea animals (like coral) and plants remove dissolved carbonate ions from water to form their chalky shells and skeletons. Perhaps more limestone will be formed as dead animals sink to the seabed and are compressed over a timescale of years. Phytoplankton are photosynthesising microscopic organisms living in the sea. Increased carbon dioxide could stimulate growth of phytoplankton, which in turn will remove more carbon dioxide.

Q1 Draw a set of labelled feedback loops showing how natural equilibriums can be disrupted. Do your examples return to equilibrium or find a new point of equilibrium?

LOW LYING AREAS OF LANDS MAY BE AT INCREASED RISK OF FLOODING

POLAR ICE CAPS MAY MELT CAUSING A RISE IN SEA LEVELS

Predicted global warming effects.

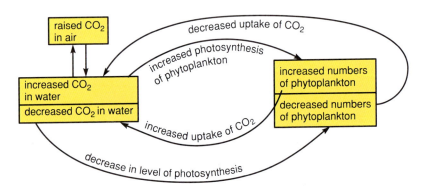

Feedback loops regulate the cycling of substances. Feedback can be either positive or negative.

Separate issues

1

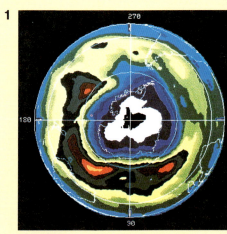

Ozone depletion over an area larger than the Antarctic continent. These data, recorded in 1987 by NASA's *Nimbus-7* satellite, registered an ozone value of 109 Dobson Units, represented by the dark area at the centre.

2

Poplar trees dead and dying from attack by acid rain.

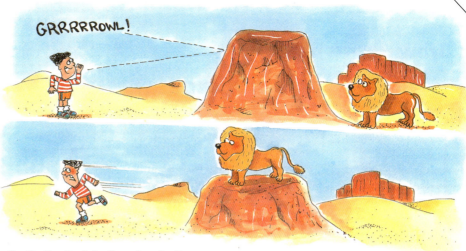

Echoes

Sound waves can be reflected off walls and other solid obstacles in a similar way to light waves being reflected off a plane mirror. We know it takes time for the sound waves to travel. This leads to a time gap between hearing an original sound and hearing its reflection off a solid object. We recognise this as an **echo**.

The Whispering Gallery in Saint Paul's Cathedral in London is famous for the echoes that it produces.

A captain of a ship may find out how close the ship is to a large iceberg at night by sounding the ship's siren and timing how long it takes for an echo to be heard. This technique is called **echolocation**. Can you think of any reasons why the captain should not rely on this method alone to locate an iceberg? (*Hint*: think of how poor weather conditions may effect the speed of sound waves — the air may be saturated with water particles, forming mist.)

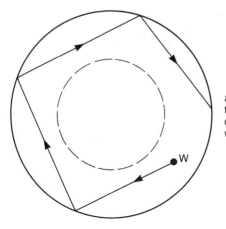

a whisper at W is reflected round to people on the other side who can hear clearly what has been whispered

The Whispering Gallery in Saint Paul's Cathedral (above) and echo formation.

Q1 An echo is heard 6 seconds after a ship's siren is sounded. Approximately how far away is the iceberg? Remember to note in your answer that this value is dependent on the conditions.

How do we hear?

Collect

- loudspeaker
- signal generator
- connecting wires
- sound meter

1 Connect a loudspeaker to a signal generator.
2 Move the pointer to produce different frequencies.
3 Keeping the volume constant, turn the pointer to the lowest frequency at which you can still hear. What happens to the sound as you do this?

4 Now turn the pointer to the highest frequency at which you can hear. Compare your results with your friends. Do you all hear the same range of frequencies?
5 Select a frequency for the whole class, and repeat the activity this time varying the volume. Measure the volume using a sound meter. Do you all begin to hear at the same volume?

Hearing problems

Almost 20% of the population suffer a degree of permanent hearing loss. Temporary hearing loss may be caused by ear infections or colds. Total deafness can be present at birth or occur later if the ear is diseased or damaged. As a person ages there is often a degree of hearing loss. A young person with optimum hearing can detect frequencies in a range of 20 Hz to 20 000 Hz. Both the loudness and frequency of a sound affects hearing.

Hearing is tested using an **audiometer**. The meter is similar to a signal generator. It emits sound of very pure tone with no overtones or **harmonics** (a tone produced by oscillating frequencies). It is calibrated in decibels. A person is asked to listen to signals from an audiometer through a pair of earphones and to indicate the level of sound at which they begin to hear. The frequency and output levels of the signal at the point the person acknowledges hearing are recorded on a graph called an audiogram. A result of 0 dB for most frequencies would be read for a young person with optimum hearing. A result of 20 dB would indicate a hearing loss of 20 dB.

A person's hearing may be improved by fitting a hearing aid. The aid contains a small microphone, an amplifier, a battery and an earphone. Aids not only make sounds louder but also have tone controls that alter the frequencies according to the need of the wearer. This is similar to the adjustments made on a graphic equaliser on a midi system.

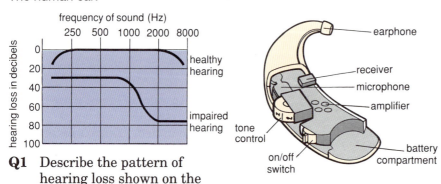

The human ear.

Key

A	sound waves enter ear and,	G	which sets the fluid in the cochlea vibrating,
B	set the ear drum vibrating,	H	the nerve endings are stimulated and electrical impulses travel to the brain
C, D, E	vibrations transferred by three small bones,		
F	to the oval window,		(the semi-circular canals are omitted)

A hearing aid.

Q1 Describe the pattern of hearing loss shown on the audiogram.

Making use of interference effects

Sound, like light and other waves, is subject to **interference** effects.

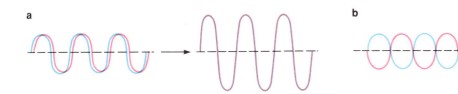

Interference effects in sound waves (a) constructive interference leads to enhanced sound, (b) destructive interference leads to no sound.

Collect

- signal generator
- loudspeakers (2)
- connecting wires (4)

Interference in sound waves

1 Set up a signal generator connected to two loudspeakers about half a metre apart as shown in the diagram.
2 Set the signal generator to 2 kHz.
3 Walk past the two loudspeakers and note the way the sound that you hear changes.

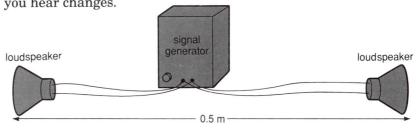

loudspeaker   signal generator   loudspeaker

◀———————— 0.5 m ————————▶

White noise silences Japanese cars

AN antinoise technology could soon make Japanese motor cars among the quietest in the world. The technology, which is often called white noise, is now standard in Nissan Bluebirds, and engineers say it can reduce the effects of engine noise by more than ten decibels.

The idea behind white noise – of cancelling out noise by generating sound waves of the opposite phase – is not new, but it was not until the development of powerful microprocessors that the system could be put into practice.

"So far the system has been used in refrigerators, aircraft and concert halls," said a spokeswoman for Nissan, "but our device is the first to be designed for cars."

After ten years of research, Nissan came up with a system that consists of four microphones placed in the ceiling of a car, which pick up the noise of the engine and feed the noise to a microprocessor in the back of the car. By analysing these sound waves the microprocessor generates a mirror image of the sound waves which cancels out the original waves. Two speakers under the front seats produce the white noise.

According to Nissan engineers, the system reduces engine noise at speeds of 4000 revolutions per minute or more, the kind of levels that are attained when the car accelerates. It also reduces the need for sound-proofing materials in cars, which can add more than 30 kilograms in weight to an average saloon.

The technique is particularly suitable for counteracting sources which produce a single, identifiable noise, such as the engine. Engineers say that more complex sounds, coming from other parts of the car, are harder to counteract.

Peter Hadfield, Tokyo

(New Scientist 28.3.1992)

Q1 Read the article on white noise and answer the following questions:

a What is white noise and why does it work?

b Where has the white noise system been used?

c What part does the microprocessor in the car play?

d What are the advantages of reducing sound insulation in cars?

e By how much is the sound level reduced in Nissan cars?

f How effective do you think the white noise technology will be at low speeds?

Microelectronic components

Input transducers

An **input transducer** is a device that converts a form of energy, for example sound waves, to electrical energy. Some devices can produce electrical energy directly from the input energy—no extra power is needed.

As electronic circuits need only small voltages and currents to operate them the following devices could be used.

A **thermocouple** consists of two wires of different metals welded together. The junction formed converts heat to electrical energy. Thermocouples operate over a wide temperature range (−200 °C to 450 °C). Thermocouples can be small and sensitive. A **thermistor** behaves in the same way as a thermocouple. However it is smaller and has a more limited temperature range of between −30 °C and 120 °C.

Solar cells, **light dependent resistors** (LDR) and **phototransistors** all convert light energy to electrical energy. The solar cell changes about 15% of light energy into electrical energy. The others vary in their cost and efficiency (depending on how bright the light is and the wavelength of the light).

Switches also act as a form of transducer. They can send small electrical impulses into a system. Push switches, reed, touch and microswitches are used.

Microphones can be of various sizes and types but all convert sound energy into electrical energy. The size of the current depends on the loudness and the frequency of the sound.

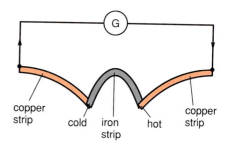

Thermocouple.

Symbol for a microphone.

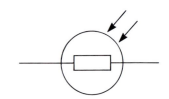

Symbol for a LDR.

Devices used in electronic circuits.

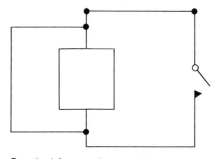

Symbol for a relay switch.

The table gives information about some input transducers.

Name of device	Output voltage	Working temperature	Size	Cost	Speed	Power
thermocouple	4 mV	−150 °C to 250 °C	4	2	4	4
rod thermistor		− 30 °C to 110 °C	2	3	2	2
bead thermistor		− 30 °C to 105 °C	3	2	4	2
LDR		− 5 °C to 40 °C	3	3	1	2
solar cell	500 mV	− 10 °C to 40 °C	1	1	2	4
phototransistor		− 5 °C to 70 °C	4	3	3	3
photodiode		− 10 °C to 45 °C	4	4	4	3
microphone 1	6 mV	− 5 °C to 60 °C	1	1	3	3
microphone 2		5 °C to 30 °C	4	4	3	2
push-switch	—	daily temperature	2	3	4	4
touch-switch	—	daily temperature	2	4	3	4
micro-switch	—	5 °C to 35 °C	2	2	3	4

1 = poor   2 = fair   3 = good   4 = very good

When designers are choosing components for a circuit they must consider the following points.

- What type of energy does it convert?
- Is it sensitive enough?
- Will it fit into the space given?
- Is it too expensive for the required task?
- Will it react quickly?
- Does it need a battery or will it make its own voltage?

Q1 Use a components catalogue to find out about some components. Which component from the above table would you use to build:

a a photographic light meter

b a bar-code reader

c an electronic thermometer

d a thermostat?

Output transducers

Output transducers work in the opposite way to input transducers. They convert electrical energy to some other form. Small components have been designed for microelectronic circuits. They replace things like light bulbs, loudspeakers and large relays.

Some are used in electric systems but are too large for microelectronic systems where size, low power, and cost are important.

Q2 Use a components catalogue to find out as much as you can about the following components:

a loudspeaker

b LED

c buzzer

d relay.

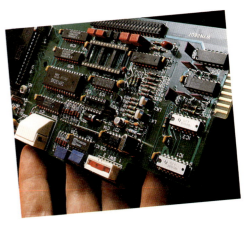

A computer circuit containing a buzzer.

True breeding

We will investigate the inheritance of a trait for flower colour. The two forms of the trait are red and white. Red is dominant over white. The two alleles can be written as R (dominant red) and r (recessive white).

RR and rr are called the **homozygous** genotypes because both alleles are the same. (*Homo* means the same.) RR is said to be homozygous dominant and rr homozygous recessive. Rr is called the **heterozygous** genotype because the alleles are different. (*Hetero* means different.)

When plants that are homozygous for the red flower (RR) are cross-fertilised, they can only produce red-flowered plants. Similarly, when homozygous recessive plants (rr) are cross-fertilised they can only produce white flowers. Homozygous genotypes are described as **true breeding** as the offspring will always show the same trait as the parent.

True breeding poppies.

Monohybrid cross

A **monohybrid cross** is carried out so that we can follow the inheritance of a single trait from different alleles of one given gene. The starting generation of the cross is called the parental generation (P).

The results of this first cross are all heterozygous red-flowered plants. They are the first generation and they are genetically and phenotypically identical. This generation is called the F_1 generation. F stands for filial, which means belonging to a son or daughter. The F_1 generation can be crossed with itself to produce the F_2 generation.

We can look at the ratios of genotypes and phenotypes produced in each generation.

	Ratio of genotypes RR : Rr : rr	Ratio of phenotypes red : white
P	2 : 0 : 2	2 : 2
F_1	0 : 4 : 0	4 : 0
F_2	1 : 2 : 1	3 : 1

female gametes

male gametes

r   R

red Rr	R
red Rr	red Rr
r	red Rr

A parental generation cross between true breeding red plants and true breeding white flower plants.

female gametes

male gametes

R   R

red Rr	r
red RR	white rr
r	red Rr

An F_1 generation cross.

We can also describe the phenotypes using fractions. There are four possible combinations of alleles in the F_2 generation and one of them gives white flowers and three give red flowers. We can say one quarter are white or three quarters are red. A ratio of 3 : 1 and three quarters describe the same outcome.

Q1 The presence of horns on Hereford cattle is controlled by one gene. The hornless condition is the recessive homozygous genotype.
  a Choose a letter to represent the two alleles.
  b What is the genotype of a true breeding hornless mother and a true breeding horned father?
  c Use a Punnet square to work out the F_1 generation of these parents.
  d Use a Punnet square to work out the F_2 generation if the F_1 generation is crossed with itself. What is the ratio of genotypes and the ratio of phenotypes?

A horned Hereford cow.　A hornless Hereford cow.

Cell division

Mitosis

Collect

- root (onion or daffodil)
- razor blade (sharp)
- microscope slide and coverslip
- filter paper (1 piece)
- chromosome stain (acetic orcein)
- dropping pipette
- bunsen burner
- microscope (low power)
- dissecting needles (2)

CARE!
The razor blade is very sharp

Chromosome squash

Just before a cell divides it must make a copy of each chromosome. This is called mitosis.

1 Put your root on a microscope slide and, with the razor blade carefully cut off and keep on the slide the end 5 mm of the root.

2 Add 9 drops of chromosome stain using the pipette and gently tease the root tip apart using the dissecting needles.

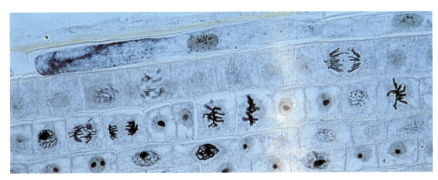

Longitudinal section through a root tip showing several stages of mitosis.

3 Gently heat the slide over a very small bunsen flame until steam rises from the stain. This helps the stain to be absorbed by the cells. It is important not to boil the stain or let it evaporate.

4 Place a coverslip over the cells. Fold the piece of filter paper. Carefully press straight down with your thumb on the filter paper on top of the coverslip to spread out the cells. Be careful not to move the coverslip.

5 Examine the root preparation under the microscope and look for any of the stages of mitosis shown on the left. Make a drawing of each stage that you find and for each, label any parts of the cell that you can distinguish.

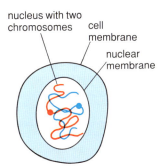

nucleus with two chromosomes — cell membrane — nuclear membrane

chromosomes are visible in the nucleus just before cell division

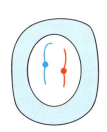

chromosomes shorten and thicken

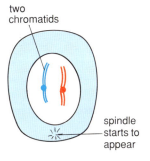

two chromatids — spindle starts to appear

each chromosome now consists of two chromatids

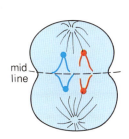

mid line

the nuclear membrane disappears and the chromatids are pulled apart by the spindle fibres

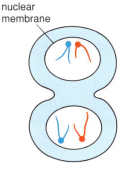

nuclear membrane

a nuclear membrane forms round each set of chromatids, and the cell starts to divide

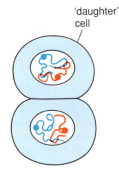

'daughter' cell

cell division is completed — two 'daughter' cells, each containing the same number of chromosomes have formed

Stages of mitosis.

Q1 Write a report of your experiment. Try to say why you treated the root tip with stain first and include your drawings in a results section.

Meiosis

Each of us began life as a zygote. The zygote is formed by the fusion of a male gamete and a female gamete, both of which have half (23) the full set of chromosomes in their nucleus. The sex cells, which produce the gametes, undergo a process where the number of chromosomes in each cell is halved. This process is called meiosis.

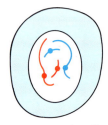

the red chromosomes are from the organism's mother; the blue ones are from its father

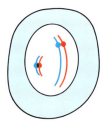

homologous chromosomes pair up

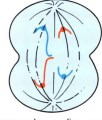

the nuclear membrane disappears and paired chromosomes move apart

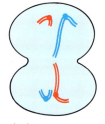

each chromosome becomes two chromatids

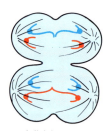

a second division separates the chromatids

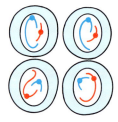

four gametes are formed — each contains only half the original number of chromosomes

Stages of meiosis.

Q2 Copy and complete the table to compare mitosis and meiosis. All the information you need is on pages 52–55 and in this extension.

	Mitosis	Meiosis
• When does the process occur?		
• How many chromosomes are passed on to each daughter cell?		
• Does the daughter cell contain the diploid or haploid chromosome number?		
• Are the chromosomes in each daughter cell identical?		
• Does the process occur during asexual or sexual reproduction? Will the daughter cells show variation?		

Genetic disorders

Some diseases are hereditary, running in families. By analysing family trees over many generations to see who has suffered from a particular inherited disease, it is possible to decide how the inheritance of the disease is controlled. If a disease is largely hereditary, it is possible that there has been a change in the DNA of the sufferer. There are 2000 diseases which are known to be caused by a single mutation in a gene or pair of mutated alleles.

Huntington's chorea

Huntington's chorea affects about five people in every 100 000 of the population. It causes uncontrollable muscle movement and mental deterioration. The affected person does not experience any symptoms until well into adulthood so a carrier may already have children before the disease is diagnosed. It is caused by a dominant gene on chromosome 4. At present there is no way of detecting carriers but scientists are investigating genetic probes which may lead to their detection in the future.

Cystic fibrosis

This is a disorder of mucus-secreting glands throughout the body, especially in the pancreas, lungs and intestines. It can cause pneumonia, blockage of the intestines and poor absorption of food. In Britain it is quite common, affecting 1 in 1600 babies. Most patients used to die at an early age but this is no longer the case due to improvements in treatment methods. Cystic fibrosis is caused by a recessive gene.

Q1 Is it possible to be a carrier of a genetic disease without actually suffering from it? What genetic conditions are needed for the disease to appear in any offspring?

Q2 Are children more likely to suffer from Huntington's chorea or cystic fibrosis if one of their parents is a carrier of the gene?

Sex-linked inheritance

Some disorders, such as red–green colour blindness are more common in males than in females. This is because the genes for these disorders are found in the part of the X chromosome which is unmatched by the shorter Y chromosome. If a male carries the gene he will show the symptoms. A female can carry the gene but not show symptoms if there is the recessive allele for the disorder on one X chromosome but a dominant allele for not having the disorder on the other X chromosome. A female will only show the disorder if there is a recessive allele on both chromosomes.

One of the best known family trees of a carrier of haemophilia is that of Queen Victoria.

Haemophilia

This is an example of sex-linked inheritance. Haemophilia is a blood disorder in which the blood fails to clot due to a lack of a substance in the blood, called Factor VIII. Patients bleed internally and externally following even minor injury. This can be very painful when it happens in joints. Some forms of haemophilia can be treated with a clotting factor isolated from donated blood. Haemophilia affects about 1 in 10 000 male babies but it is very rare in females.

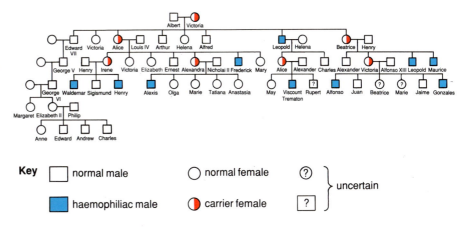

Queen Victoria's family tree.

Q3 How many children did Queen Victoria have? Do not include her sons- or daughter's-in-law.

Q4 By working out which gametes the parents may be carrying and the possible combinations of them we see that statistically one quarter should be normal females, one quarter carrier females, one quarter normal males and one quarter haemophiliac males. Is this true for Queen Victoria's children?

Earth shattering

Approximately half a million earthquakes are recorded each year. Of these, only one in five is felt and in only one in 500 is damage caused. A very severe earthquake struck Anchorage in Alaska in 1964. The quake measured 8.5 on the Richter scale and caused a **tsunami** (long and high ocean wave) 67 metres in height. In 1976, 750 000 people died because of an earthquake (7.9 on the Richter scale) in Tangshan, China. Six years later the city was still a prohibited area.

Earthquake damage in Anchorage, Alaska.

A large crack appeared in the ground during the 1964 earthquake in Anchorage, Alaska.

The Richter scale

The strength of an earthquake can be quantified using the Richter, or Gütenberg–Richter scale, introduced in 1954. The scale runs from 0 to 10 and measures the amplitude of the surface wave. Scale 1 would be similar to a person jumping down from a one metre high table. Each subsequent scale point has ten times the energy. Other scales are used to quantify earthquake waves, for example the Modified Mercalli scale. However, in 1977 a more satisfactory scale, based on seismic movement called the Kanamori scale, was devised in Japan, but usage, particularly by the media, tends to be with the well-known Richter scale.

Richter scale	
Number	Effect of an earthquake
1	Detected only by instruments
2	Feeble — felt by people at rest
3	Slight — hanging objects swing, similar to a light lorry passing
4	Moderate — felt by people walking
5	Moderately strong — sleeping people woken up, windows break
6	Strong — trees sway, some damage to buildings
7	Very strong — walls crack, it is difficult to stand
8	Destructive — chimneys fall, branches break off trees
9	Ruinous — many buildings damaged, cracks in the ground
10	Disastrous — many buildings destroyed, large cracks appear in the ground

Read the two extracts.

On 8th February 1750 London was startled by a sudden jolt. The tremor was not that strong, but it rattled windows, shook furniture and sent people hurrying into the streets. It was made particularly disturbing by the fact that in nearly two centuries London had experienced only one minor tremor. 'O, that our repentance may prevent heavier marks of His displeasure,' cried the Evangelist John Wesley. But Wesley's prayers went unanswered. Exactly one month later a second and more powerful shock hit London. This one knocked down chimneys, rang church bells, toppled some buildings and threw the city into a full blown religious panic. During the next several months, three more tremors shook the British Isles, causing no great damage but vast dismay.

(*Earthquakes*, Time-Life Books Inc., 1989)

Small earthquake stirs Peterborough

Tim Radford
Science Editor

IT WAS only a small earthquake, but it still managed to shake Peterborough. The energy released was about the same as 10 tons of exploding TNT.

The shock — the second in the region in 12 months — occurred at 1.23am yesterday about four kilometres south-east of the Cambridgeshire town. Police reported about 70 calls from alarmed citizens, but no damage or injuries.

"It was like a slow train coming, making a rumbling noise increasing in intensity. I felt the bed lift, the floor shake and the rafters creak, but then it went away as quickly as it came," said one resident.

But Akhtar Hussain, owner of Royal Taxis in Peterborough, said: "It wasn't mild. It was a big bang. We all ran out of the office thinking a that lorry had hit the building."

There are about 100,000 earthquakes of equivalent size worldwide every year, and about six in the UK and surrounding waters, according to Dr David Redmayne of the Geological Survey in Edinburgh. The most recent seismic shock was in the Welsh borders in April 1990. Some tiles were lost and chimneys dislodged. That one was 200 times more powerful, measuring 5.1 on the Richter scale.

Dr Roger Musson, of the Geological Survey in Edinburgh has been studying the history of British earthquakes since 1700, and is wondering about including a death in 1940 during a seismic shock in North Wales.

"One usually thinks of deaths as being in falling buildings. But during this one an elderly lady got up and fell down the stairs and was killed in the fall. So few people have ever been killed in British earthquakes I'm inclined to stretch a point."

(*Manchester Guardian* 18.2.1992)

Q1 Compare the descriptions of the earthquakes mentioned in the two extracts.

Q2 Use the Richter scale on page 188 to estimate the power of the shocks mentioned in the extracts.

Q3 Explain why there was vast dismay in the 'year of the earthquake' as 1750 came to be known.

Q4 Write a 'newspaper article' about the tremors in 1750.

Q5 How do you think the dangers from earthquakes would differ in a city, in a mountainous area, and by the coast?

Q6 Why do you think Japan has developed an advanced method of recording earthquakes?

Geological time

Geologists have used many methods to date rocks over the years. Methods in use today include measuring radioactive decay, looking at fossils in sedimentary rocks, and comparison with other rocks nearby.

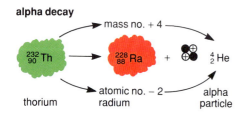

alpha decay

thorium → radium + alpha particle

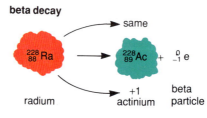

beta decay

radium → actinium + beta particle

Radioactive decay.

Key

→ salt collected from rocks and taken to the sea

Deltas provide evidence for geologists.

The passing of time

Collect

- coins (100)
- plastic container

A model of radioactive decay

This model, whilst not accurate, gives a general idea of a constant decay process.

1 Shake the coins in a container and spread them on a table.
2 Remove those which come down heads (these represent decayed atoms).
3 Note the number of tails left.
4 Repeat steps (1) to (3) until all the coins are discarded.
5 Plot on a graph the number of tails left after each set of coins has been tossed. Or you could use a computer simulation.

Use the information on the resource sheet to answer the following questions.

Q1 Sketch a graph of a candle burning. How does this compare to the shape of your graph from tossing coins?

Q2 How old do present-day geologists estimate the Earth to be?

Q3 Why is the method John Joly used to date the Earth likely to be totally inaccurate?

Q4 Collect a copy of the graphs showing radioactive decay. The rate of decay of radioactive isotopes (see page 154 for a definition of an isotope) is similar to the graph produced by tossing coins. Over a fixed period of time half the atoms decay. This is called the **half-life** of the isotope and it is different for different isotopes. The half-life of isotopes can be measured in a laboratory. When uranium decays it changes to lead. See the resource sheet that shows graphs of radioactive decay for iodine-128 and protactinium-234. In a rock sample such as granite the amounts of uranium and lead present can be compared and as uranium decays to lead the age of the rock can be estimated. Study the graphs on the sheet and work out the half-life for each substance using the equation on the resource sheet to help you.

Collect

- resource sheet

Save the planet!

The Earth Summit, Rio de Janeiro, Brazil, 1992

Repeated warnings from scientists resulted in this summit. It was attended by more than 100 countries. The aim of the Earth Summit was to begin a system of planetary 'housekeeping' in an attempt to preserve the Earth's atmosphere, soils and the life that exists on it.

Some of the problems the delegates (each country's spokespersons) may have discussed at the summit are shown.

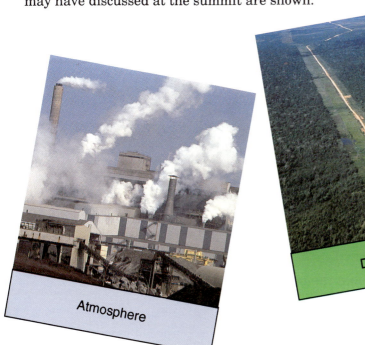

Atmosphere

Deforestation

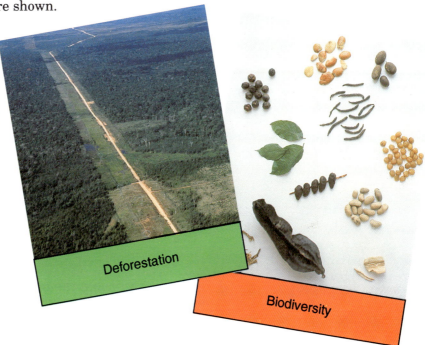

Biodiversity

Collect

● resource sheet

Stage your own conference

Work individually or in groups. Each group should elect a spokesperson.

1 Choose a topic from the three above.
2 Read the resource sheet and find out more on your topic using information from books in the classroom or library.
3 Make notes about the factors involved in the damage processes. Remember to include any economic factors and also to consider the situation from all points of view.
4 If you consider the problem to exist, suggest a plan of action that could be taken.
5 Prepare a talk to be presented at your conference. You will need to state the problem clearly, give evidence, reasons for and against, and suggest possible ways in which to improve the situation. Include pictures and flow diagrams where you think they will help the other delegates at your conference to understand.

Space debris

The use of satellites is of great benefit to the human race. They provide greatly improved communication and valuable weather data and images. They assist in locating land resources and in monitoring the spread of crop diseases and they also aid navigation processes. However, the increasing number of satellite launches are posing a potential threat to the safety of manned space stations and manned spacecraft. This is because debris from old rockets and satellites which have either exploded or collided poses serious danger. This 'space junk' is now found in low-Earth orbit.

Space debris.

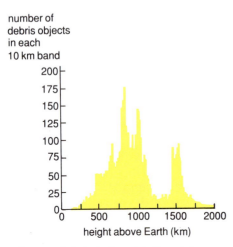

number of debris objects in each 10 km band

Space debris in low-Earth orbit.

Damage caused by space debris

In 1983 a fleck of paint measuring 0.2 mm across struck the window of the space shuttle *Challenger* and left a crater 2.5 mm in diameter. Imagine what would happen if a piece the size of a filing cabinet struck a shuttle travelling at the same speed. Space agencies estimate that there are about 3.5 million pieces of debris presently in orbit around the Earth.

An object stays at rest, or if it is moving continues to move with uniform velocity, unless an external force acts on it. Space junk is often the result of an explosion or a collision. The object will then continue to move at very high speeds until it collides with another object.

The **momentum** of an object depends on its mass and its velocity and can be represented by the following equation. It is measured in units of kg m/s.

$$\text{momentum} = \text{mass} \times \text{velocity}$$
$$\text{kg m/s} \qquad \text{kg} \qquad \text{m/s}$$

When two or more moving bodies meet, their total momentum remains constant providing there is no external force acting (for example, friction).

So, during a collision:

total momentum before collision = total momentum after collision

This is also true of an explosion.

The force of collisions can be calculated using the change in momentum of the objects involved:

$$\text{force} = \frac{\text{change in momentum}}{\text{time}} = \text{rate of change of momentum}$$

Rockets and jets use the momentum of high velocity gases produced by burning fuel to provide an equal and opposite forward momentum. You can see this principle in action when you blow up a balloon and then release it. The momentum of the air leaving the balloon gives it momentum in the opposite direction.

Q1 What is space junk and where does it come from?

Q2 What would be the most dangerous height for a manned spacecraft to orbit? What would be a safe height?

Q3 Most of the world's telecommunication satellites orbit at a height of 36 000 kilometres. How much space debris would you expect to find at this height?

Q4 Suggest ways in which space could be 'cleaned up'.

Q5 If a piece of space junk has a mass of 10 g and a velocity of 50 000 km/h, what is its momentum?

Q6 A rocket is launched vertically sending out 60 kg of exhaust gases every second with a velocity of 200 m/s. What is the momentum of the rocket?

Identifying plastics and fibres

Keys can help us to identify systematically unknown plastics and fibres.

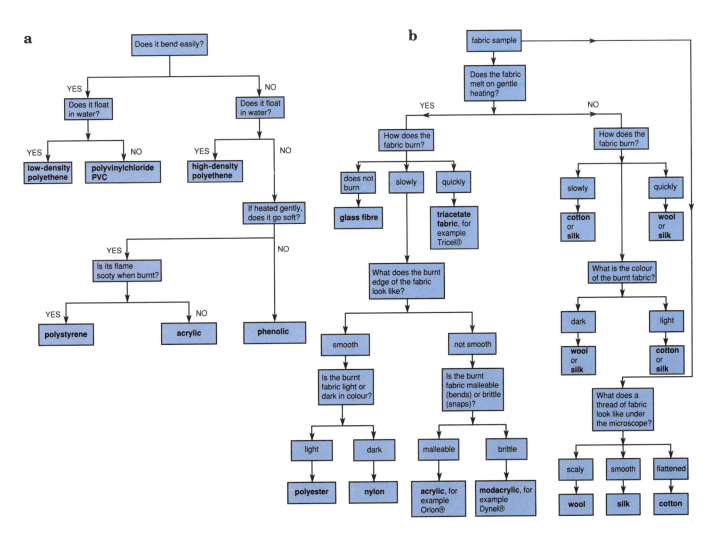

Keys that can be used to identify (a) plastics and (b) fibres.

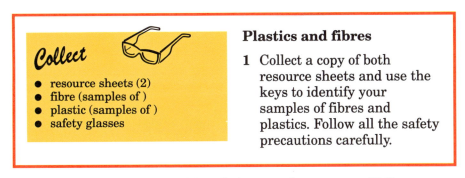

Collect

- resource sheets (2)
- fibre (samples of)
- plastic (samples of)
- safety glasses

Plastics and fibres

1 Collect a copy of both resource sheets and use the keys to identify your samples of fibres and plastics. Follow all the safety precautions carefully.

Q1 Did the keys work well for all the samples you tested? Can you suggest any improvements to either of the keys?

Nitrogen and plant growth

Plants use nitrogen to make proteins. Fertilisers are applied to the soil to improve its nitrogen content so that plants can make proteins at an optimum rate, therefore maximising growth.

Unfertilised and fertilised plant growth.

Collect

- glass rod
- test tube
- clamp stand
- bunsen burner and heat-proof mat
- activated charcoal
- mineral wool
- soda lime
- protein sample (soya bean)
- spatula
- universal indicator paper
- safety glasses

CARE!
Use soda lime carefully

Test for nitrogen

This experiment demonstrates that proteins contain the element nitrogen.

1 Mix, using the glass rod, a half-spatula measure of soya bean with one spatula measure of soda lime.
2 Set up the apparatus as shown in the diagram.
3 Heat the test tube.
4 After the mixture has reacted, dismantle the apparatus and test any gas produced.

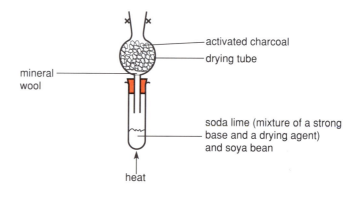

Q1 Record the steps of the experiment and note all your observations.

Q2 Name the gas produced.

Q3 Why does the formation of this gas prove that proteins contain the element nitrogen?

Calculating coulombs

The amount of electrical energy that flows during an electrolysis
experiment is measured in coulombs. The number of coulombs can be
calculated by using the following equation:

current × time = amount of electrical energy
(amps)   (seconds)   (coulombs)

Collect

- ammeter
- resistor (variable)
- power pack (low voltage)
- copper strips (2)
- beaker
- connecting wires
- sandpaper
- clock
- tile
- safety glasses

Find the number of coulombs needed to deposit one mole of copper

163

1 Rub both copper strips with sandpaper.
2 Scratch on one strip 'A' and on the other 'C'.
3 Set up the apparatus shown in the diagram and switch on the
power supply. Adjust the resistor to give a reading of 0.5 amps.

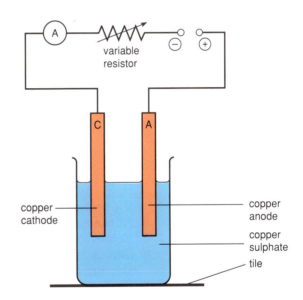

4 Switch off the power supply after 15 minutes.
5 Remove and wash the cathode gently and then leave it to dry in a
warm oven.
6 Reweigh the cathode.

Q1 For your experiment calculate:
  a the number of coulombs used
  b the mass of copper deposited on the cathode
  c the number of coulombs needed to deposit 1 g copper
  d the number of coulombs needed to deposit 1 mole (64 g) copper.

Q2 The reaction $Cu^{2+} + 2e^- \rightarrow Cu$ occurs at the cathode. This means
163 2 moles of electrons are needed to deposit 1 mole copper. Use the
results of your experiment to calculate the number of coulombs
which are equivalent to 1 mole electrons. This amount is known
as the **Faraday constant**.

Q3 Look up the theoretical value
of the Faraday constant in a
data book.

Q4 Calculate the amount of
electrical energy needed to
deposit:
  a 1 mole of silver atoms
  b 1 mole of aluminium
  atoms
  c 1 mole of calcium atoms.

Making a cold cream

Cold creams have a dual affect on skin. A moisturising component restores moisture to dry skin and an oil component helps to prevent further moisture loss.

Q1 What type of colloidal dispersion is cold cream?

Q2 What type of substance should a manufacturer add to stop the oil and water from separating?

Collect

- measuring cylinder
- beaker (100 cm³)
- evaporating dish
- thermometers (2)
- bunsen burners and heat-proof mats (2)
- tripod and gauze
- liquid paraffin (50 g)
- beeswax (16 g)
- borax (1 g)
- distilled water
- glass rod
- tile
- safety glasses

CARE!

This cream must not be used on your skin in case you are sensitive to it

Make a cold cream

1 Put the beeswax into the evaporating dish.
2 Add the liquid paraffin to the beeswax.

CARE!
Liquid paraffin is flammable

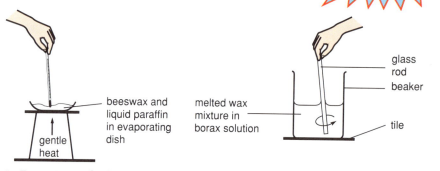

beeswax and liquid paraffin in evaporating dish

gentle heat

melted wax mixture in borax solution

glass rod

beaker

tile

3 Pour 33 cm³ of distilled water into the beaker.
4 Add the borax to the water.
5 Heat the evaporating dish gently until the wax has melted and the temperature is 75 °C as shown in the diagram.
6 At the same time heat the borax solution to 75 °C.
7 Remove both from the heat.
8 Slowly pour the melted wax mixture into the borax solution, stirring constantly with the glass rod.
9 Keep stirring until the mixture is almost cold.

Q3 In what ways could a manufacturer test the cream to find out if it was likely to cause an allergic reaction? Would you do the same? Why?

Cold creams.

Investigating concrete and cement

Collect

- concrete and cement (pieces)
- flame-test wire
- filter paper and funnel
- conical flask
- test tubes, bungs (4) and rack
- spatula
- glass rod
- beakers (2, 100 cm³)
- measuring cylinder
- tripod and gauze
- bunsen burner and heat-proof mat
- nitric acid (2 M)
- barium chloride (0.02 M)
- calcium hydroxide (1 M) (limewater)
- silver nitrate (0.02 M)
- concentrated hydrochloric acid (from your teacher)
- dropping pipette
- distilled water
- tile
- safety glasses

1. Place a small piece of concrete in a beaker and add 50 cm³ nitric acid.
2. Squeeze the rubber end of a dropping pipette and lower it to just above the surface of the acid in the beaker. When you stop squeezing the end, gas is drawn into the pipette. Now put the end of the pipette into the limewater and squeeze the end so that the gas bubbles through the limewater as shown in the diagram. Does the limewater turn cloudy?
3. Gently warm the acid and concrete in the beaker while stirring with the glass rod.
4. When no more gas is given off, stop heating.
5. Add 50 cm³ distilled water.
6. Filter the contents of the beaker, keeping the filtrate and residue.
7. Wash the residue with distilled water and leave to dry.
8. Separate the residue into any distinctive parts.
9. Pour about 1 cm³ filtrate into a test tube. Divide the remaining filtrate into two parts and test one part with barium chloride solution and test the remaining part with silver nitrate solution.
10. Carry out a flame test with the fragments of residue and the filtrate you saved in the test tube, cleaning the wire each time with hydrochloric acid.
11. Repeat steps (1) to (10) using cement pieces.

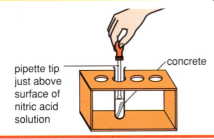

pipette tip just above surface of nitric acid solution — concrete

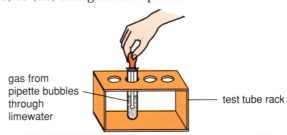

gas from pipette bubbles through limewater — test tube rack

Copy the two tables below and record your results.

	Cations present		
cement			
concrete			

	Anions present		
	sulphate	carbonate	chloride
cement			
concrete			

The human eye

The eye is an energy transducer. (See page 40 for an example of a non-biological transducer.)

High intensity light can damage the retina. Mountaineers climbing at a high altitude can suffer from snow-blindness where the retina of their eyes is 'burnt' by the reflection of bright light off the snow.

The iris controls the amount of light entering the eye and so helps to protect the retina from receiving too much light. It is made up of two antagonistic muscles (see page 134) called circular and radial muscles.

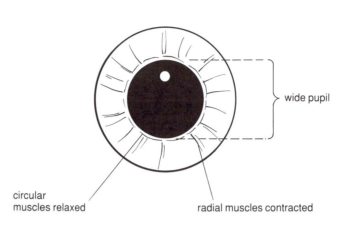

dim light

wide pupil

circular muscles relaxed

radial muscles contracted

Iris muscles of the human eye in dim light conditions.

Q1 Redraw the diagram above to show what happens in bright light conditions using labels to explain.

Structure of the eye

Vision

Light from an object produces a focused image on the retina. This is very similar to the way an image is focused on to film in a camera.

The back of the retina is made up of about 120 million light-sensitive cells. There are two types of cell — **rods** and **cones**, which are named after their shapes. The cones are responsible for colour vision. There are thought to be three different types of cone cell; reacting to red, green and blue light. When all three types are stimulated simultaneously the sensation of white light results. Rods can only distinguish black and white but they are more sensitive to low light intensity than cone cells are. This is why in a darkened room objects appear black, white or grey.

Cones are concentrated in the area of retina called the fovea, with rods further round the retina.

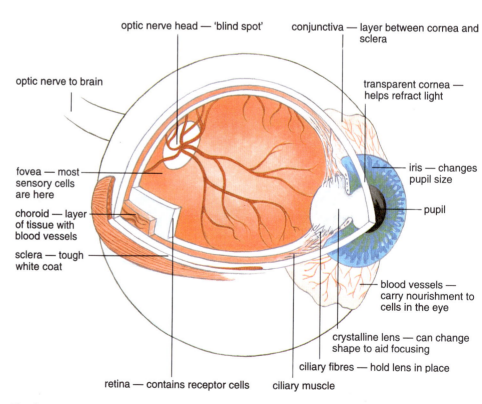

optic nerve head — 'blind spot'

conjunctiva — layer between cornea and sclera

optic nerve to brain

transparent cornea — helps refract light

fovea — most sensory cells are here

iris — changes pupil size

choroid — layer of tissue with blood vessels

pupil

sclera — tough white coat

blood vessels — carry nourishment to cells in the eye

crystalline lens — can change shape to aid focusing

ciliary fibres — hold lens in place

retina — contains receptor cells

ciliary muscle

The human eye.

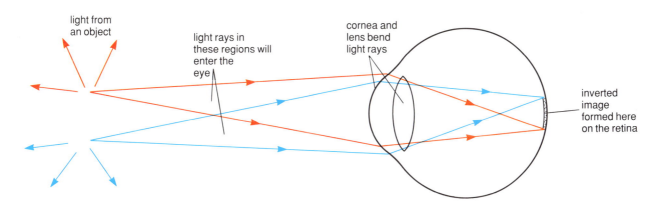

How an image forms on the retina of the eye.

Collect

- resource sheets (2)
- white card
- metre rule
- colour test cards

Compare vision

1 Study resource sheet A.
2 Draw two parallel lines one millimetre apart on the white card.
3 Looking at the lines, gradually move away until they appear to merge as one.
4 Record your distance from the card.
5 Collect the class results and draw a graph. What is the average distance from the card when the lines appear to merge? (Do the mean, median and mode vary?)

Investigate colour vision

1 Carefully follow the instructions on resource sheet B.
2 Compare notes with the rest of the class. Can everyone see the colours normally? Is anyone colour blind? If so are they totally colour blind or can they see some colours?
3 Collect a red card and a green card.
4 Look at one of the cards out of the corner of your eye.
5 Repeat with the other card.
6 Can you say which colour is which? How can you explain your observations?

Q1 Why do some people wear half-moon spectacles?

Q2 Why is it more difficult to see colours at dusk?

Q3 Explain why we can sometimes see a faint star by looking just beyond it.

Q4 Cats have both rods and cones in their eyes but they have many more rods than humans. What does this tell you about the eyesight of a cat and its way of life?

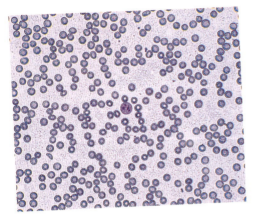

Normal blood. One white cell can be seen at the centre surrounded by many red cells and clusters of platelets, × 236.

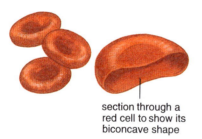

section through a red cell to show its biconcave shape

Red blood cells.

The blood and immunity

On average an adult has about five litres of blood (about a bucketful). Blood is a very special kind of tissue. It is made of many cells suspended in a fluid called plasma.

There are two main types of blood cell — red cells (erythrocytes) and white cells (leucocytes). Platelets are very small fragments of cells which help the blood to clot. They collect at a wound site, acting as a plug to stop bleeding.

Transport

Red cells are present in blood in much greater numbers than white cells. There are approximately five million red cells per cubic millimetre of blood! Their function is to transport oxygen to and carbon dioxide from all cells in the body. They are disc shaped which gives them a large surface area to maximise the exchange of gases by diffusion. The part of the cell which gives it its red colour is a pigment called haemoglobin. Haemoglobin is a protein containing iron at its centre. It is the iron in a haemoglobin molecule that enables oxygen to be carried. Red cells are unusual cells in that they do not have a nucleus — they function only as oxygen transporters.

People who do not have enough haemoglobin in the red cells tend to feel tired and are pale around their eyes. They suffer from anaemia.

Red cells only live for about four months in humans so new ones have to be made constantly in the bone marrow, at a rate of about two million every second.

Fighting disease

White cells fight disease. They do not contain haemoglobin and they do have a nucleus. Like red cells, most white cells are produced in the bone marrow. There are 700 times fewer white cells than red cells in humans. White cells protect the body from disease and kill bacteria entering the body. There are two main types of white cell — **phagocytes** and **lymphocytes**. Phagocyte means *cell eater*. Lymphocytes are made in the lymphatic system. They produce special proteins called antibodies.

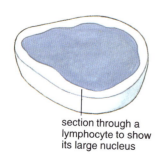

section through a lymphocyte to show its large nucleus

White blood cell.

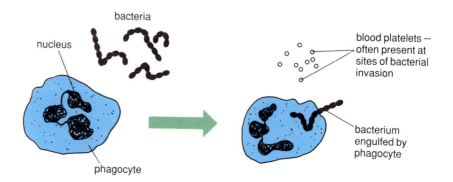

bacteria

nucleus

blood platelets — often present at sites of bacterial invasion

phagocyte

bacterium engulfed by phagocyte

A phagocyte engulfing a bacterium.

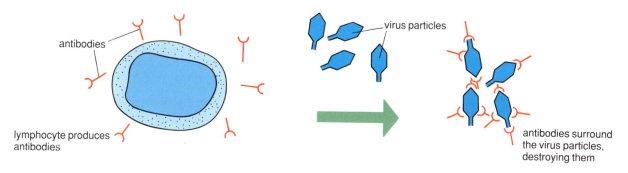

A lymphocyte destroying virus particles.

Immunisation

If the body is invaded by bacteria or viruses it usually responds by making antibodies. When a doctor immunises a person against a specific disease, a vaccine containing a small amount of dead or inactivated disease fragments (for example the polio vaccine contains dead fragments of poliomyelitis virus), is given to the person. The antibodies that are made remain in the blood and are able to 'recognise' a possible future invasion by the live bacteria or virus. This means the dead fragments have stimulated the body to protect itself. A remarkable feature of the immune system is its ability to build-up a 'memory' of past infections, giving protection for the future. Most babies and young people are immunised against polio, diphtheria, measles and tetanus. Smallpox, which was once a widespread and often fatal disease, has been entirely wiped out due to many years of worldwide immunisation. Since October 1992 babies are immunised against the most common forms of meningitis. Scientists are trying to develop a vaccine to protect against the human immunodeficiency virus (HIV) which can develop into acquired immunodeficiency syndrome (AIDS).

Collect

- artificial blood
- flasks (2)
- oxygen generator
- carbon dioxide generator
- vacuum pump

Investigate blood

1 Pour 1 cm³ blood into each flask and label them A and B.
2 For each of the steps (a) to (d) note any colour change.
   a Bubble oxygen through flask A and carbon dioxide through flask B.
   b Bubble oxygen through flask B.
   c Bubble carbon dioxide through flask A.
   d Draw air out of flask B with a vacuum pump.

Collect

- blood resource sheet
- AIDS fact sheet

Q1 Write a report of your results and try to explain the colour changes.

Q2 Construct a table showing the differences in structure and function of white cells, red cells and platelets.

Q3 How does a vaccine work?

Q4 Collect the AIDS fact sheet.
   a What does AIDS stand for?
   b What is the name of the virus which causes it?
   c How is the virus thought to be spread?
   d How can a person reduce their chance of catching AIDS?

The properties of enzymes

- Enzymes are proteins.
- They are specific — they control a single chemical reaction. For example the enzyme sucrase only acts on its substrate, sucrose.
- They are denatured by heat. This means they are structurally damaged and stop working.
- They are sensitive to pH. Enzymes that function inside cells prefer neutral conditions (pH7), whereas enzymes in the stomach prefer an acidic environment.
- They catalyse over and over again because they are not used up by the reaction they control.

Enzymes

Enzymes are proteins that catalyse reactions in every cell of the body. Some enzymes, such as DNA polymerase, function inside cells, whilst others, such as pepsin, a digestive enzyme, function outside cells.

Digestive enzymes are produced either by intestinal cells, or by glands which secrete the enzymes into the digestive system. The salivary gland is an example of a digestive gland.

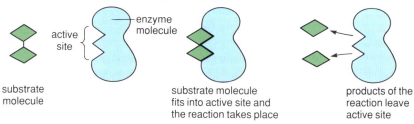

Mode of action of a typical digestive enzyme.

Uses of enzymes

Enzymes can be extracted from organisms and purified for use in industry. Proteases are used to digest protein stains in clothes. They operate at low temperatures so save fuel. However some people can develop allergies, such as skin rashes, to the enzymes in biological washing powders. Other uses of proteases include tenderising meat and skinning fish. Amylases, which break down starch molecules, are used in chocolates, fruit juices and syrups.

Collect

- test tubes (2)
- beaker (25 cm³)
- stewed apple
- pectinase
- bunsen burner, tripod and gauze
- thermometer
- muslin
- clock
- safety glasses

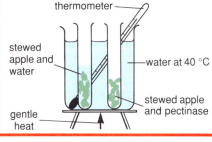

Investigate the activity of pectinase on apple

1 Put a little apple and about 1 cm³ water into a test tube, and about the same amount of apple and about 1 cm³ pectinase into a second test tube. Warm both test tubes to 40°C in a beaker of water.

2 Leave the tubes to stand for 10 minutes.

3 Filter each of the two tubes through muslin. (Do not squash the pulp.)

4 Record the height of the juice in each tube every 2 minutes for 10 minutes.

5 Design an experiment to investigate a change in one of the variables. You could alter the temperature, use different kinds of apple or other fruits. Show your teacher the design and perhaps carry out your design.

Q1 Prepare a report of your observations.

Q2 What difference did you find between the two tubes?

Q3 Why do you think manufacturers of apple juice add pectinase?

Q4 Why do manufacturers use enzymes in washing powders?

Q5 Why are enzymes called biological catalysts?

Q6 Enzymes are present in all plants and animals. When living things die their own enzymes start to break down their tissues. Explain how the use of heat, freezing and refrigeration, and vinegar help to preserve food.

The human endocrine system

There are two main types of gland.

- Exocrine (digestive) glands release enzymes via ducts into the digestive system where they break down food molecules.

- Endocrine glands are ductless glands that release hormones directly into the blood. The hormones act on target organs.

The endocrine system is made up of several different glands. Hormones and nerve impulses are responsible for coordinating the body but they work in different ways. The nervous system can be compared to a telephone where a message goes directly to one person. Hormones are 'broadcast' like a radio message so everyone can hear but only those people concerned with the message actually respond to it.

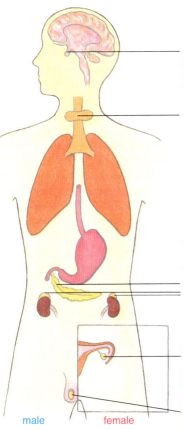

pituitary gland (often called the 'master gland') — produces stimulating hormone and growth hormone (GH). Too little GH causes dwarfism. Too much causes giantism

thyroid gland (sometimes called the 'butterfly gland' after its shape) — produces thyroxine which controls metabolic rate. Too little in childhood causes cretinism (physical and mental growth is stunted). Too little in adults causes overweight and slow mental and physical actions. Too much causes mental instability, restlessness and weight loss

pancreas — produces insulin and glucagon which act antagonistically to regulate the level of sugar in the blood. Too much insulin causes overweight (too little sugar in the blood). Too little can lead to diabetes mellitus

adrenal glands — produce adrenaline (often called the 'flight or fight' hormone), which prepares the body for action. Adrenaline acts very quickly

ovaries — produce oestrogen which controls the secondary sexual characteristics, prepares the uterus to receive a fertilised egg and nourish it. Progesterone is also produced and aids this process

testes — produce testosterone which controls sexual development

male   female

The human endocrine system.

1 Use the diagram to construct a table, with the following headings: *Hormone, Gland function, Effects of too much hormone, Effects of too little hormone, Temporary or permanent effect*.
2 Using the different coloured pens, highlight on a copy of the body:
   a hormones found mainly in males
   b hormones found mainly in females
   c those hormones concerned with physical growth and development after birth.

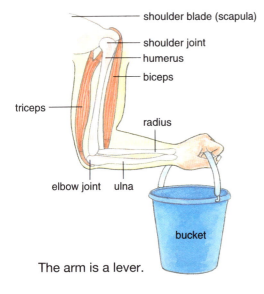

The arm is a lever.

Helpful machines

The arm is a lever. A small movement of the muscle pair in the arm causes a large upwards or downwards movement of the hand. The arm is a machine which increases movement and decreases the force. The elbow is the fulcrum, the muscle pair makes the effort and the hand lifts the force. A hand whisk also works by increasing movement to decrease the force. These are two examples of movement magnifiers.

$$\text{work} = \text{force} \times \text{distance moved}$$

Some machines increase the force and decrease the movement. These are called force magnifiers. The car jack shown is an example of a force magnifier.

Moments

It would be very difficult to open a door if it had no handle. All the objects illustrated have a fitment which acts to increase the turning effect of the hand. The turning effect of a force is called a **moment**. A see-saw is a lever which demonstrates moments.

$$\text{moment} = \text{force} \times \text{distance moved from the turning point}$$

A car jack is a force magnifier.

All these objects act to increase the turning effect.

What happens when there are more than two forces on a see-saw?

Use the diagram below to plan an investigation. Design a table to record your results. What do you conclude from your investigation?

- the lever principle:
  $W_{big} \times X = W_{small} \times Y$

Q1 List ten machines that you might find in the kitchen or outside in the garage. Explain how two of the machines work and say if they are distance or force multipliers.

Q2 A nut can be turned with a spanner. Explain why it is easier to turn the nut if the spanner handle is long.

Q3 The arm is a hinge joint and acts as a lever. Name another hinge joint in the body.

Extracting metals from their ores

Metal ores are compounds of metals found in the ground mixed in with many rocky impurities. Many metal ores are oxides of metals, and some are sulphides which can be converted to the oxide by heating.

Reactivity series

Potassium (K)
Sodium (Na)
Lithium (Li)
Calcium (Ca)
Aluminium (Al)
[Carbon (C)]
Zinc (Zn)
Iron (Fe)
Tin (Sn)
Lead (Pb)
Copper (Cu)
Silver (Ag)
Gold (Au)
Platinum (Pt)

The thermic reaction

This is a reduction process involving aluminium powder and a metal oxide, usually Fe_2O_3. The reaction is used to produce heat for processes such as welding. Your teacher may demonstrate the following reaction.

$$Fe_2O_3 \ + \ 2Al \ \rightarrow \ Al_2O_3 \ + 2Fe$$
iron oxide + aluminium → aluminium oxide + iron

Iron oxide loses its oxygen to aluminium, so is reduced to iron. Of course, reduction always goes hand-in-hand with oxidation. A substance is oxidised when it combines with oxygen.

Q1 What has been oxidised in the above reaction?

We can also list metal elements in order of their ability to remove oxygen from oxides of other elements. This ability is ordered in the reactivity series. In theory, this reaction could be used to extract iron from its ore. The thermite reaction is used to extract chromium and manganese from their ores.

Q2 Can you think of reasons why the thermite reaction is not used on an industrial scale to extract iron from its ore?

Carbon, of course, is a non-metallic or organic element but it does remove oxygen from certain metals. It can be added to the reactivity series just above the level of zinc. A very high temperature is needed for carbon to reduce iron ore. On an industrial scale, iron is extracted from its ore in a blast furnace. Several reactions are involved in contrast to the single thermite reaction. Iron ore, coke (carbon) and limestone (calcium carbonate) are fed in to the furnace near its top. Molten iron and slag are tapped from the bottom of the furnace. The reactions take place in three main stages.

$$C_{(s)} \ + \ O_{2(g)} \ \rightarrow \ CO_{2(g)}$$
carbon + oxygen → carbon dioxide

166

$$CO_{2(g)} \ \ \ \ \ C_{(s)} \ \rightarrow \ 2CO_{(g)}$$
carbon dioxide + carbon → carbon monoxide

$$Fe_2O_{3(g)} \ + \ 3CO_{(g)} \ \rightarrow 2Fe_{(l)} + \ 3CO_{2(g)}$$
iron oxide + carbon monoxide → iron + carbon dioxide

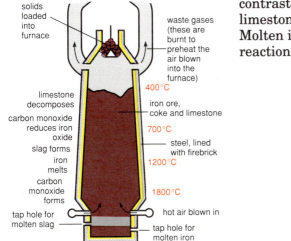

solids loaded into furnace

waste gases (these are burnt to preheat the air blown into the furnace)

400°C

limestone decomposes

iron ore, coke and limestone

carbon monoxide reduces iron oxide

700°C

slag forms

steel, lined with firebrick

iron melts

1200°C

carbon monoxide forms

1800°C

tap hole for molten slag

hot air blown in

tap hole for molten iron

An iron ore blast furnace.

Metals that are above carbon in the reactivity series cannot be extracted using carbon. Can you think why? Reactive metals are extracted by electrolysis of their molten halide (chloride or fluoride).

Extraction of aluminium by electrolysis

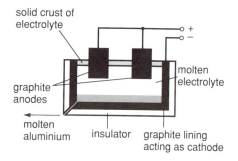

The electrolysis of molten cryolite and bauxite.

Aluminium ore is called bauxite. It contains a high concentration of aluminium oxide. The bauxite is purified to obtain pure aluminium oxide (Al_3O_3). This is heated with cryolite (a compound of sodium, aluminium and fluorine, Na_3AlF_6) to form a molten mixture of cryolite and bauxite. This is because the electrolysis of pure molten aluminium oxide is impossible due to its very high melting point (above 2000 °C) and the liquid is a poor conductor. The molten cryolite and bauxite mixture has a lower melting point (900 °C) and also conducts electricity well. It is essential to melt compounds before you electrolyse them. The molten mixture contains positively charged aluminium ions (Al^{3+}) and negatively charged oxide ions (O^{2-}). When the electric current is passed through the cell, the aluminium ions travel to the cathode and the oxide ions travel to the graphite (carbon atoms) anode. At the cathode the Al^{3+} ions pick up electrons to form aluminium atoms (Al). The oxide ions lose electrons at the anode to form oxygen molecules (O_2). Because of the intense heat the oxygen immediately reacts with the carbon atoms in the anode to produce carbon dioxide ($CO_{2(g)}$).

Rolls of aluminium.

Group II metals

Make sure you know the position of alkali earth metals in the Periodic Table.

Collect

- magnesium (strip)
- calcium (strip)
- tongs
- bunsen burner, tripod and gauze
- test tubes (4)
- spatula
- distilled water
- pH paper or universal indicator
- data sheet
- glass rod
- safety glasses

The alkali earth metals

1 **a** Burn a small piece of magnesium and a small piece of calcium using tongs.
   b Collect a small amount of the 'ash' from each metal in separate test tubes.
   c Add a small amount of distilled water to each one and test the pH as shown in the diagram.

2 **a** Add a small piece of each metal to some water in a test tube.
   b Identify any gas that is produced.
   c Test the pH of the contents of the test tube.

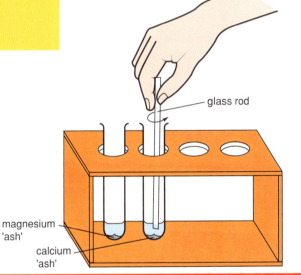

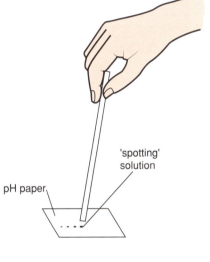

Your teacher may demonstrate this experiment.

Q1 Calcium hydroxide is formed when calcium reacts with water. Look up the formulae of the reactants and products for all the reactions. Write a balanced equation for each reaction.

166

Q2 Write a report of your experiment. Use your results and the data sheet to summarise the physical and chemical properties of alkali earth metals. Describe any trends you have noticed.

Ionisation energy

When an atom of an element loses one electron, an ion with a positive charge of one is formed.

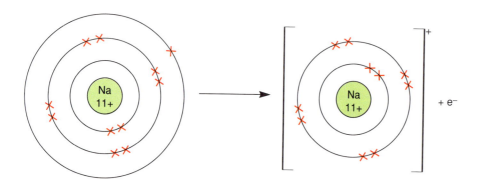

When an ion is formed energy is used. It is possible to calculate or measure the amount needed to remove one mole of electrons from one mole of atoms of an element. This is called the **first ionisation energy**. It is measured in kilojoules per mole (kJ/mole), and can be represented as

$$M_{(g)} = M^+_{(g)} + e^-$$

H									He
1310									2370
Li	Be			B	C	N	O	F	Ne
510	900			799	1090	1400	1310	1680	2080
Na	Mg			Al	Si	P	S	Cl	Ar
494	736			577	786	1060	1000	1260	1520
K	Ca								
418	590								

Key
element
ionisation energy

1. Plot a graph of first ionisation energy against atomic number for the elements up to calcium. Connect all the straight lines. Remember to label the axes with the correct units.
2. On your graph label each point with its chemical symbol.

Q1 Describe the pattern in first ionisation energy. Does it vary periodically? Explain your answer in terms of the electronic configurations of the elements.

Q2 Using a coloured pen pick out the plot for the noble gases. Describe the pattern in reactivities for the noble gases. Think about what you know of the noble gases and try to explain the pattern in these terms. Is the pattern what you would expect? Is there a trend in first ionisation energy?

Q3 On your graph, pick out the plot linking Group I metals in a different colour. Describe and explain the pattern in first ionisation energy. Is the trend what you would expect? Why?

Beta particle decay

When a beta particle is emitted, the mass number stays the same but the atomic number increases by one. This is because the beta particle is an electron.

This is usually written as:

$$^{14}_{6}C \rightarrow {}^{14}_{7}N + {}^{0}_{-1}e \text{ (beta particle)}$$

Alpha particle decay

When an alpha particle is emitted, the equivalent of two neutrons and two protons are emitted. (That is the nucleus of a helium atom.) The mass number falls by four units and the atomic number falls by two units.

This is usually written as:

$$^{238}_{92}U \rightarrow {}^{234}_{90}Th + {}^{4}_{2}He \text{ (alpha particle)}$$

Notice that:

● the mass number to the left of the arrow (238) equals the sum of the mass numbers to the right of the arrow (234 + 4).

● the atomic number to the left of the arrow (92) equals the sum of the atomic numbers to the right of the arrow (90 + 2).

Radioactive decay

What happens to a nucleus when it undergoes radioactive decay? A nucleus can eject a beta particle or an alpha particle.

Isotopes with atomic numbers over 82 normally emit alpha particles while isotopes with atomic numbers below 82 normally emit beta particles.

When uranium-238 decays, a series of transformations gives rise to new elements all of which are radioactive except the last, which is an isotope of lead.

Q1 Write down the decay transformations when uranium decays to thorium. You will need to work out what type of particle is emitted and write an equation for each step in the decay pathway.

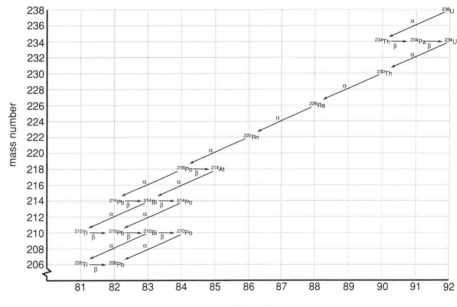

The series of transformations in decay of uranium-238 to lead.

Q2 Remember that the half life of a radioactive isotope is the time taken for half the atoms in a given sample to decay. How long do we have to wait before an isotope has decayed completely? How many half-lives must pass before 99.9% of the original mass of a given sample has decayed? (*Hint*: after one half-life 50% is left. After two half-lives half of 50% is left, that is, 25% and so on.)

Radon is one of the substances formed in the complete radioactive decay of uranium-238 to lead. Radon is also found in the atmosphere. In some places (such as Cornwall), radon builds up in buildings due to radioactive decay of rocks in the Earth's surface.

Q3 What element does radon decay to?

Q4 What kind of element forms when radon decays?

Q5 When radon decays what element forms?

Glossary

abiotic   Describes the non-living part of the environment, such as rocks and streams.

acidic oxide   A compound of oxygen and another element which has acidic properties. An acidic oxide reacts with bases to form salts. Examples include sulphur dioxide and phosphorus pentoxide.

addition polymer   An unsaturated compound with multiple bonds such as C=C, C=O. It can be saturated by adding a molecule across the multiple bond to form an addition polymer.

addition reaction   An addition reaction is one in which molecules add together to form a single product.

aerobic respiration   Cellular respiration which uses oxygen. Food molecules in the body are combined with oxygen or oxidised. The products are carbon dioxide, water and energy.

alkanes   Saturated compounds found in crude oil. They are hydrocarbons with the general formula C_nH_{2n+2}.

alkenes   Unsaturated compounds with the general formula C_nH_{2n}. Ethene, C_2H_4, is the simplest and most well known.

alkyd resin   Any synthetic resin used widely in adhesives and coatings (particularly paints). A product of a reaction involving condensation of alcohols and dicarboxylic acids.

alleles   Alternative forms of genes occupying the same position in the chromosomes, for example, tall or short in pea plants.

alpha particle (α)   Helium nucleus containing two neutrons and two protons. Alpha particles are emitted during some radioactive transformations.

amalgam   An alloy of mercury and another metal, for example silver. It has been used widely in dentistry.

amino acid   An organic compound containing one or more amino groups ($-NH_2$) and one or more carboxyl groups ($-COOH$). There are several hundred naturally occurring amino acids but only 20 are needed to make proteins. When proteins are digested, amino acids are released.

amniocentesis   The removal of a small amount of amniotic fluid surrounding a fetus. It is possible to diagnose some illnesses or conditions of the unborn baby at an early stage.

amphoteric oxide   An oxide that can react as a base or an acid. It can form a salt from either a base or an acid. Zinc oxide is amphoteric.

amplifier   An electronic device used to increase the strength of the current or voltage fed into it. Amplifiers are used to, for example, amplify or increase sound in a radio or music system.

amplitude   The magnitude or displacement from zero of a curve. In a sound wave this indicates the volume of the sound.

anaerobic respiration   Cellular respiration which takes place in the absence of oxygen. Fermentation is a form of anaerobic respiration.

analogue signal   An analogue signal is one which copies the original. Sound can be transduced to electricity and then back to sound by copying the shape of the waves.

analogue-to-digital converter (ADC) A device that changes analogue to digital signals. These are found in many modern electronic systems such as computers and compact disc players.

AND gate   A logic circuit that has two inputs and one output. It only operates if both inputs are high.

Andromeda Galaxy   This is a spiral galaxy lying about 2.2 light years from Earth.

angina   Correctly called *Angina pectoris*. This is a sudden and intense chest pain caused by a momentary lack of oxygen to the heart muscle.

angiosperms   Any flowering plant.

antagonistic muscles   Muscles that are mutually opposed — one relaxes whilst the other contracts. The biceps and triceps in the upper arm are an example of an antagonistic muscle pair.

anther   The top of the stamen (male part of a plant) containing pollen sacs. Male gametes in pollen grains are produced in the pollen sacs by cell division.

arteries   The blood vessels that carry oxygenated blood away from the heart to the body.

asexual reproduction   Reproduction that does not involve gametes. Taking a cutting from a plant is a form of asexual reproduction.

asteroid   A small body or minor planet that moves around the sun.

asteroid belt   The group of asteroids found between the orbits of Mercury and Mars. Their diameters range from two kilometres to 670 kilometres.

atmospheric pressure   The pressure of the atmosphere on the Earth's surface. One atmosphere is a unit approximately equal to 760 mgHg, $101\,325\ Nm^{-2}$, or roughly $1 kgcm^{-2}$.

atrium   One of the heart's upper cavities. There are two, one on each side of the heart.

Avogadro constant   The number of particles in one mole is approximately equal to 6×10^{23}. Named after its discoverer.

axon   The long, thread-like part of the neurone that carries nerve impulses away from the nerve cell body to tissues and organs in the body.

background radiation   There is constant bombardment of low intensity radiation from the Sun's rays on Earth. Naturally occurring radioisotopes are found in rocks, soil and air. These all contribute to a background radiation. Britain has some areas where background radiation is considered to be high.

balanced diet   A balanced diet should contain carbohydrates, fats, proteins, minerals, vitamins, water, roughage, and enough food to provide for our needs.

basalt   A fine-grained, igneous rock. It is the most common volcanic rock and is usually extrusive.

basic oxide   A base is the opposite of an acid. A base will neutralise an acid to form a salt. Most metals form basic oxides.

Beaufort scale   This is an internationally used scale of wind velocities ranging from 0 (calm) to 12 (hurricane force). It is named after Sir Francis Beaufort, the nineteenth century Admiral who devised it.

bedrock   Solid unweathered rock that lies below the loose deposits on the surface of the Earth.

beta particles (β)   Electrons that are emitted from a nucleus as a result of radioactive decay. The atomic number changes but not the mass number.

Big Bang   This is the most popular theory concerning the creation of the Universe. It is suggested that all matter was packed into a small super-dense mass. When a monumental explosion took place fragments were hurled in all directions forming galaxies and stars.

binary system This is a system based on just two numbers: 0 and 1. It is used extensively in electronic systems, including computers.

Caledonian mountains A mountain range in Scotland.

capacitor A device that stores electric charge. It usually consists of two conducting surfaces separated by a dielectric material. It used to be called a condenser.

capillaries Small, thin-walled blood vessels. They form an interconnecting network between arteries and veins.

cathode ray oscilloscope (CRO) An instrument containing a cathode ray tube that produces a beam of high energy electrons. A representation of a rapidly changing quantity is given on its screen.

chain reaction A chain reaction occurs when a neutron collides with an atomic nucleus, causing the ejection of more neutrons. These neutrons collide with more nuclei and the reaction continues to increase.

cholesterol This is a pale yellow or white substance which is found in all animal tissues, blood, bile and fat. There is some evidence to suggest that a high level of cholesterol in the body is associated with an increased risk of heart disease.

chromatogram When a mixture is separated in chromatography, a chromatogram is produced. The chromatogram is analysed and the substances in the mixture identified.

chromosomes These are thread-like structures found in the nucleus of a cell. They are responsible for the transmission of hereditary characteristics. A human body cell has 46 chromosomes. A human gamete has 23 chromosomes.

composite A compound of two different materials. Bone is a composite. In industry composites are often made by reinforcing a plastic matrix with fibres of, for example, glass, boron or graphite. These high performance materials are used in aircraft, spacecraft, car components, sports goods and machinery.

condensation polymerisation A reaction in which a polymer is made by splitting off a small molecule, often water. Nylon and polyester are made by this process.

cytotoxic Poisonous to living cells.

DDT A powerful and persistent insecticide. Whilst it is harmless to plants it remains in the bodies of the animals which eat the insects affected by it and so its concentration is built up in the food web. *See also* persistent insecticide.

decibel (dB) One tenth of a Bel. The unit used to measure the intensity of sound. Zero decibels is the lowest sound audible to humans.

denitrifying bacteria Bacteria that cause nitrogen in plants to be released.

digital-to-analogue converter (DAC) A device that converts digital signals to analogue signals. For example a CD player needs a DAC to convert the laser beams to sound.

denatured Change the nature of something. For example, proteins can be changed by either physical or chemical means, such as excess heat, or acid, resulting in the loss of solubility or biological activity.

dendrites Short thread-like projections on the end of a nerve cell. They conduct impulses towards the nerve cell body. The name comes from the Greek for 'tree-like'.

electrically neutral Does not carry a charge.

elliptical orbit An orbit shaped like a flattened circle. Planets have elliptical orbits.

empirical formula The simplest formula of a chemical substance. It shows the ratio between the numbers of each type of atom in a molecule or giant structure. *See also* molecular formula.

emulsifying agent A substance that produces an emulsion from chemicals that do not normally mix, such as oil and water. Soaps and detergents are emulsifying agents.

emulsion A colloid in which both phases are liquid.

energy Anything that can be harnessed to do some kind of work. Examples are light, heat, sound, electrical, movement and many others.

enzymes Enzymes are proteins that act as catalysts. They are specific in their action and work best at a particular temperature and pH.

exothermic reaction This is a reaction that gives out heat. All combustion reactions are exothermic.

exponential decay The decrease of a physical quantity over time. The longer the decay takes the faster it decays. Radioactive decay is an example.

flaccid Soft and limp, lacking firmness.

front The dividing line between warm and cold air masses in weather. The line at which the two air masses meet.

fundamental frequency The frequency of the principal or lowest note in a complex vibration.

galaxy A star system which is held together by gravitational attraction. The Solar System is part of the Milky Way galaxy.

gamete A sperm or ovum that can undergo fertilisation.

groups The vertical columns of elements in the Periodic Table. For example, Group I is called the alkali metals and Group O is called the noble gases.

hermaphrodite An individual animal or flower that has both male and female reproductive organs. A worm is a hermaphrodite.

homeostasis The maintenance of the physical and chemical properties of the body.

homologous series Organic compounds that have the same general formula. The compounds are related to each other in that there is a constant structural difference between one member and the next. Alkanes and alkenes are examples of homologous series.

hydrocarbons Compounds containing the elements hydrogen and carbon only. Oil derivatives are hydrocarbons.

hypertension Blood pressure that is higher than that usually found for a person, compared to others of the same sex, age and fitness.

integrated circuit (IC) A very small electronic circuit. It is a complete circuit manufactured in a single package. The circuits are used extensively in computing technology.

intensity A measure of the strength of waves such as sound or shock waves.

ions Ions are atoms which have lost or gained one or more electrons. They are charged particles. Metal ions are positively charged. Most non-metal ions are negatively charged.

isobars Lines on a weather map connecting places of equal atmospheric pressure.

isotope Atoms of the same element that have different numbers of neutrons in their nuclei are called isotopes. They also have a different mass number.

leguminous plants Belonging to the family of plants which has pods, for example, peas and beans.

light year Unit of distance used in astronomy. It is equal to the distance travelled by light in one solar year, 5.8784×10^7 m.

logarithmic Numbers based on raising to a power. The points on a scale are proportional to the logarithms of the numbers.

malnutrition The lack of adequate nutrition due to insufficient food or an unblanced diet.

mass spectrometry Measuring the relative amounts of isotopes in a sample by using controlled magnetic fields and the positive ion currents that arrive at a fixed point.

metabolic rate The speed at which physical and chemical changes take place within living organisms.

metabolism The total of all the chemical processes that occur in living organisms.

metalloid *See* semi-metals.

molecule A group of atoms joined together by covalent bonds, for example, H_2O, Cl_2.

molecular formula The number of each kind of atom in a molecule. For example the *empirical* formula for ethanoic acid is CH_2O; the molecular formula is $C_2H_4O_2$. *See also* structural formula.

mutation A change or alteration in the chromosomes or genes of a cell. This may affect the structure or development of offspring.

myco-protein Protein made from a fungus, for example, which is used as a meat replacement.

nitrifying bacteria Bacteria that convert ammonium compounds into nitrates, by oxidation.

nitrogen-fixing bacteria Bacteria in the soil that convert nitrogen in the atmosphere into nitrogen compounds that can be used by the root nodules of plants such as peas and beans. *See also* leguminous plants.

nodules A small lump or outgrowth on a plant root.

obesity More than 20% overweight.

optimum conditions The conditions that produce the best results.

organic compounds Carbon compounds that are derived from or relate to living things.

overtones Musical tones, apart from the fundamental, which contribute to the sound and quality of music. The frequency of each overtone is a multiple of that of the fundamental.

palaeontological Concerning the study of fossils to determine the structure and evolution of extinct animals and plants. The age and conditions of the surrounding rock layers are also studied.

period A horizontal row of elements in the Periodic Table.

persistent insecticide An insecticide that stays in the body of animals which eat insects and can therefore build up to dangerous levels.

photocell A device that produces a current or voltage when exposed to light. It is used in exposure meters and burglar alarms, for example.

pigments A substance found in paint or animal cells that produces a characteristic colour. For example, haemoglobin in blood and chlorophyll in plants.

plastics Synthetic materials, usually made from oil derivatives, which have a polymeric structure. They can also be moulded when soft and then set.

positive feedback In electronic systems an increase in the output energy systems reinforces the input energy.

pressure The exertion of one force on the surface of another. Force per unit area. Units are Pascals or N/m^2, Nm^{-2}.

pure substance A substance that is made of one type of chemical and is not mixed with anything else.

quartz A hard, glossy mineral composed of silicon dioxide in hexagonal crystalline form. It is found in most rocks especially sandstone and quartzite. Impure coloured varieties include semi-precious stones, such as agate, chalcedony, and amethyst.

radiation sickness Illness caused by over-exposure of the body to ionising radiation produced by radioactive material or X-rays. The symptoms include vomiting and diarrhoea. In severe cases, cancer or sterility can result.

radioactive A substance that gives off any or all of alpha, beta and gamma rays.

radiotherapy The treatment of diseases, such as cancers, by bombardment with alpha or beta particles.

reflex action An automatic response to a situation, involving no conscious decision.

relative atomic mass (RAM) This is the mass of an atom compared to one twelfth of a carbon atom.

relative formula mass The relative mass of a molecule on the same scale used for the relative atomic mass. It is the sum of the individual mass of the atoms that make up the molecule.

resonance   Vibrations produced by a body vibrating in sympathy with the nearby source of sound or vibrations.

respiration   The chemical breakdown of complex substances, such as fats and carbohydrates, taking place in the cells and tissues of plants and animals, in which energy is released and carbon dioxide produced.

salt   An ionic compound made when an acid is neutralised by a base. The hydrogen part of the acid is replaced by a metal ion in the salt.

saturated   Compounds containing only single bonds are saturated. Alkanes are examples of saturated compounds. A solution is saturated when it contains the maximum amount of solute at a given temperature.

scree   A build up of weathered rock fragments at the base of a hill. It often forms a slope.

seismic surveying   Surveying using artificially produced tremors in the Earth.

seismograph   An instrument that registers and records the features of earthquakes.

semi-conductors   A substance, such as silicon or germanium, which has an electrical conductivity between that of a metal and an insulator. Conduction increases with temperature and the presence of impurities.

semi-metals   Elements with physical and chemical properties that are between those of metals and non-metals. They are semi-conductors and form amphoteric oxides. They are boron, silicon, germanium, arsenic, selenium and telerium and they form a diagonal band in the Periodic Table.

sensors   Anything that receives a signal and responds to it. For example, the retina or a photoelectric cell.

sexual reproduction   Reproduction involving the fusion of a male and female gamete.

spiral   A winding or twisting form or shape.

stroke   The rupture of a blood vessel in the brain causing loss of consciousness. Sometimes paralysis results, especially down one side of the body.

structural formula   This shows the way in which the atoms are arranged, for example, ethanoic acid (CH_3COOH):

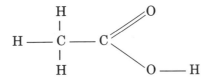

substrate   The substance upon which an enzyme acts.

supernova   A star that explodes catastrophically following the exhaustion of its nuclear fuel. For a short time it is 100 million times brighter than the Sun. The debris expands forming a nebula that radiates radio waves, X-rays and light, for hundreds or thousands of years.

target organ   A hormone is usually specific to a particular organ so is said to target the organ.

thalassaemia   Correctly called thalassaemia major. It is a form of anaemia that occurs in people from Mediterranean countries. It is hereditary and affects both sexes equally. It is caused by an abnormality in haemoglobin which causes the red cells to break down too easily. There is no cure and transfusions are the main treatment.

trait   Another word for characteristic.

transducer   A device that converts different forms of energy to or from electric energy.

translocation   The movement of one part of a chromosome to another part of the same or a different chromosome.

Tyndall effect   The phenomenon where light is scattered by particles of matter in its path. Used to test for colloidal properties.

ultrasound   Sound waves above those that can be heard by humans. The sound waves have a frequency above 20 kHz.

unsaturated   Unsaturated compounds contain double or triple bonds. The spare bonds can be used during addition reactions. Alkenes, such as ethene, are unsaturated compounds.

ventricle   A lower chamber of two in the lower half of the heart that receives blood from an atrium and pumps it to the arteries.

vitamins   Substances that are essential for the efficient functioning of body metabolism. Most cannot be synthesised by the body, but only very small quantities are needed.

zygote   The cell that results from fertilisation and the organism during the first two months of pregnancy.

Index

A

addition polymers   94
adolescence   131
aerobic respiration   132
agrochemicals   96–9
air, movement   78–80
alcohol, effects   119
alkali (Group I) metals   146–8, 152
alkaline earth (Group II) metals   152, 207
alkanes   92, 93
alkenes   93
alleles   53, 55
alpha particles   154, 155, 160, 209
aluminium, extraction   206
amalgam   102
amino acids
    in human diet, essential   125
    in plants, transport   19
ammonia
    manufacture   168
    in nitrogen cycle   25
ammonium nitrate, manufacture   99
amniocentesis   65
amplifiers   36, 40, 44
    transistors as   44, 45
amplitude of waves   33, 34
anaerobic respiration   132
analogue signals and systems   42–3
analogue-to-digital converter   43
AND gate   46, 47
angiosperms   10
anthers   22
aphids   176
arm, movement   134, 204
arteries   120, 121, 122
    diseased   122
arthritis   135
asexual reproduction, plant   20
asteroids   83
astronomy   82–7
atmosphere, Earth's   78, *see also* air
atmospheric pressure   80
atom(s)   143, 162–3
    masses of   162, 163
    numbers of   162–3, 209
atom bombs   157
audio systems   40–2
Avogadro number   163
axon   118

B

babies, birth   131
bacteria
    denitrifying   25
    nitrifying   25
    nitrogen-fixing   25
basalt   74
bauxite   206
Bernoulli effect   80
beta particles   154, 155, 160, 209
Big Bang   82–3
binary system   42
biodegradable plastics   95
biotechnology   60–3
    food   126
birth   131
bistable circuits   47
blood   200
    circulation   120–1
blood pressure, high   122
blood vessels   120–1, 122
    narrowed/blocked   122
bones   133
brain   117–19
breeding
    selective   57
    true   184

brown dwarfs   86
bulbs   20

C

cancer, radiation and   155, 157
capacitors   48
capillaries   120
carbohydrate, dietary   124
carbon, metal extraction employing   205
carbon cycle   26–7
carbon dioxide
    global warming and   27, 178
    manufacture   112
    plant take up/use of   10, 13
    tests for   13
carpels   21
cathode ray oscilloscope   33, 34
CDs   42
cell (electrolytic)   102
cell (living), division   54, 185–6
cement   111, 197
ceramics   110
chemical industry   91–114
chemical weathering   76
chemistry   161–73
    calculations in   161–73
    equations   166–9
    Periodic Table   139–60
    reactions *see* reactions
childhood   131
chlor-alkali industry   101–3
chlorine, manufacture   101, 102
chlorophyll   15, 175
chloroplasts   15
chromatography   141
chromosomes   54, 55, 56–9, 66
    squashes   185
circuits   44, 46–7, 182
circulation, blood   120–1
clinker, in cement   111
cold cream, making   196
colloids   104–7, 196
colour vision   199
comets   87
communication, sound   40–3
communication satellites   86
compact disc   42
composites, glass   109
compression of waves   32, 41
concentration of solutions, expressing   170
concrete   111, 197
condensation polymers   94
construction materials   108–11
consumers
    primary   24
    secondary   24
continents
    collision   73
    drift   70–1, 72
continuous phase in colloids   104
convection currents   78
copper, purification   100, 195
copper sulphate, manufacture   112
core, Earth's   70
Coriolis effect   79
corms   20
coronary arteries   122
coulombs   195
crust, Earth's   68, 70
cystic fibrosis   187

D

Darwin, Charles   58
DDT   24
decibels   39

decisions
    by brain   119
    in electronics   44
decomposers/decomposition   24, 25
deforestation   27, 29
dendrites   118
deoxyribonucleic acid   56–9, 60
deposition, mechanical   77
depressions   80, 81
development, human   128–31
diabetes   61
diaphragm, in microphone   40
diaphragm cell   103
diet   124–7
    balanced   124–6
    unbalanced   127
digestion   127
digital signals and systems   42–3
digital-to-analogue converter   43
diploid number of chromosomes   54
disease
    fighting   200–1
    genetic   187
disperse phase in colloids   104
distillation, fractional   92
DNA   56–9, 66
dominant allele   54
drug abuse   137

E

ears   180
Earth   68–81
    origin   82–3
    saving   191
Earth Summit (1992)   191
earthquakes   68, 69, 72, 188–9
echoes   179–81
ecosystems, plants and   24
egg, human   129
electricity, storage   48
electrolysis   100–3, 195
electron(s), arrangement   151–3
electronics, micro-   44–7, 182
electrostatic attraction   153
elements
    classifying   143
    families of   144
    investigating   158
    trace, plants and   177
embryo
    human   129
    plant   23
empirical formulae   164
emulsifying agents   105
emulsions   105
endocrine system   128, 203
energy, *see also* fuel
    food as source of   126
    ionisation   208
    nuclear *see* nuclear reactions
    sound and   40
energy value of food   126
environment, plastics in   95
enzymes   127, 202
    digestive   127
equations, chemical   166–9
erosion of rock   76–7
exercise   132, *see also* fitness
    heart in   123
eye   198–9

F

factory, chemical, setting up   113
Faraday constant   195
farming, chemicals in   96–9
faults, plates and   72

fertilisation 55
  in humans 129
  in plants 21, 23
fertilisers 25, 98–9
  genetic engineering and 62
  manufacture and analysis 99
fetus, health of 130
fibres, identifying 193
finches, Darwin's 58
fitness 120–3, *see also* exercise
flower, reproductive organs 21
flowering plants, photosynthesis 10
food 124–6
  energy value 126
food chains, plants and 24
forests, destruction 27, 29
formula(e), chemical 164–5
formula mass, relative 162
fossil(s) 70
fossil fuels, global warming and 27
fractional distillation 92
frequency (of waves) 32, 33
  fundamental 36
  natural 36
fridge, acoustic 49
fronts, weather 80
froth flotation 100
fuel, food as 124, *see also* energy
fundamental frequency 36
fungicide, copper sulphate as 112

G
galaxy 82
gametes 55
  human 128, 186
  plant 21
gamma rays 154, 155, 160
gas(es)
  atmospheric 78
  moles of 172–3
  noble 149, 152
gas giants 53
gas–liquid chromatography 141
gel 104
gene(s) 53, 54
  mapping 62
  mutations in 57, 155
  therapy using 62
genetic disorders 187
genetic engineering 60–3
  dangers of 63
genetics 51–9, 64, 65, 184, 187
genotype 53, 54
geology 68–77, 88, 188–90
  sound used in 38
glass 108–9, 110
  laminated 109
glass ceramics 110
global warming 27, 178
glucose in plants
  manufacture 10
  transport 19
granite 74, 75
grasses, wind-pollination 22
greenfly 176
greenhouse effect (global warming) 27, 178
groups in Periodic Table 145
growth, plant 20–3, 28, 177, 194
guard cells 14
gum disease 136
gypsum 111

H
Haber process 96–7, 168
haemophilia 187
half-life 156

halogens 148–9, 152
haploid number of chromosomes 54
headphones 41
hearing 180
heart 117, 120–3
heredity 51–9, 64, 65, 184, 187
hermaphrodites, plant 21
Hertzsprung–Russell diagram 86
homeostasis 117
hormones 128, 203
human biology 115–38, 198–201
Huntington's chorea 187
hydrocarbons
  saturated 93
  unsaturated 93
hydrogen
  in Haber process 96, 97, 168
  manufacture 101, 102
hydroponics 177
hypertension 122

I
igneous rocks 74
immunity 200–1
industry, chemical 91–114
inheritance 51–9, 64, 65, 184, 187
input transducers 182–3
insecticides 24
insects, cross-pollination by 22
insulators, glass/ceramic 110
insulin 61
integrated circuits 44, 46
interference effects 181
iodine, purification 142
ionisation energy 208
ionising radiation *see* radioactivity
iris 198
iron oxide 205
isobars 80
isotopes, radioactive 176
  decay 156, 190, 209

J
jet stream 78
joints 134, 135

K
kwashiorkor 127

L
lactic acid 132
laminated glass 109
latch 47
leaves
  chlorophyll extraction from 175
  starch in, testing for 11
  structure 14–16
light
  communication using 40, 42
  photosynthesis/chlorophyll and 13, 175
  waves and 32
light-dependent resistors 46, 47, 182
light year 85
lignin 16
logarithmic scales 39
logic gates 46
longitudinal waves 32
loudness 34, 39
loudspeakers 41
lungs 117

M
magma 74

malnutrition 124, 127
mantle, Earth's 68, 70
mass
  of atoms 162, 163
  of molecules 162, 163
mass spectrometry 162
materials 91–114
  manufacture 91–114
  purifying 140–2
medicine, genetic engineering in 61
meiosis 54, 186
membrane cell 103
Mendel, Gregor 53
Mendeleev, Dimitri 144
mercury cell 102
mesophyll layer 14
metabolism and metabolic rate 126
metal(s) 143
  alkali (Group I) 146–8, 152, 207
  alkali earth (Group II) 152
  extraction from ore 206–7
metal halides 149
metalloids 143
metamorphic rocks 75
microchips 44
microelectronics 44–7, 182
microphones 40, 182
Milky Way 82
minerals, *see also* trace elements
  dietary 125
  plant growth and 177
mitosis 55, 185
moisturising cream, making 196
mole(s), of atoms/molecules 163, 170–3
  in gas 172–3
  in solutions 170–2
molecules
  formulae of 164
  masses of 162, 163
  numbers of 163
moment 204
monohybrid cross 184
motor effect 41
muscles 117, 134–5
music, making 36–43
mutations 57, 155
myco-protein 126

N
NAND gate 47
natural selection 58–9
natural variation 57
nervous system 117, 118
neurones 118
nitrogen 25, 96–9
  in Haber process 96–7, 168
  plants and 25, 96–9, 194
nitrogen cycle 25
noble gases 149, 152
noise 39
NOR gate 47
NOT gate 46, 47
nuclear reactions
  in industry 157, 159
  in Sun 83
nutrition 124–7
nylon 94

O
obesity 127
ocean floor, movements 72
oil, chemicals from 92–5
optical fibres 40
OR gate 46, 47
ore, metal extraction from 206–7
organic compounds, definition 26

oscilloscope, cathode ray 33, 34
osmosis, plants and 16, 17
output transducers 183
overtones 36
oxides 151
   metal 147, 205
   period 3 151
oxygen, plant production of 10, 12, 13
ozone layer 49
   depletion 178

P
paint 107
palisade layer 15
pedigree analysis 64
pendulums 37
peppered moth 58
period (in Periodic Table) 145, 160
   properties across 150–1
Periodic Table 139–60
periodicity 144
pesticides 24
petrochemicals 92–5
phenotype 54
phloem cells 15, 19
photocells 42
photosynthesis 10–15
pitch (in music) 32, 34
placenta 130
planets 83–5, 90
plants 9–30, 175–7
   growth 20–3, 28, 177, 194
   importance 10–13
   nitrogen and 25, 96–9, 194
   photosynthesis 10–15
   and recycling 24–7
   reproduction 20–3
   transport in 16–19, 176
plaque, dental 136
plasmids 60
plasmolysis 16
plastic(s) 95
   glass-reinforced 109
   identifying 193
plate tectonics 72
pollination 21, 22
   cross- 22
   self- 22
polymers 93–5
   addition 94
   condensation 94
   natural 93, 94
   synthetic 94–5
potometer 18
precipitation 81
pregnancy 129
pressure 79
   atmospheric 80
producers, primary, plants as 24
proteins
   dietary 125, 127
   manufacturing 60–2
purifying materials 140–2

Q
Quorn 126

R
radioactivity (ionising radiation) 154–7, 160
   dangers 155
   decay 156, 190, 209
   uses 157
radiolabelling 124, 176
rainfall 81
rainforest, destruction 27, 29

rarefaction 32, 41
reactions, chemical
   electron arrangement and 151–3
   equation 166–9
   halogens in 149
   product, calculating amount of 168–9
receivers 41, 43
recessive allele 54
red giant 83
reed switches 45
reflexes 118
refractory ceramic materials 110
relays 45
reproduction 20–3, 55, 128–30, 186
   human 128–30
   plant 20–3
resistors 45
   light-dependent 46, 47, 182
resonance 36
resonance tube 37, 38
   disadvantages 38
respiration
   animal/human 132
   plant 10, 13
retina 198
Richter scale 68, 188
rocks
   dating 190
   erosion 76–7
   formation 74–5, 90
   identifying 88
root hairs 17

S
satellites 86
scurvy 125
sedimentary rocks 75
seed
   dispersal 21, 23
   formation 21, 23
seismic surveying 38
semi-conductors 44
semi-metals 143
sensors 43
sex-linked disorders 187
sexual intercourse 129
sexual reproduction 21–3, 55
   human 128–9
   plant 20, 21–3
skeleton 133
sodium chloride solution, electrolysis 101–3
sodium hydroxide manufacture 101, 102
soil formation 77
sol 104
solar cells 182
Solar System 82, 83
solutions, moles in 170–2
sound 31–50, 179–81
   communication with 40–3
   helpful 38, 180
space, outer 82–7
   debris/junk 192
   travel/exploration 86, 89
speed of sound 34, 35
sperm 129
sport 132–5
stamens 21
starch, testing leaves for 11
star(s) 82, 85–6
stem tubers 20
stigma 22
stomatal pore 14
stroke 122
style (plant) 23
substances 140–5
   composition 143
Sun 82, 83

supernova 86
switches 182
   bistable 47
   reed 45
   transistors as 44, 45

T
tape, audio, and tape recording 41, 42
telephones 40
telescopes 87
temperature, global rises in 27, 178
thalassaemia major 62
thermic reaction 205
thermistors 45, 182
thermocouple 182
thermoplastics 95
thermoset plastics 95
tofu 126
tooth decay 136
trace elements, plants and 177, *see also* minerals
transducers 40, 182–3
transistors 44–5, 182
translocation in plants 19
transmitters 40
transpiration 17, 18
transverse waves 32
troposphere 78
tubers, stem 20
turbulence 79
turgor, plant cell 16
Tyndall effect 104

U
ultrasound 38
Universe, birth of 82–3

V
vaccines 201
variation, species 52
   natural 57
vascular bundles in plants 19
vegetative reproduction in plants 20
veins 120, 121
vibration 32, 36
vision 198–9
vitamins 125
   deficiency 125
volcanoes 68, 69

W
water, in plants
   conservation 19
   movement 16–19, 177
water vapour 81
wavelength 32, 33, 34
waves, sound 32–4
   interference in 181
weather 80–1
weathering of rock 76–7
white dwarf 83
wind 78, 79
   cross-pollination by 22

X
xylem vessels 15, 16, 17, 19

Z
zygote 55
   human 129, 186
   plant 23